MUSIC
OF THE OLD SOUTH:
Colony to Confederacy

MUSIC
OF THE OLD SOUTH:
Colony to Confederacy

Albert Stoutamire

Rutherford • Madison • Teaneck
Fairleigh Dickinson University Press

Associated University Presses, Inc.
Cranbury, New Jersey 08512

ISBN: 0-8386-7910-2
Printed in the United States of America

To
A N N E

Contents

Preface

I first must express my appreciation for the encouragement and inspiration provided by Wiley Housewright, Dean of the School of Music, The Florida State University. Without his influence the research for this publication would not have materialized. Next, I acknowledge that only because of the patience, consolation, and assistance of my wife, Anne, to whom this book is dedicated, the work came to fruition first as a doctoral dissertation and now, ten years later, in its present form.

The original purpose of the research was to make precise historical knowledge concerning a small segment of American music more readily available to scholars. The locales chosen were centers of culture in Virginia from the beginnings of its colonization through the Civil War. Williamsburg and Richmond, the principal sites of the Virginia State Capitol, were the two places from which the events unfold.

In my writing I make the assumption that these two cultural centers also reflect the cultural tastes and pursuits, from the best to the worst, of a larger area, the South, which became a political entity of the Confederate States of America as the era drew to a close. Therefore, I use the "Old South" in referring generally to the geographical locale that became the Confederacy. But I refer more particularly to the customs and culture—the way of life—of its people during the era from colony to Confederacy.

I believe that the cultural activities of Williamsburg and Richmond were exemplary—the epitome of fashion—in the Old South. I do not imply that events in Williamsburg were grander than all others in the southern colonies, because it is well known that many of the large southern plantations served as cultural centers of high esteem. Nevertheless, leaders from various cultural centers journeyed to Williamsburg or read the *Williamsburg Gazette* to learn of the latest fashions from London.

Similarly, I do not presume that all musical events in Richmond outshone those in Charleston, New Orleans, Mobile, and Memphis. But I do assume that cultural events in those and other Southern cities shared a common bond in musical tastes, and I point out that London, Paris, and New York set the standard for fashion in urban areas throughout the United States up to the advent of the Confederacy. Since Richmond offered political leadership to the South, it is reasonably assumed that cultural leadership was also in evidence in the city.

As the histories of culture in other Old South urban centers become available to us through efforts of music scholars, it will be interesting to note what they report regarding Richmond's role in cultural leadership.

Primary sources of information presented in this book were found in the files of newspapers in the Virginia State Library in Richmond, various historical records in the Valentine Museum in Richmond, and music and rare book collections in the Library of Congress in Washington. These sources were supplemented by materials from the Virginia Historical Society in Richmond and the Baptist Historical Association at the University of Richmond. The libraries of the University of Virginia, the University of Pennsylvania, the University of North Carolina, and

LaGrange College in Georgia also provided services and materials essential to the writing of this book. I am gratefully indebted to many persons from the above institutions for the assistance given me in my research.

The illustrations were made possible for inclusion in this volume through efforts of many persons to whom I am also most gratefully indebted. Katherine Smith of the Virginia State Library in Richmond worked diligently, drawing on her expert knowledge of Richmond history to locate many of the photographs and to help me obtain copies of them. Various other members of the Virginia State Library staff were also most helpful in finding and preparing illustrations. Charles Hardin and Hugh DeSampler of Colonial Williamsburg, Incorporated, provided the superb photographs of Williamsburg scenes. Phillip Flourney of the Virginia State Chamber of Commerce provided a copy of his beautiful photograph of Richmond's St. John's Church. The Confederate Museum, The First Baptist Church, and the Valentine Museum, all of Richmond, helped make pictures available. And finally, two Richmond residents and close friends of mine, Carol Wash and James Walthall, provided most valuable assistance in collecting the illustrations.

Albert Stoutamire

MUSIC
OF THE OLD SOUTH:
Colony to Confederacy

Chapter 1

Music in Colonial Virginia

Introduction

Although the site at the falls of the James River was selected as a place for future settlement as early as 1607, and settlements were soon made there, it was not until 1737 that Richmond town was laid out by William Byrd II. The town received its charter in 1742 but developed slowly. At the end of the colonial period, Richmond consisted of about 300 houses, most of them crude, wooden structures on streets that were muddy in the rainy season and dusty in the dry season. Virginia, like every other colony in America, was a rural, agrarian country, and its centers of culture were the large plantations and a few larger settlements. In his *Notes on Virginia,* written in 1782–83, Thomas Jefferson wrote:

> We have no townships. Our country being much inter-sected with navigable waters, and trade brought generally to our doors, instead of being obliged to go in quest of it, has probably been one of the causes why we have no towns of any consequence. Williamsburg, which, till the year 1780 was the seat of our government, never contained above 1,800 inhabitants; and Norfolk, the most populous town we ever had, contained but 6,000. . . .

Secondary to this place (i.e., Norfolk), are the towns at head of the tide waters, to wit, Petersburg on Appomattox; Richmond on James' River; Newcastle on York river; Alexandria on Potomac, and Baltimore on Patapsco.[1]

Therefore it is clear that Richmond, which became the seat of the Virginia government in 1780, was chosen as the capital not because it was a center of trade, industry, or culture but primarily because it was a safe distance from the British by sea, yet at the head of a navigable body of water. Also, since the colony was growing westward, a more central location was desired.

Music Activities Before 1750

The known records and artifacts left by the seventeenth-century settlers and adventurers in Virginia reveal only a small amount of information about the music of those people. Some references to music were found in the writings of the seventeenth-century historians; and historians of subsequent centuries, writing about the seventeenth century, cite events that include musical activities. However, a compilation of references to musical activities cited in the standard histories of seventeenth-century Virginia would give neither an extensive nor a conclusive account of the musical lives of the people. By assuming that the principal town of the colony would also have been a center for the cultural activities of the colony, the writer has taken the following statements concerning seventeenth-century Jamestown as a reliable summary of that period:

At the site of the early settlement at Jamestown, Virginia, a large assortment of iron and brass Jew's harps (also known as Jew's trumps) have been found. . . .
As there is no record of spinets, or Virginals, having been

1. Adrienne Koch and William Peden, eds., *The Life and Selected Writings of Thomas Jefferson* (New York: Random House, Inc., 1944), p. 227, cited hereafter as Koch, *Writings of Jefferson.*

used at Jamestown, we have no way of knowing whether such wire-stringed, keyboard instruments were used in the homes of the more prosperous planters, together with other musical instruments of the period.

It is quite certain, however, that the Jamestown settlers knew the songs and ballads which were sung in Great Britain in those days. They were also familiar with English, Irish, Welsh, and Scotch dances. A few contemporary accounts reveal that the Virginia colonists enjoyed merry tunes and ditties, as well as lively dances. Although living in a wilderness, there were times when they could enjoy a few leisure-hour activities and amusements, including singing and dancing.[2]

The above quotation refers only to seventeenth-century America, since, although Jamestown was burned at the time of Bacon's rebellion in 1676, the Statehouse was not completely destroyed by fire until 1698, and the seat of government was removed to Williamsburg during the year 1700. After 1700, Jamestown was no longer a place of importance, and "its residents drifted away, its streets grew silent, its buildings decayed, and even its lots and former public places became cultivated fields."[3]

Although most of the seventeenth-century music activities of colonial Virginians were left unrecorded, the eighteenth-century writers left many records from which historians could piece together a comprehensive account of music in that era. Matthew Page Andrews presents the following account of festivities that included music during the early eighteenth century.

In the midst of Spotswood's term the colony was called upon to mourn the passing of Queen Anne and the accession to the British throne of George I, November 1714. Public mourning in the Dominion rivaled that of the mother country. Previously, the death of William III had furnished the

2. John L. Cotter and J. Paul Hudson, *New Discoveries at Jamestown* (Washington, D. C.: U. S. Government Printing Office, 1957), p. 84.
3. *Ibid.*, Preface (n.p.).

occasion for an elaborate ceremonial. On May 18, 1702 Governor Nicholson had called to Williamsburg not only the colonial militia, but a number of Indian chiefs. Reviewing stands and batteries were placed in front of the college. In the upper balcony were buglers from warships; in the second balcony were placed oboeists, and below those were violinists, who separately and together played "very movingly." Men in somber black bore flags covered with crepe, followed by the governor seated upon a white horse caparisoned in black.

After the "funeral sermon" by Dr. James Blair, the governor withdrew, to return in blue uniform and gold braid, whereupon the bugles, violins and oboes struck up lively airs, and Queen Anne was proclaimed with artillery salutes, and the rattle of "musquetry."[4]

Unlike a more somber group of fellow Englishmen who were colonizing New England, the Virginians were gay, fun-loving people. They took pride in their cultural and religious activities, and while the settlers to the north opposed theatrical ventures and resisted innovations in the music of their churches, Virginians accepted both. Freedley and Reeves relate that a "pastoral colloquy" was acted by the students of the College of William and Mary in Williamsburg in 1702, and that in 1716, "a playhouse was erected for Charles and Mary Stagg, who were to secure their supporting cast, music, and scenery from England."[5] William Byrd II made the following entry in his diary under the date of April 1721: "After dinner we walked to see Mrs. Grymes just come to town and from thence we went to the play which they acted tolerably well."[6] Byrd's writings are of interest because of his role in the founding of Richmond and because he participated in

4. Matthew Page Andrews, *Virginia, The Old Dominion* (Richmond: The Dietz Press, Inc., 1949), p. 191.

5. George Freedley and John A. Reeves, *A History of the Theatre* (New York: Crown Publishers, Inc., 1955), p. 297.

6. Louis B. Wright and Marion Tinling, eds., *The London Diary and Other Writings of William Byrd* (New York: Oxford University Press, 1958), p. 522.

the colonists' musical life, having an interest in all cultural activities of the day. He was not an amateur musician.

Judging from William Byrd's entries in his diary of ten years prior to the play reference, the new way of singing the Psalms, which was such a controversial subject in the New England colonies, was more readily accepted in Virginia. His entry of December 15, 1710 states: "In the afternoon I went . . . to the church to hear the people sing Psalms and there the singing master gave me two books, one for me and one for my wife."[7] This entry of the next day states: "In the afternoon my wife and I had a quarrel about learning to sing Psalms, in which she was wholly in the wrong, even in the opinion of Mrs. Dunn who was witness to it."[8] A little over a week later, on December 24, 1710, he stated simply: "We began to give in to the new way of singing Psalms."[9] The "new way" referred to singing by music notation, that is, singing the tune according to a published version rather than according to a rote version that may have been passed down through several generations of singers. The rote versions of the tunes were so diverse that seldom could two church congregations sing together without resulting in cacophonous sounds.

Eighteenth-century Virginians were quite fond of dancing to the music of fiddles. During the years 1709 and 1710 William Byrd attended nine or more social gatherings where there was dancing and merriment.[10] He recorded that on February 6, 1711, "the company went in coaches from the Governor's house to the capitol where the Governor opened the ball with a French dance with my wife. Then I danced with Mrs. Russell and then several others . . . then we danced country dances for an hour."[11] In addi-

---

7. Louis B. Wright and Marion Tinling, eds., *The Secret Diary of William Byrd of Westover* (Richmond: The Dietz Press, 1941), p. 272.
8. *Ibid.*
9. *Ibid.*, p. 276.
10. *Ibid.*, pp. 10–264, *et passim.*
11. *Ibid.*, p. 297.

tion to his references to French dances and country dances, Byrd gives several accounts of having danced the minuet. Other references are made to having heard singing and playing on instruments and to having attended a "concert of music at the Governor's" in 1720.[12] Although Byrd's references identify neither the performers nor the music, they do give an early date for a concert that is not generally cited in the standard histories of American music.[13]

Interest in Music

The intelligentsia of the colonies apparently enjoyed reading a column in the *Virginia Gazette,* which consisted of contributions from subscribers. In the column, a contributor known as "Zoilus" laments his having entered into a literary controversy with other contributors over the value of music. The exact nature of the controversy is not clear because some issues of the newspaper are missing, but it is interesting to note that the witty reply of "Zoilus" was in ballad style.

> The Monitor *Admonished:*
>   A new Song:
> to the tune of, *To all ye Ladies now at Land.*

> I, who long since did draw my Pen
>   In Injur'd Wit's Defence,
> Am now alass! compell'd again
>   To succor common Sense:
> For sure it never suffer'd more,
> Than lately by the *Monitor,*

---

12. Wright and Tinling, eds., *The London Diary* . . . , p. 400.
13. The concert attended by Byrd was probably given at a private social gathering. The first public concert in America is generally cited as being given in Boston in 1731. *See:* John Tasker Howard, *Our American Music* (New York: Thomas Y. Crowell Co., 1956), p. 22; and G. G. Sonneck, *Early Concert Life in America* (Leipzig: Breitkopf and Haertal, 1907), p. 10.

with a fa la.
. . . .[14]

In the four ensuing verses "Zoilus" inferred that he regretted having written to the Monitor since so many persons had entered the musical controversy in opposition to him. The next issue of the *Gazette* contained a parody on the above parody and was dedicated to "Zoilus." Not to be outdone, "Zoilus" wrote another five-verse "song" beginning as follows:

I knew that the song, which I lately did send,
Wou'd give me great trouble and Pain, in the End;
I meant not to Answ'ring, mistake me not quite,
But in Reading the Stuff, which their Worships
    wou'd write.
Derry down, &c.[15]

Other literary interests in musical themes were found in the *Gazette*. Reprinted from a London source were the words to an "Ode for his Majesty's Birth-Day, 1736. By Colly Cibber, Esq; Poet-Laureat. Set to Musick by Dr. Green."[16] Another writer who recalled a conversation with some gentlemen reported to the paper as follows:

Nothing can be more unjust, than to imagine that the sole Pleasure of Hearing Good Musick, consists in the Sound; or that it is nothing but the tickling of the Ear, and a mere

---

14. *The Virginia Gazette*, January 21, 1736. The Monitor was the headline for the column. Throughout this book quotations are capitalized and italicized as found in the original source. Spellings are retained except for obvious errors in the original printing.

15. *Ibid.*, February 4, 1736.

16. *Ibid.*, February 11, 1736. Colly Cibber, a well known writer and librettist of the day, tells of the reaction against Italian opera in favor of ballad opera in his "An Apology for His Life." Cibber wrote "Love in a Riddle," a ballad opera popular in England *ca.* 1729. Maurice Greene (*ca.* 1695–1755) was one of Handel's friends and later his rival. Greene was organist at St. Paul's, professor of music at Cambridge, and in 1735 was appointed Master of the King's Band of Music, in which capacity he probably composed the music to Cibber's *Ode*.

Delight of Sense, as they were pleas'd to call it. . . .

I would therefore advise those Gentlemen that find themselves unmov'd by Harmony, (which I take for granted are but few,) to look upon Musick as a Thing out of their Province; and I warn them from intermedling with it in any Manner whatsoever. . . .[17]

Two replies to the above statement were printed later. One of these, written by a Virginia gentleman who had spent some time in England, gives an interesting viewpoint of an attempt to acquire a gentleman's musical education.

Upon the Perusal of your Paper upon Music, I find, that unless a Man is to sit like an Animal, void of all Symptoms of Reason, for Three or Four Hours, for Sake of giving Pleasure to the Organs of Hearing, Music is thrown away on him.

I confess, I was once fashionable enough to be led away by the Stream; and at my first going to *London,* was inclinable to learn to play upon some instrument, and my Father, to indulge me, brought me a Drum; I must acknowledge this Instrument gave me a World of Pleasure for some Time; but the *Italian* Singers, were just arrived, and my Companions soon laugh'd me out of my Drum, and to refine my Taste, carried me to the *Opera.*

In short from *Tuesday* to *Saturday,* and from *Saturday* to *Tuesday,* the Topick of every Conversation ran upon the beautiful Passage of a Chromatik Song of Signora Cuzzoni, and the Lively Division of Signora *Faustina.* Then the pathetick Song of Senefino was ravishing, and tho' not a Hundredth Part of the Audience either understood Musick, or Italian; yet, when a *Connoisseur* gave the Word, 'twas Tinder to the Soul. *O Cara! Bravo! Bravissimo! &c.* I attended this August Assembly for a Whole Winter, except one Night, for which Neglect I was near forfeiting my Understanding: But, at last, I grew tir'd of the Expence, and asham'd at my Folly, for throwing away so much Money, and more Time, upon a Jargon of Sounds, without Sense.

And, Folly as it grows in Years,
The more extravagant appears![18]

---

17. *Ibid.,* October 22, 1736.
18. *Ibid.,* November 6, 1736.

Another item illustrating the colonist's interest in music was published under the general classification of "foreign intelligence" and was identified as "News from London."

> On Tuesday Night last, Mr. Handel had an Oratorio for his Benefit, at the Opera house in the Hay market; their Royal Highnesses the Prince and Princess of Wales were present; there was the greatest and most polite Audience ever seen there; and 'tis thought Mr. Handel could not get less that Night than 1500 [Pounds]. It's imagin'd there will be no more Operas after this Season, and the Italian Strowlers will be sent home; for now, the People of Quality seem to prefer Sense, to Sounds and Nonsense.[19]

The newspapers of the eighteenth century printed little news of local events. Examples of two types of items printed have been cited—letters from subscribers and "foreign intelligence." Advertisements constituted a third general classification of items published. From this third classification came the information that was most helpful in determining the activities of the colonists. Before 1750, no advertisements of concerts or theatrical entertainments are to be found, but other forms of advertisements often offer clues to the musical activities of the time.

Musical Entertainment
Judging from an advertisement in the *Virginia Gazette*,

---

19. *Ibid.*, July 28, 1738. Handel was yielding to the tastes of the day by writing oratorios in English rather than operas in Italian, but he doggedly refused to lower the quality of his musical works to comply with the newly acquired taste for the ballad opera.

John Christopher Pepusch (1667–1752) was the composer responsible for setting the music to the *Beggar's Opera,* first performed in 1728 in London, and thereby establishing a precedent out of which grew the style of writing used by later composers such as Shield, Dibdin, Arnold, and Storace whose works were heard by late eighteenth-century and early nineteenth-century Richmond audiences. Although Pepusch was a Prussian by birth, he spent the last 50 years of his life in England as an organist and composer of odes, masques, motets, theatrical works, and instrumental music. His best known work was his selection and adaptation of the tunes for the *Beggar's Opera.*

there were a number of fiddle players and singers who could come to country fairs and display their talents.

> We hear, from *Hanover* County, that on *Tuesday* next, (being St. Andrew's Day,) some merry-dispos'd Gentlemen of the said County, design to celebrate that Festival, by setting up divers Prizes to be contended for in the following Manner, (*to wit*,) A neat Hunting Saddle, with a fine broadcloth Housing, fring'd and flowr'd &c. to be run for (the Quarter,) by any Number of Horses and Mares: A fine *Cremona* Fiddle to be plaid for, by any Number of Country Fiddlers, (Mr. Langford's Scholars excepted:) With divers other considerable Prizes, for Dancing, Singing, Foot-ball-play, Jumping, Wrestling, &c. particularly a fine pair of Silk Stockings to be given to the Handsomest Maid upon the Green, to be judg'd of by the Company.
>
> At *Page's* Warehouse, Commonly call'd *Crutchfield* in the said County of *Hanover,* where all Persons will find good Entertainment.[20]

No evidence was found that the above event actually took place, nor could Mr. Langford be further identified, but on St. Andrew's Day of the next year (1737), a similar advertisement appeared in the *Virginia Gazette*. The advertisement stated that, "if permitted by the Hon. William Byrd,"

> a Violin be played for by 20 Fiddlers and to be given to him that shall be adjudged to play the best: No Person to have the Liberty of playing, unless he brings a Fiddle with him. After the prize is won, they are all to play together, and each a different tune; and to be treated by the Company. . . .
> . . . Drums, Trumpets, Hautboys, &c. will be provided to play at the said Entertainment.
> . . . A Quire of Ballads be sung for, by a Number of Songsters; the Best Songster to have the prize, and all of them to have Liquor sufficient to clear their Wind-Pipes. . . .[21]

A news item in the *Gazette* indicated that this event

20. *Ibid.,* November 26, 1736.
21. *Ibid.,* October 7, 1737.

was held, and although the music contests were not included in the report, the item stated that "Drums were
beating, Trumpets sounding, and other Musick playing,
for the Entertainment of the Company. . . ."[22] Thus it
may be concluded that gay events found little opposition
and were generally encouraged in Virginia, whereas in the
colonies to the north the Pilgrims, Puritans, and others
fervently opposed such activities.

Instruction in Music

Two previous citations indicate the nature of musical
instruction given in the first half of the eighteenth century
in Virginia. The first concerns William Byrd and the singing master, and the second concerns the contest in which
"a fine *Cremona* Fiddle" was to be "plaid for by any Number of Country Fiddlers, (Mr. Langford's scholars excepted) ."[23] The writer suspects that Langford's scholars
were violinists and would be considered unfair competition for untutored fiddlers.

Two additional references have a bearing on what was
to follow in the second half of the century. The earliest
involves the first advertisement of instruction in dancing
found in the *Virginia Gazette*.

> This is to give Notice, that this Day the Subscriber has
> opened his School at the College, where all Gentlemens
> Sons may be taught Dancing, according to the newest French
> manner, on Fridays and Saturdays once in Three Weeks by
> William Dering, Dancing-Master[24]

The writer infers that if dancing instruction were given
music instruction was also likely to be available since the
dancing master was frequently a musician and played the
music for dancing lessons on a "kit" or small violin. The

---

22. *Ibid.*, December 9, 1737.
23. *Ibid.*, November 26, 1736.
24. *Ibid.*, November 26, 1737.

other reference concerned Samuel Davies, who "in 1748 went from Pennsylvania to the Scotch-Irish Presbyterians of Virginia," where he began teaching music to the Negro slaves.[25] Since most of Davies' work concerned the second half of the century, the report on his work has been placed in the latter part of this chapter.

Musicians

Sufficient evidence was found to indicate that there were many musicians in Virginia before 1750, and although musicians played and sang at various celebrations and were teachers, the evidence that any permanent resident enjoyed more than an avocational interest in music is negligible. It is known that there were some professional musicians and much musical activity in Charleston, South Carolina, and in the colonies to the north of Virginia. It is reasonable to assume that professional musicians traveled through and performed, taught, and settled in Virginia. With the exception of Peter Pelham, who is reported to have moved to Virginia in 1749, the research carried out in connection with this writing has not uncovered the name and details of any long-term resident of Virginia who "made a living" as a musician in Virginia before 1750. Pelham's career in Virginia is discussed in the latter part of this chapter with the events of the second half of the eighteenth century. William Byrd's singing master, his fiddlers, and musicians who gave the concert he attended, as well as Mr. Langford (who may or may not have been a violinist and a teacher) and the musicians in the St. Andrews celebration, might possibly have been professional musicians, but no evidence has been found to support this contention.

Being a musician by avocation was not unusual, however, and the study of music was considered a necessary

---

25. Miles Mark Fisher, *Negro Slave Songs in the United States* (Ithaca, New York: Cornell University Press, 1953), p. 29.

part of a gentleman's education. Later references show that gentlemen amateurs joined the semiprofessional talent available and presented concerts. Although no reference was found relating to such activities in Virginia before 1750, an assumption that they existed is not unreasonable. That this avocational interest in music was not limited to gentlemen is shown by the advertisements about slaves and indentured servants who had run away from their masters. The fact that these persons were musicians was an important part of their identification as runaways. Five advertisements about slave musicians were found from before 1750:

> Ran away from the Subscriber in Lancaster County, . . . a dark Mulatto Fellow, named Will: . . . he carried with him, a white Fustian Jacket, a lopping Ax, and a Fiddle. . . .[26]

> Ran away from the Subscriber, in Charles City County, . . . a servant Man, named Thomas Sellers. . . . He . . . plays well on the Fiddle. . . .[27]

> Ran away from the Subscriber, in Prince George County, . . . an Irish Servant Man, nam'd Thomas Hoy. . . . He . . . plays very well on the Violin, and pretends to teach Dancing. . . .[28]

> Ran away . . . , a likely young Negroe Man. . . . He . . . plays very well on the Violin.[29]

> Ran away . . . , a Negroe Man, named Harry. . . . He plays upon the Fiddle. . . .[30]

It is apparent that during the first half of the eighteenth century there was a time and a place for every kind of music to be performed and enjoyed by colonial Virginians from all social ranks—gentleman, freeman, indentured servant, and slave.

---

26. *The Virginia Gazette,* May 5, 1738.
27. *Ibid.,* May 19, 1738.
28. *Ibid.,* September 26, 1745.
29. *Ibid.,* December 5, 1745.
30. *Ibid.,* March 27, 1746.

Mid-Eighteenth Century Through the Revolution

As in the first half of the century, the newspapers of the second half continued to print three kinds of material: news from outside of Virginia, letters, and advertisements of local interest. It may be assumed that news of local interest was carried verbally or, in some instances, by playbill or by broadsides. Occasionally, the essential information from a playbill appeared in a newspaper in the form of an advertisement. Rarely were news items, reviews, or criticisms of musical events printed in the newspapers. However, certain items that were published reveal the nature of the colonists' interests in music.

Interest in Music

An article from England stated that "musick was never so much in vogue as at this time," and that this fact could be attributed to "our gracious Queen [Charlotte], who in a very masterly manner plays on the organ, harpsichord, and piano forte. . . ."[31] Another news item told of "a specimen of a newly invented type for printing music. . . ."[32] Readers in Virginia were informed that "a scheme is on foot, and will be proposed this season of Parliament, to tax all the public diversions throughout the kingdom, such as operas, plays, . . . balls, concerts, &c."[33] News of social

---

31. *The Virginia Gazette* (Printers: Purdie and Dixon), September 28, 1769.

Between 1765 and 1780 there were sometimes two or more newspapers printed in Williamsburg, Virginia, under the name of *The Virginia Gazette*. References to specific issues of *The Virginia Gazette* issued between 1765 and 1780 are hereafter identified by the printer or printers as follows:

(C) Clarkson and Davis
(D) Dixon and Hunter or Dixon and Nicholson
(P) Purdie
(PD) Purdie and Dixon
(Pi) Pinkney
(R) Rind

32. *The Virginia Gazette* (R), March 30, 1769.
33. *Ibid.*, May 3, 1770.

events in England such as "The Ball this Evening will be
opened by the Prince of Mecklenburg, and it is thought
with the Dutchess of Grafton, . . ." was offered to the Virginia readers of the *Virginia Gazette*.[34] At the height of the
American Revolution, in 1780, the *Virginia Gazette* subscribers were presented with a series of "historical anec-
dotes on bards and musick in Briton."

Musical Instruments

Table 1 presents a summary of advertisements concerning musical instruments found in the *Virginia Gazette*
from 1751 through 1779.

TABLE 1
MUSICAL INSTRUMENT REFERENCES FROM *VIRGINIA
GAZETTE* ADVERTISEMENTS
1751–1779

Printer and Date of Issue   Item[a]

September 5, 1751	To be sold . . . "A Spinett"
June 25, 1752	Meeting to consider the church "or-gan to be sent for."
February 12, 1762	For Sale—Jew's harps & violins
(PD) April 11, 1766	For sale—fiddles & Roman strings
(PD) July 25, 1766	For sale—violins, German flutes, violin bows, bridges, pegs, and strings (in Norfolk)
(PD) June 4, 1767	For sale—bugles, Roman strings, and long fiddle sticks
(PD) January 8, 1767	"Spinets and harpsichords made and repaired"
(PD) September 17, 1767	For sale—"A very neat hand organ"
(PD) December 3, 1767	For sale—hunting horns, Roman fiddle strings, and long fiddle sticks
(R) July 14, 1768	Lottery for raising money to build a new church and the purchase of an organ (in Fredericksburg)

---

34. *Ibid.* (PD), April 23, 1772.

(R)   March 3, 1768 . . . . For sale—large and small fiddles

(PD) September 28, 1769 . . . For sale—complete sets of spinet wire, hunting horns, fiddles, long fiddle sticks, and Roman fiddle strings

(PD) November 29, 1770 . . For sale—Cremone and Steiner's violins, with best screw bows . . . Roman strings, German and common flutes of different sizes

(R)   July 18, 1771 . . . . Lost—the top part of a German flute

(PD) April 11, 1771 . . . . . For sale—hunting horns tipped and plain, German flutes and fifes, spinet wire and hammers, fiddles, Roman fiddle strings & fiddlesticks

(PD) August 29, 1771 . . . . . . For sale—German flutes, violins

(PD) November 5, 1772 . . . For sale—toy fiddles (in Richmond)

(PD) April 8, 1773 . . . . For sale—spinnet (in Manchester)

(PD) January 7, 1773 . . . . . For sale—a church organ (in King and Queen County)

(PD) May 27, 1773 . . . . For sale—spinet

(PD) June 10, 1773 . . . . For sale—German flutes and violins, violin strings, and bridges

(PD) July 8, 1773 . . . . Lost—the lower part of a German flute

(Pi) September 28, 1775 . . . Notice by the Committee of Safety: Recommended that drums and fifes be provided the troups

(Pi) April 20, 1775 . . . . For sale—a second hand guitar

(D)   July 29, 1775 . . . . For sale—Regimental fifes

(P)   August 16, 1776 . . . . . . For sale—Fifes, Jew's Harps (in Gloucester)

(P)   January 3, 1777 . . . . . . Stolen—Two German flutes (in Fredericksburg)

(D)   November 14, 1777 . . . . For sale—German flute and guitar

(D)   November 28, 1777 . . . . For sale—fiddlestrings

(P)   October 17, 1777 . . . . . . For sale—a spinet and a guitar (in Westmoreland County)

(D)   January 23, 1778 . . . . . For sale—"a good fiddle"—a German flute (in Yorktown)

(F)   April 3, 1778 . . . . For sale—Jew's harps (in Alexandria)

(D)   October 9, 1779 . . . . . . For sale—"a genteel spinet" (in Hanover County)

(D)   October 16, 1779 . . . . . For sale—fiddle strings

---

a. Advertisements pertain to Williamsburg and vicinity unless a location in parentheses indicates otherwise.

The above summary of advertisements indicates that violins, spinets, harpsichords, organs, and German flutes were popular instruments that were in general use in the colony. References to spinets, harpsichords, and organs were found only in the second half of the eighteenth century. The reference to "A Spinett" for sale in 1751 (Table 1) was the first to that instrument found in the eighteenth century, but it is likely that earlier references could be found. Howard states that an organ at the Smithsonian Institution, said to have been imported in 1700 to Port Royal, Virginia, "cannot be substantiated, and this particular instrument probably dates from at least a half a century later."[35]

"The organ to be sent for" (Table 1), which was possibly put into regular use in 1755, may have been the first permanent church organ in Virginia.[36] Maurer reports that Peter Pelham was instrumental in the installation of the organ in Bruton Parish Church at Williamsburg in 1755 and that Pelham played that organ for almost 50 years thereafter.[37] The House of Burgesses of Virginia passed "a resolve for paying a salary to the organist" in 1773.[38] No reference was made as to the location of the organ for which an organist was to be paid, and there were several church organs in the colony at that time. One was in St. Mary's Parish, Caroline County, and an advertisement for an organist to be employed there was printed in the *Virginia Gazette*.[39] Another organ had been installed in Straton Major Church and was used for the first time in 1768.[40]

35. Howard, *Our American Music*, p. 17.
36. *Ibid.*, p. 23.
37. Maurer Maurer, "The 'Professor of Musick' in Colonial America," *The Musical Quarterly*, XXXVI, 4 (October, 1950), 511–24. Pelham moved to Richmond at the turn of the century but apparently was inactive as a musician in Richmond [*William and Mary Quarterly*, XI, 2 (1931), 264–66].
38. *The Virginia Gazette* (R), March 18, 1773.
39. *Ibid.* (PD), March 11, 1773.
40. *Ibid.* (R), June 23, 1768.

References in Table 1 indicate that the violin was a popular instrument of the Virginia colonists. Numerous references to runaway slaves who played the violin suggest that the instrument was perhaps equally popular among the slaves as among the freemen, and perhaps slaves provided dance music for their masters.[41] Thomas Jefferson wrote that the "instrument proper to them [the Negro] is the Banjar, which they brought hither from Africa."[42] The banjo is seldom mentioned in the advertisements of runaway slaves. Perhaps the instrument was so common that knowing a slave played the banjo would have been of little avail in identifying him.

German flutes were also popular with the gentlemen amateur musicians, and the counterparts to the German flute were guitars for the ladies.

> About 1756–58 there was introduced in England from the Continent the Italian form of *cetra* referred to as the English Guitar. . . .
> In spite of its feeble quality, the English wire strung guitar had considerable popularity, being the feminine substitute for the German flute, then in such favour with the male amateur.[43]

The first advertisement reference to a German flute was

---

41. *The Virginia Gazette,* March 27, 1752; October 27, 1752; (PD) May 7, 1767; (PD) August 4, 1768; (PD) August 18, 1768; (PD) November 3, 1768; (PD) March 9, 1769; (PD) May 4, 1769; (PD) December 21, 1769; (PD) March 8, 1770; (PD) July 19, 1770; (R) November 1, 1770; (R) July 18, 1771; (PD) July 18, 1771; (R) July 18, 1771; (PD) May 7, 1772; (PD) May 14, 1772; (R) April 15, 1773; (R) May 20, 1773; (PD) June 24, 1773; (PD) July 22, 1773; (PD) February 17, 1774; (PD) June 16, 1774; (R) June 30, 1774; (Pi) December 1, 1774; (D) January 28, 1775; (Pi) January 20, 1776; (P) April 26, 1776; (D) May 9, 1777; (P) May 9, 1777; (P) May 23, 1777; (D) May 20, 1779; (D) March 19, 1779; (D) June 12, 1779. Each citation listed apparently refers to a different person. Duplicate and repeated advertisements are not cited.

42. Koch, *Writings of Jefferson,* p. 258.

43. Eric Blom, ed., *Grove's Dictionary of Music and Musicians,* 5th ed. (New York: St. Martin's Press Inc., 1955), II, 947.

printed in 1766, and a second-hand guitar was advertised for sale in 1775 (Table 1).

A few Jew's harps are listed in Table 1, but only one of the many references to bugles is listed. Because the word "bugle" appeared in lists of ladies' merchandise for sale, but was unrelated to any other musical merchandise, the writer suspects that in those instances the word meant "bead"—an ornament of the ladies' wearing apparel. Several references to drums and fifes were found. They were the principal instruments used in playing martial music during the American Revolution. "Yankee Doodle" and "Chester" were the most popular tunes of the Revolution.[44]

It is reasonable to assume that a majority of the instruments used in Virginia during the eighteenth century were never mentioned in advertisements. It is likely that most persons would have had instruments shipped to them from England or elsewhere and would not have waited for an advertisement to appear in the paper. A reference was found citing a letter that acknowledged receipt of a fiddle in Northampton, Virginia, shipped from John Norton, Merchant in London, in 1766.[45] Before 1780, references were made to French horns, trumpets, hautboys, and bassoons being played by professional musicians, amateurs, or slaves, but these instruments were probably either ordered from Europe or brought to America by the performers.

Three of the references listed in Table 1 and mentioned here were thought to be of special interest. The first advertisement was the earliest reference to a spinet found in Virginia. The other two give descriptions and other information about the importing and selling of instruments.

---

44. For details of these and other tunes of the Revolutionary period, see O. G. Sonneck, *Miscellaneous Studies in the History of Music* (New York: The Macmillan Company, 1921) and other general histories of American music listed in the Bibliography.

45. Frances Norton Mason, ed., *John Norton & Sons, Merchants of London and Virginia* (Richmond: The Dietz Press, 1937), pp. 15–16.

To be SOLD, for ready Money or short Credit, a Great Variety of Household Furniture, of the newest Fashions, London Make, viz.
Mahogony Chests of Drawers
Ditto Dressing Tables
Ditto Card Ditto
Ditto Claw Ditto
Ditto Chairs
. . .
A Spinett
Sundry Pictures, done by good Hands
John Mitchelson[46]

King and Queen, January 1, 1773.
I intend to leave the Colony immediately, for a few months. I have for sale a CHURCH ORGAN, which, for Elegance and Sweetness of Tone, is inferiour to none on the Continent. The whole case is polished Mahogany, the Pipes gilt, and the Imagery which adorns it striking, and as large as the Life. The Price is two Hundred Pounds, which is vastly under prime cost. The Payment will be made quite easy to the Purchaser. It now stands in *Stratton Major* Church. Apply to John Tayloe Corbin, Esquire, or the Subscriber.
William Dunlap[47]

For SALE, at Mr. JOHN PRENTIS'S Store, in Williamsburg,
An Exceeding Elegant
S P I N E T ,
in genteel Mahogony Case, with a Musick Desk, spare Wires, Quills, &c. This instrument is entirely new, and just imported in the *Virginia,* Captain *Esten.* The lowest Price is twenty two Pounds Currency.[48]

Philip Vickers Fithian, a plantation tutor in Virginia during 1773 and 1774, mentioned many musical instruments in his journal. In the following reference, the Colonel was Charles Carter, master of the plantation and father of several children who were being tutored by Fithian.

---

46. *The Virginia Gazette,* September 5, 1751.
47. *Ibid.* (PD), January 7, 1773.
48. *Ibid.* (PD), May 27, 1773.

The Colonel told me last Evening that he proposes to make the vacant End of our School-Room, . . . a Concert-Room, to hold all his instruments of Music—As he proposes to bring up from *Williamsburg* his *Organ*, & to remove the *Harpsichord, Harmonica, Forte-piano, Guittar, Violin, & German-Flutes*, & make it a place for Practice, as well as Entertainment.[49]

The harmonica was described as "the musical glasses without water, framed into a complete instrument, capable of through bass and never out of tune."[50] Also known as Franklin's Armonica, named after its inventor, Benjamin Franklin, the instrument was "very popular both in England and America."[51] Fithian described the festivities at a social gathering, which included a ball for which "the Music was a French-Horn and two Violins."[52]

Music Scores

References to specific compositions, composers, and tunes were frequently found in the materials of the second half of the eighteenth century in Virginia. In the spring of 1756, Samuel Davies, a Presbyterian minister, "sent thanks to the London Society for Promoting Christian Knowledge for sending the Negroes Song Books."[53] The books were *Watts Psalms and Hymns*.[54] Not so specific was a letter dated 1769 from Ro. C. Nicholas of Williamsburg to John Norton of London ordering "six dozen in Octavo neatly bound with the new Version of Singing Psalms & the Virginia Arms impress'd on one of the Covers."[55] Other references, such as found in a letter written by Thomas Jefferson in 1762, gave only a vague idea of the

49. Hunter Dickinson Farish, ed., *Journal & Letters of Philip Vickers Fithian* (Williamsburg: Colonial Williamsburg, Inc., 1957), p. 51.
50. *Ibid.*, p. 243.
51. Sonneck, *Early Concert Life* . . . , p. 23.
52. Farish, ed., p. 57.
53. M. M. Fisher, *Negro Slave Songs* . . . , p. 9.
54. *Ibid.*
55. Mason, *John Norton* . . . , pp. 84–85.

types of music used in colonial Virginia: ". . . The cursed rats . . . carried away . . . half dozen new minuets I had just got, to serve, I suppose, as provision for the winter."[56]

Table 2 indicates that by 1770 a wide selection of music that was popular in England could be purchased from merchants in Virginia. Instrumental method books, instrumental sonatas and selections from operas, songs for the voice with instrumental accompaniment, and collections of hymns were among the popular offerings. The first advertisement of music for sale found in the *Virginia Gazette* does not identify specific compositions, but those advertisements beginning in 1771 present a more satisfactory list (Table 2) of music that was for sale in Virginia.

Table 2
VOCAL AND INSTRUMENTAL COMPOSITIONS: REFERENCES FROM *VIRGINIA GAZETTE* ADVERTISEMENTS 1766–1776

Printer and Date of Issue	*Music Advertised for Sale*[b]
(PD) July 25, 1766	Miller's solos
	Dothel's, Bate's Battma's, and Berg's duets
	airs
	Spanish and Italian duets, marches, minuets
	a choice collection of the newest airs and songs
	ruled books
	Tutors for . . . instruments (sold in Norfolk)
(PD) November 29, 1770 . .	Instructors for the violin and flute
	Beggars Opera
	Love in a Village
	The Padlock

b. Advertisements pertain to Williamsburg and vicinity unless a location in parentheses indicates otherwise.

---

56. Koch, *Writings of Jefferson*, p. 351.

A great variety of other musick by the best masters

Blank musick books

(PD) December 13, 1770 ...Musical Dictionary

(PD) August 29, 1771 .....Instructions for the Harpsichord, violin, and German flute

Pasquali's Thorough Bass for the Harpsichord

Baccherini and Burgess Senior's Lessons for the Harpsichord

Midas, the Padlock, and Love in a Village; for the Harpsichord, Voice, German Flute, and Hautboy

Periodical Overtures for the Harpsichord, Piano Forte &c.

Eight Italian Sonatas for two violins or Flutes, with a thorough bass for the Harpsichord, by several eminent composers

Fisher's Minuets, with Variations for the Harpsichord

Pasquali, Campioni, . . . Pugnani, Florio, Lates, and Richter's Sonatas

Stamitz's Concertos, Duets, and grand orchestra trios.

Gasparini's trios

Vivaldi's cuckoo concertos

(PD) April 23, 1772 ......New Music, both dances and songs

(PD) December 3, 1772 ...The Storer, or the American Syren; being a collection of the newest and most approved SONGS

(PD) June 10, 1773 ....Several choice Pieces of Musick

(D) December 9, 1775 .....The Masque, a new Collection of the best English, Scotch, and Irish Songs, Catches, Duets, and Cantatas

The London Songster, or polite Musical Companion, to which are added a genteel collection of the various Toasts, Sentiments, and *Hob Nobs* now in Fashion

The Robin, or Ladies polite Songster

Allan Ramsay's collection of Scotch Songs

(D) February 24, 1776 . . . . . Harmonia Sacra, or a choice Collection of Psalm & Hymn Tunes
(P) August 16, 1776 . . . . *Watt's* Hymns and Psalms Psalters
(sold in Gloucester County)
(D) December 20, 1776 . . . . Watt's and Wesley's Hymns

That music was also ordered from England was shown by a letter and "invoices of Goods to be sent to York River on Acct. of Cole Digges Senr." in 1771, which included the following music: "Martini's Sonatas, Campioni's Sonatas, —do—Solo—, Lampugani's Sonatas, . . . and Handel's Water Piece."[57]

Fithian mentioned several compositions that were performed by the Carters in their home where he was a tutor.[58] Mentioned twice was "Water Parted from the Sea," by Thomas Arne and from the opera *Artaxerxes.*[59] A dance tune called "Felton's Gavotte" and another called the "Trumpet Minuet" were also mentioned by Fithian.[60] William Felton, composer of the Gavotte, was "an English clergyman . . . well known in the eighteenth century as a composer and performer on the harpsichord and organ."[61] Fithian wrote that "Mr. Carter is Learning 'Bedford,' 'Coles Hill,' and several other Church Tunes, and . . . the Colonel [Carter] shew'd me a book of vocal music which he has just imported, it is a collection of Psalm-Tunes, Hymns, & Anthems set in four parts for the Voice."[62] Fithian catalogued all of Carter's Library, but the music was listed only as "17 Volumes of Music by various Authors."[63]

57. Mason, *John Norton* . . . , pp. 156–57.
58. Farish, ed.
59. *Ibid.,* pp. 37, 132.
60. *Ibid.,* pp. 30, 71.
61. *Ibid.,* p. 425.
62. *Ibid.,* pp. 42, 127. A version of "Bedford" may be found in hymnals of today. Two are: *The Hymnal of the Protestant Episcopal Church in the United States* (Norwood, Mass.: The Pimpton Press, 1943) , hymn number 116; *At Worship, A Hymnal for Young Churchmen* (New York: Harper Brothers, 1951) , hymn number 7.
63. Farish, ed., p. 221.

Periodically, the *Virginia Gazette* printed poetry in a column called "Poet's Corner." Table 3 lists those poems that were called songs and that designated a tune to be used in singing.

Table 3
REFERENCES TO TUNES USED BY BALLAD WRITERS:
FROM THE *VIRGINIA GAZETTE*

Printer and date of issue	Title and Tune
(PD) May 14, 1772	"Song, Ad Infinitum Tune, Which Nobody can deny"
(P) October 6, 1774	"The Glorious Seventy Four, A new Song to the tune of Hearts of Oak" "An American Parody on the old Song of 'Rule Britannia'"
(P) January 12, 1775	"A Song, to the tune of 'Last Sunday Morning We sail'd from Cork'"
(P) February 23, 1775	"A new Song, to the tune of the Prussian Hero"
(P) June 15, 1775	"A Song to the tune of 'The Echoing Horn'"
(P) July 6, 1775	"Liberty, A new Song, to the tune of Hearts of Oak"
(D) July 15, 1775	"Fish and Tea, A New Song to an old tune"[c]
(P) July 27, 1775	"An extempore Song, composed by a jovial company, to the tune of 'A Light heart and a thin pair of breeches through the world, brave boys.'"
(D) July 29, 1775	"A New Song on the present critical times, by J. W. Hewlings, to the tune of 'Hearts of Oak.'"[d]
(P) August 17, 1775	"A Junto Song to the tune of a begging we will go, we'll go, &c."
(D) February 24, 1776	"A New Song to the tune of the British Grenadiers."

c. The words are those of "What a Court Hath Old England" from *Ballads of the Revolution Sung by Wallace House With Guitar* (Folkways Records Album Number FP48-1, 48-2, FP5001 Copyright 1953 by Folkways Records and Service Corp., 117 W. 46 Street, N. Y. C.).

d. The words are those of the "Liberty Song," from *Ballads of the Revolution Sung by Wallace House. . . .*

(D) November 22, 1776 ....."American Song, to the tune of 'The
                                Watery God.'"
(D) March 14, 1777 ...."A New War Song by Sir Peter Par-
                                ker written, and printed in London.
                                Tune—'Well met, Brother Tar.'"

The tune "Hearts of Oak" is listed three times in Table
3, each of the other tunes is mentioned only once.[64] Fithian
described the singing of ballads such as those in Table 3.

> About Seven the Ladies & Gentlemen begun to dance in the
> Ball-Room. . . . But all did not join in the Dance for there
> were parties in Rooms made up, some at Cards; some drink-
> ing for Pleasure; some toasting the Sons of America; some
> singing "Liberty Songs" as they call'd them, in which six,
> eight, ten or more would put their heads together and roar,
> & for the most part as unharmonious as an affronted—[65]

The practice of printing ballads in the newspapers continued throughout the eighteenth century, and ballads that
were printed in the Richmond newspapers after 1780 are
included in Chapter 2.

Instruction in Music

At one end of colonial Virginia's social structure were
the ladies and gentlemen who employed itinerant music
masters to visit their homes to give instruction in music,
and at the other end were the slaves who received instructions in singing church music.

Cuthbert Ogle, who advertised in the *Virginia Gazette*
in 1755, was one of the mid-eighteenth-century music
tutors in Virginia.

---

64. "Hearts of Oak" by William Boyce and various versions of the
other tunes may be found in William Arms Fisher, *The Music that
Washington Knew* (Boston: Oliver Ditson Company, Inc., 1931); and in
William Chappell, *Popular Music of the Olden Time* (London: Cramer,
Beale, and Chappell, 1859).
65. Farish, ed., p. 57. Fithian terminates the sentence with a dash
and does not apprize the reader of the object being affronted.

The Subscriber, living at Mr. Nicholson's, in Williamsburg, proposes to teach Gentlemen and Ladies to play on the Organ, Harpsichord or Spinett; and to instruct those Gentlemen that play on other Instruments, so as to enable them to play in Concert. Upon having Encouragement, I will fix in any Part of the Country.

Cuthbert Ogle[66]

Maurer found that Ogle died less than a month after the above advertisement appeared in the *Gazette*.[67]

Ogle possessed a library that was distinctly English. Much of it was not "great" music, but it was the music that was being played and sung by English amateurs and professionals. Ogle had Handelian classics but he also had catches by Purcell and Blow, music for a Harlequin pantomime, and songs by Granom and Leveridge.[68]

He also owned much music by the organist-composers of eighteenth-century England, and his library included music by Alberti, Corelli, Hasse, and others.[69]

During the 1770s, Francis Russworm taught "young Gentlemen" in and about Williamsburg . . . "the Violin, German and Common Flutes," and he taught the "young Ladies . . . to dance a Minuet after the newest and most fashionable method."[70] Mrs. Neill proposed to teach the "young Ladies . . . Reading, Needle work, . . . and the Guittar" in Williamsburg.[71] Thomas Sterling and Thomas Hookins advertised that they "would willingly learn any Number of Boys the MILITARY MUSICK of the FIFE and Drum . . ." in Alexandria, Virginia.[72]

---

66. *The Virginia Gazette,* March 28, 1755.
67. Maurer Maurer, "The Library of a Colonial Musician, 1755," *The William and Mary Quarterly,* III (October, 1950) , 39–52.
68. *Ibid.*
69. *Ibid.*
70. *Ibid.* (PD) , May 16, 1771.
71. *Ibid.* (D) , December 20, 1776, and July 4, 1777.
72. *Ibid.* (D) , June 17, 1775.

Philip Vickers Fithian, the previously mentioned tutor to the Carter family at Nomini Hall plantation in Northern Virginia, was an amateur flutist. In his journal Fithian left an intimate record of the musical life in the Carter home. The music master who periodically came to instruct the Carter children in music for several days at a time was referred to only as "Mr. Stadley." Stadley also taught in a number of other homes in the Northern Neck of Virginia, and before coming to Virginia, he had taught music in New York and Philadelphia. Stadley was apparently held in high esteem by his associates. Fithian wrote: "After breakfast Mr. Stadley left us; I feel always Sorry when he leaves the Family; his entire good-Nature, Cheerfulness, Simplicity, & Skill in Music have fixed him firm in my esteem. . . ."[73] Stadley taught the violin, flute, harpsichord, and pianoforte. One of the Carter children learned the guitar under the direction of her father rather than from Stadley because, as Fithian expressed it, "Mr. Stadley does not understand playing on the Guitar."[74] Fithian wrote that his own playing and the playing of one of Carter's sons was "like Crows among Nightingales" when compared with Stadley.[75] Fithian also compares the playing of a visiting young lady with other amateur ladies of his time and gives his impression of the attitude of Virginia girls toward playing music.

> Miss Washington [Niece of George Washington, daughter of Colonel John Augustine Washington] is about seventeen. . . . She plays well on the Harpsichord, & Spinet; understands the principles of Musick, & therefore performs her Tunes in perfect time, a Neglect of which always makes music intolerable, but it is a fault almost universal among young ladies in the practice; She sings likewise to her instrument, has a strong, full voice, & a well-judging Ear; but most of the Virginia-

---

73. Farish, ed., p. 189.
74. *Ibid.*, p. 79.
75. *Ibid.*, p. 82.

Girls think it labour quite sufficient to thump the Keys of a Harpsichord into the air of a tune mechanically, & think it would be Slavery to submit to the Drudgery of acquiring Vocal Music. . . .[76]

Judging from Fithian's comments, excellent instruction was being given in Psalm and hymn singing, and the congregational participation was quite different from that of his home in Cohansie, New Jersey.

I rode to Ucomico-Church, I was surprised when the Psalm begun, to hear a large Collection of voices singing at the same time, from a Gallery, entirely contrary to what I have seen before in the Colony, for it is seldom in the fullest Congregation's, that more sing than the Clerk, & about two others! —I am told that a singing Master of good abilities has been among this society lately & put them on the respectable Method which they, at present Pursue—[77]

Some young gentlemen from the colony went to England to study. The "Rev. B. Booth's Academy . . . at Woolton, five miles from Liverpool" advertised in the *Virginia Gazette* in 1766 that young gentlemen were taught "English, Latin, Greek, Writing, Arithmetick, . . . Musick, Dancing, and Fencing."[78]

Previously, mention was made of Samuel Davies who came to Virginia in 1748 and began evangelistic work with slaves. He is said to have "utilized music to encourage Negroes to cheerfulness and to counteract their militancy."[79] Reports on Davies' teaching indicate that he was highly successful and received much personal satisfaction from his work. He was reported to have said that "the Negroes . . . have an ear for music, and a kind of ecstatic delight in Psalmody; and there are no books they learn so soon, or take so much pleasure in, as these used in that

76. *Ibid.*, pp. 123–24.
77. *Ibid.*, p. 195.
78. *The Virginia Gazette* (PD), November 27, 1766.
79. Fisher, *Negro Slave Songs* . . . , p. 29.

heavenly part of divine worship."[80] The origin of the spiritual, "Lord, I want to be a Christian," has been attributed to the slaves who received Christian and musical instruction from Davies during the 1750s in Virginia.[81]

Thomas Jefferson indicated that he too was impressed by the Negroes' musical talents. "In music they are generally more gifted than the white. . . ."[82] The Hanover Presbytery of Virginia seriously considered utilizing the Negroes' musical talent by "purchasing slaves and having infant slaves baptized for choir duties," but there is no record of action taken beyond the original consideration of the idea as recorded in the Presbytery's journal of October 26, 1780.[83]

Since it is known that slaves were given instruction in the singing of church music, it is not surprising that an advertisement was printed in a Richmond newspaper in 1782 as follows:

Ran away from the subscriber, in Chesterfield County, . . . on the 1st of May, 1781, when the British troops were there, . . . Daniel, . . . and Dinah. . . . The above Negroes much given to singing hymns.[84]

The Theatre
Research for this study has disclosed the existence of a close alliance between the theatre and music partially because records of theatrical events have been preserved, whereas other events were either not recorded or records have been lost. Therefore, the following sketch of the development of the theatre in America was found to be useful in understanding the events of the pre-revolutionary

---

80. *Ibid.*
81. *Ibid.*, p. 30.
82. Koch, *Writings of Jefferson*, p. 258.
83. Fisher, *Negro Slave Songs . . .*, p. 38.
84. *The Virginia Gazette, or, the American Advertiser,* June 22, 1782.

period in Virginia and the post-revolutionary period in Richmond.

Sonneck indicates that the introduction of plays to American audiences was probably made in 1703 in Charleston, South Carolina, and that the first opera advertised for performance was also at Charleston in 1735.[85] *Flora, or Hob in the Well* and *The Devil to Pay* were both performed in Charleston in 1736, and other than a brief episode there the following year, "no further references to theatrical affairs appear in the old sources until 1749 . . ." with the exception of those acted in Philadelphia "by changeable figures two feet high."[86] There were plays by live actors in Philadelphia in 1749, and these actors moved to New York in 1750.[87] Apparently the same group of actors, who were known as the New York Company of Comedians, moved to Williamsburg in 1751, where they built a play house and held performances.[88]

In 1752 the *Virginia Gazette* announced:

We are desired to inform the Publick. That as the Company of Comedians, lately from London, have obtain'd His Honor the Governor's Permission, and have, with great Expense, entirely altered the Play-House at Williamsburg to a regular theatre, fit for the Reception of Ladies and Gentlemen, and the Execution of their own Performances, they intend to open on the first Friday in September next, with a Play, call'd The Merchant of Venice, (written by Shakespear) and a Farce, call'd the Anatomist, or Sham Doctor. The Ladies are desired to give timely Notice to Mr. Hallam, at Mr. Fisher's, for their places in the Boxes, and on the Day of Performance to send their Servants early to keep them, in order to prevent Trouble or Disappointment.[89]

85. O. G. Sonneck, *Early Opera in America* (New York: G. Schirmer, Inc., 1915) , pp. 5–12.
86. *Ibid.,* p. 14.
87. *Ibid.,* p. 13.
88. *Ibid.,* p. 17.
89. *The Virginia Gazette*, August 21, 1752.

The London Company of Comedians received their financial backing from William Hallam of London and were
under the management of Lewis Hallam, brother of the
London financier. This same London Company later became the American Company and still later the Old American Company that played in Richmond after the American Revolution. Sonneck states that the London Company
of Comedians stayed in Williamsburg 11 months during
the years 1752–53, and that Peter Pelham was their
Harpsichordist.[90]

Since the London Company is known to have performed
opera and music between the acts of plays in New York
in 1753 and 1754, it is reasonable to assume that some of
the same musical performances were given in Virginia.
However, the first orchestra known to have accompanied
an opera in America was made of a "Set of Private Gentlemen" in upper Marlborough, Maryland, in 1752; and
having found no additional evidence concerning the Williamsburg performances, the writer assumes that the Virginia opera of the 1750s was accompanied by a lone harpsichord. Few records exist that give clues to the nature and
identification of the musician accompanists for two reasons: first, the newspaper advertisements that have been
preserved neglect many of the details of the performances,
and second, the playbills that might have carried such
information have not been preserved.

David Douglass assumed the leadership of the London
Company on the death of Hallam, and at the end of the
1760–61 season, Douglass left Virginia with "a recom-
mendation signed by the Governor, Council, and one hundred of the principal gentlemen of Virginia. . . ."[91]
Douglass' company was again in Virginia in 1762 and in
1763. Sonneck found that "a Virginia Company performed

90. Sonneck, *Early Opera* . . . , p. 19.
91. *Ibid.*, p. 31.

in Williamsburg in 1768 with Mr. Pelham and others to conduct the orchestra."[92] Little is known about the Virginia Company of 1768, but it was apparently unrelated to the Virginia Company that played in Richmond and other southern cities during the last decade of the eighteenth century. The American Company (formerly the London Company) was in Williamsburg again and also in Fredericksburg in 1771.

Sonneck lists a large number of English operas that were performed in the key cities in eastern America during the eighteenth century, and it is known that musical entertainment between the acts of plays was part of the standard fare of theatrical companies during the century. In 1772 the theatre in Williamsburg advertised "A CURIOUS SET OF FIGURES," which were to "appear on the stage as if alive, and . . . a set of WATERWORKS representing the SEA, and all manner of SEA MONSTERS sporting on the waves. . . ." The advertisement concluded with:

N.B. Between the acts will be instrumental music, consisting of *French* horns and trumpets.[93]

Theatrical and musical entertainments were curtailed in Virginia during the Revolution but were resumed after the war, at which time Richmond became a center for cultural and entertainment activities.

Concerts and Musicians

Beginning in 1766, several concerts were advertised in the *Virginia Gazette*. Each concert was to be followed by a ball. The first of these affairs offered "a genteel Supper, and Liquor suitable for such an occasion" in addition to the concert and ball. The newspaper advertisement stated that the event was to take place in Fredericksburg, and

92. *Ibid.*, p. 44.
93. *The Virginia Gazette* (R), November 19, 1772.

"several of the best Hands in Virginia" were to "assist in the Concert."[94] The advertisement also listed the instrumentation as "3 violins, 1 Tenor, 1 Bass, 2 Flutes, 1 Hautboy, 1 Horn, and 1 Harpsichord."[95] A similar advertisement of a concert and ball was printed a year later, but supper and liquor were not part of the fare.[96] The next two concerts advertised in the *Virginia Gazette* had obvious similarities, each being "a concert of instrumental music by Gentlemen of note, for their own amusement," and each was to be followed by a ball.[97] One was to be at King William courthouse in October 1768 and the other at Hanover Town in May 1769. The advertisement of the latter concert stated: "It is requested by the Ladies, that the company may be governed by a becoming silence and decorum, during the performance."[98]

Virginia's Peter Pelham, Junior, was the son of the Peter Pelham whose concert in Boston in 1731 was "the first public concert in any of the English speaking colonies."[99] Pelham's name is frequently mentioned in the musical records of the pre-revolutionary era, and he may have been considered the most prominent of the Virginia musicians of his day.

Peter Pelham is a fine example of the type of musician who contributed much to the social and cultural life of the American people in the eighteenth century—yet could not make a living at music alone. He played the organ in the church and the harpsichord in the theatre, gave lessons, sold music, and helped Virginia families select instruments for their homes. But, despite Virginia's wealth and love of music, all these activities did not give him a living. Thus Williamsburg's leading musician served as a committee clerk for the House of Burgesses, helped supervise the printing of notes

94. *Ibid.* (R), December 11, 1766.
95. *Ibid.*
96. *Ibid.* (R), December 24, 1767.
97. *Ibid.* (R), October 27, 1768, and (R), May 11, 1769.
98. *Ibid.* (R), May 11, 1769.
99. Howard, pp. 22–23.

and currency, kept a store . . . and he was Keeper of the
Public Gaol for many years.[100]

Several other musician-teachers mentioned before were
Samuel Davies, Cuthbert Ogle, Frances Russworm, and
Mrs. Neill. Not previously mentioned was Francis Alberti, teacher of Thomas Jefferson and his family. The
same Alberti may have played in the concert at Fredericksburg in 1769. The advertisement stated: "Tickets to be
had, at a dollar each, of Mr. Thomas Tinsley in Hanover
Town, Mr. Lewis Jordan at Hanover court-house, and of
Francis Albertie."[101] Even though the concert was advertised as being played by gentlemen for their own amusement, the possibility that professional musicians were assisting the gentlemen is not unlikely, and perhaps Tinsley
and Jordan were also musician-teachers. In 1778, Thomas
Jefferson wrote a letter from Williamsburg to Alberti
who had returned to Italy. In the letter Jefferson berated
all music in his country.

> . . . If there is a gratification, which I envy any people in
> this world, it is to your country its music. This is the favorite
> passion of my soul, and fortune has cast my lot in a country
> where it is in a state of deplorable barbarism.[102]

Jefferson's primary purpose in writing this letter appears
to have been to inquire about the possibilities of hiring
a group of servant musicians from Italy.

> . . . The bounds of an American fortune will not admit the
> indulgence of a domestic band of musicians, yet I have
> thought that a passion for music might be reconciled with
> that economy which we are obliged to observe. I retain
> among my domestic servants a gardener, a weaver, a cabinet-
> maker, and a stone-cutter, to which I would add a *vigneron*.

---

100. Maurer Maurer, "The 'Professor of Musick' in Colonial America,"
The Musical Quarterly, XXXVI, 4 (October, 1950), 511–24.
101. *The Virginia Gazette* (R), May 11, 1769.
102. Koch, *Writings of Jefferson*, pp. 262–64.

In a country where, like yours, music is cultivated and practiced by every class of men, I suppose there might be found
persons of these trades who could perform on the French
horn, clarinet, or hautboy, and bassoon, so that one might
have a band of two French horns, two clarinets, two hautboys,
and a bassoon, without enlarging their domestic expenses.
A certainty of employment for a half dozen years, and at the
end of that time, to find them, if they chose, a conveyance
to their own country, might induce them to come here on
reasonable wages.[103]

This writer has found no evidence that Jefferson was successful in his venture to form an Italian servant band.

Among the renegade musicians in Virginia was Charles
Love, singer, violinist, and "hautboisist," who was wanted
in Virginia in 1757 "for running away from . . . Philipp
Ludwell Lee with a . . . very good bassoon."[104] Also Vin-
cent Hudson, a lad who "sounds the fife well, for which
he was enlisted," was wanted as a deserter from "the 7th
Virginia regiment of continental forces. . . ."[105] Soldier
musicians may have been scarce during the first phases of
the Revolution. There were advertisements for "a DRUM-
MER and FIFER, who can teach others the Duty," and a
"Person, well qualified, who will undertake to be FIFE-
MAJOR" to a regiment.[106]

The St. Cecilia Society of Charleston, South Carolina,
evidently thought there were some good musicians in Virginia who might accept the Society's offer to engage "a
first and second Violin, two Hautboys, and a Bassoon."
The advertisement, placed in the *Virginia Gazette,* stated
that the Society "will engage with, and give suitable Encouragement to, Musicians properly qualified to perform
at their Concert. . . ."[107]

---

103. *Ibid.*
104. Sonneck, *Early Opera* . . . , p. 26.
105. *The Virginia Gazette* (P), June 13, 1777.
106. *Ibid.* (Pi), September 28, 1775, and (P), July 19, 1776.
107. *Ibid.* (PD), July 18, 1771.

At the end of the Colonial period, Virginia's population had begun to move westward, and a new site for the capital city had been chosen. Richmond, the new capital, was destined to inherit a role of leadership of the culture acquired by the colonists and was to become a center for cultural activities of Virginians, many of whom would be immigrants of various European lineages.

Chapter 2

The Emergence of a New Center of Music Culture, 1780-1799

When Richmond was chartered as a city in 1782, it comprised about 300 houses. In reality it was a village. The first United States census taken nine years later showed that the city of Richmond had a smaller population than most counties in the state, its population being given as 3,716 persons, nearly half of whom were slaves.[1] Up to that time, the most practical public transportation was by water, and for many years thereafter, most of the entertainers and musicians who visited the city came on shipboard. Planters, with or without their ladies, came by boat, on horseback, or by horse and carriage from the surrounding areas for business; and with Richmond residents they attended the races, the balls, the theatre, the taverns, and perhaps church services. On those occasions they heard or sang old familiar tunes, some with new words

1. *The Virginia Gazette and General Advertiser,* September 28, 1791. All newspaper citations in Chapters 2 through 5 are Richmond publications unless otherwise specified.

printed on broadsides, and they heard new music brought from England in a relatively short time after the first English performance. The popular music of that day is said to be "now recognized as the only vital and truly native aspect of English eighteenth-century music."[2]

Music on Social and Public Occasions

Virginians were fond of dancing, and a celebration or social gathering was frequently concluded with a ball. The first large formal social affair noted in a Richmond newspaper was held to celebrate the official termination of the American Revolutionary War.

> On Thursday evening last an elegant Ball was given by the Hon. GENERAL ASSEMBLY, to celebrate the arrival of the Definitive Treaty, to which was invited a large and respectable company, who made a very brilliant appearance; and it is with pleasure that we communicate the regularity and good order by which it was conducted, and the satisfaction that was so expressive in every countenance.[3]

Celebrations in honor of St. John the Evangelist and St. John the Baptist held by the Masons included processions between their lodge and the church and were concluded with a ball in the evening.[4] By 1788 the Masons were accompanied on their processions by a "band of music."[5] St. Patrick's Day was celebrated in 1787 with "an elegant Ball at the Capitol, where there was a brilliant assembly of upwards of 400 Ladies and Gentlemen from the City and its vicinity, and the evening was spent in the utmost decorum and festivity."[6]

2. Paul Henry Lang, *Music in Western Civilization* (New York: W. W. Norton and Company, Inc., 1941), p. 683.

3. *The Virginia Gazette, or the American Advertiser*, December 20, 1873.

4. *Ibid.*, January 3, 1784, and *The Virginia Gazette and Weekly Advertiser*, January 3 and June 26, 1788.

5. *The Virginia Gazette and Weekly Advertiser*, June 26, 1788.

6. *The Virginia Independent Chronicle*, January 10, 1787.

The customary fall races had been discouraged but not altogether discontinued during the war. In 1784, races were held from Tuesday to Thursday during a week in October and were concluded with a ball at the Capitol.[7] By 1789 a ball and a supper were given each night of the races, and by the next year "a commodious house" built to accommodate visitors to the races had been so arranged that ladies might "attend the Balls without going out."[8]

Mordecai devotes several pages to descriptions of the "Race Ball" and the Negro musicians, Sy Gilliat and London Brigs, who were the principal performers for those events before and after the turn of the century.[9] Gilliat played the fiddle; Brigs played the clarinet and the flute. Gilliat is described as "the most prominent member of the black aristocracy" of Richmond, holding the position of sexton in the Episcopal Church until he was "impelled to resign it in a fit of unrighteous indignation, excited by hearing that he was suspected of partaking of the wine without the other ceremonies of the sacrament."[10] The *minuet de la cour,* contra dances, and sometimes a congo or a hornpipe were played and danced at the Race Ball, according to Mordecai.

Washington's birthday became an occasion for exuberant celebration. Yearly, beginning in 1788 or earlier, the day was ushered in by the firing of cannon. Parades during the day were followed by feasts and toasting in the taverns. The celebrations usually concluded with a "grand" ball, with most of the eighteenth-century Washington's birthday balls being held in the Eagle Tavern, but the new Capitol

7. *The Virginia Gazette, or the American Advertiser,* October 30, 1784.
8. *The Virginia Gazette and Weekly Advertiser,* October 8, 1789; and the *Virginia Gazette and General Advertiser,* September 29, 1790.
9. Samuel Mordecai, *Richmond in By-Gone Days,* Republished from the Second Edition of 1860 (Richmond: The Dietz Press, 1946), pp. 253-57.
10. *Ibid.*

also became a ballroom for the occasion in 1789.[11]

Balls were also held as social functions with no special cause to celebrate. Citizens of Richmond were invited to meet at the Eagle Tavern "in order to establish rules, and to appoint managers" for the dancing assemblies to be held during 1794–1795.[12] The assemblies were reorganized yearly throughout the decade.

Singing enjoyed a popularity perhaps equal to that of dancing. The writing and singing of ballads for social gatherings was an eighteenth-century and early-nineteenth-century gentlemanly pastime. Persons professing talent for writing poetry had their verses published on broadsides so that their patriotic, humorous, sentimental, or political expressions could be disseminated through song. Hymn writing was analogous to ballad writing, the subject being sacred rather than secular. Whereas hymns were sung in the home, in church, and at the turn of the century at camp meetings, ballads were sung in taverns and at political meetings. Writers of ballads and hymns sometimes specified tunes to be used in singing their poetry, but frequently no tune was indicated. A common procedure of hymn writers was to indicate the meter only, the tune being left to the discretion of the person who led the singing.

Ballads were sometimes sung throughout America within a few weeks after they had been written. In connection with an article on Washington's birthday, a Richmond newspaper published a ballad copied from the *New York Gazeteer*. The ballad is of interest because the meter fits "God Save the King" and suggests that the tune now known in this country as "America" was adopted by American patriots soon after the end of the Revolutionary War.

---

11. *The Virginia Gazette and Weekly Advertiser*, February 12, 1789.
12. *The Virginia Gazette and General Advertiser*, December 10, 1794.

Tune—"God Bless America"

Americans rejoice,
While song employ each voice,
    Let trumpets sound.
The thirteen stripes display,
In flags and streamers gay,
'Tis Washington's birth day,
    Let joy abound.

   . . . .[13]

While the United States Constitution was being formulated, a Richmond newspaper published an item in its
poetry column that begins as follows:

To the tune of a Cobler there was and he liv'd in a stall.

A plan is propos'd and it comes from Great-Britain,
The prettiest scheme that ever was hit on!
Our Minister there has told us fine things
Of the Parliament House and advantages of Kings.
    Derry down, down, down derry down.

   . . . .[14]

The poetry continued as a political satire intimating that
John Adams favored a monarchy over the form of government then being formulated for the United States.

One ballad published in a Richmond newspaper was "A
Hymn composed for the 19th of February, 1795—recommended to those who may approve of it." The poetry was
signed and dated: Robert Symmetrian, Richmond, February 15, 1795.

---

13. *The Virginia Gazette, or American Advertiser,* March 20, 1784.
14. *The Virginia Independent Chronicle,* August 8, 1787. Several versions of this tune are given by William Chappell, *Popular Music of the
Olden Time,* 2 vols. (London: Cramer, Beale, and Chappell, 1859).

> Look to the Lord, Americans,
> And bless His name, Republicans,
> For all his mercies here below
> Which he continues to bestow.
>
> . . . .[15]

In addition to patriotic and political topics, the news-papers published sentimental and comic songs written by both professional and amateur writers. When *The Poor Soldier* was performed in Richmond's Academy Theatre in 1787, the *Virginia Gazette and Weekly Advertiser* published the words to all of the songs of that ballad opera.[16]

Some tunes that were used in singing ballads may be traced with reasonable accuracy, but for some titles there are numerous variations of melodies. The better-known ballad and dance tunes of eighteenth-century America are published in a collection by William Arms Fisher.[17] Other sources for identifying English, Irish, and Scotch tunes that may have been sung in eighteenth-century Richmond are compilations by Chappell, Moffat, O'Neill, and Pittman.[18]

Music Merchantry and Instruction

A knowledge of the availability of music instruction, music scores, and instruments gives some indication of

---

15. *The Virginia Gazette and General Advertiser*, February 18, 1795.
16. March 8, 1787, March 15, 1787, March 22, 1787, and March 27, 1787. The score of Shield's *The Poor Soldier* is held by the Music Division of the Library of Congress.
17. W. A. Fisher, *The Music That Washington Knew* . . . .
18. William Chappell, *National English Airs*, 2 vols. (London: Chappell, Music-Seller to Her Majesty, 1840) ; William Chappell, *Old English Music*, 2 vols. (London: Chappell and Co., 1893) ; William Chappell, *Popular Music of the Olden Time* . . . ; Alfred Moffat, *The Minstrelsy of Ireland* (London: Augener and Co., 1897) ; Francis O'Neill, *Irish Folk Music* (Chicago: The Regan Printing House, 1910) ; and J. Pittman *et al.*, *Songs of Scotland* (London: Boosey and Company, 1877) .

music activity to be found in a locality. The lack of evidence indicating that music instruction and musical merchandise were available in Richmond until several years after the Revolutionary War suggests that the city lacked even the fundamental music supplies and services of a cultural center. Residents of Richmond apparently considered Williamsburg and Fredericksburg the closest sources of musical supplies, and ordering materials from London had been a common practice in Virginia before the war.

Merchantry

Other than an advertisement of toy violins for sale in Richmond in 1772, no musical instrument merchandise was offered for sale through newspapers until 1784.[19] In 1783 Thomas Brend, a bookbinder and stationer, had books and paper "fit for music" in his shop.[20] Matthew Wright, "at his store near the Capitol," possibly had the first supply of instruments in Richmond offered on the public market.[21] Wright advertised recently imported German flutes for sale. In the fall of that same year (1784), Montgomery and Allen imported and offered for sale: "German flutes and fiddles, fiddle strings, and music books, one Florio and Tacet's new [sic] invented German flute, with extra joints, silver keys and a neat mahogany case."[22] "A very fine toned Forte Piano, approved," could be had "for forty pounds currency" in 1784, and prospective buyers were instructed to "inquire of the printer."[23] Mr. Hayes' Printing office sold "song books, &c." during the

---

19. *The Virginia Gazette* (Williamsburg) (PD), November 11, 1772; and *The Virginia Gazette, or the American Advertiser*, April 3, June 26, and October 9, 1784.
20. *The Virginia Gazette, or the American Advertiser*, August 2, 1783.
21. *Ibid.*, April 3, 1784.
22. *Ibid.*, October 9, 1784.
23. *Ibid.*, June 26, 1784.

ensuing year.[24] Thomas Nicholson, printer of the *Virginia Gazette and Weekly Advertiser* placed the following notice in his paper for several months:

Just Published,
The Poor Soldier
A Comic Opera,
In two acts.[25]

Nicholson also advertised "one elegant violin, with case and spare strings—Twenty four dances and cotillions—also a variety of songs, set to music" just imported from London.[26] Included in a list of "an extensive and well selected fall assortment of goods" just imported from London were "Harpsichords, a Spinnet, and a Piano Forte, and Books of music for ditto" for sale by Warrington and Keene "on very reasonable terms, for CASH, TOBACCO, WHEAT, and PUBLIC SECURITIES at their current value."[27]

Apparently during the last decade of the eighteenth century, Richmond's amateur and professional musicians could find an adequate supply of pianofortes, spinets, harpsichords, violins, clarinets, hautboys, guitars, strings and other accessories, as well as music scores for instruments and voices. Several general merchandise stores and some individuals who were not merchants advertised keyboard instruments for sale during the last decade of the century. William Prichard opened a book store in Richmond in 1789. Selling a few instruments and music at first, he soon had a complete line of music and instruments. Prichard and Davidson, with whom he formed a partnership in 1795, operated the principal music store in Richmond until 1799.[28]

24. *Ibid.*, July 9, 1785.
25. May 17, 1787, *et al.*
26. *The Virginia Gazette and Weekly Advertiser*, April 3, 1788.
27. *Ibid.*, October 8, 1789.
28. *The Virginia Gazette and General Advertiser*, November 23, 1791, *et al.*

Instruction

Opportunities for music instruction in Richmond developed over a period of time chronologically corresponding to the growth of music merchantry in the city. The first person to advertise music lessons in Richmond was A. M. Quesnay, who had embarked on an ambitious plan in which he envisioned his Richmond Academy of Arts and Sciences as becoming the intellectual center of the South. Before an academy hall was built, Quesnay held classes in a home in Richmond.

> The different SCHOOLS of the ACADEMY are at present attended by M. Quesnay, next door to Capt. Mitchell's opposite to the Bridge. DRAWING, FRENCH, MUSIC, &c. are kept in the forenoon; the DANCING SCHOOLS in the afternoon. . . .[29]

In a year's time, the first building of the academy had been built, and Mr. R. Morris was "appointed a master to teach the young Ladies Tambour, Embroidery, Patterns, and all sorts of Needle work, also Vocal Music."[30] The academy hall was used not as a school room, but rather as a theatre, and the classes continued to meet in Quesnay's home—a situation that had been anticipated by Quesnay in his projected plans for developing the academy.

> As one chief encouragement to the Masters who shall be employed by Mr. Quesnay in the Academy, must flow from the public entertainments to be promoted therein, the price of teaching, from time to time, will greatly depend on the success of such entertainments, and the public favor that is extended to them.[31]

Supplies for the academy including "instruments of music and music books" were ordered and had arrived from Lon-

---

29. *The Virginia Gazette, or, the American Advertiser*, September 27, 1785.
30. *Ibid.*, August 30, 1786.
31. *Ibid.*, May 17, 1786.

don in November 1786, but the academy hall was still being used as a theatre.[32] Quesnay went to England and France seeking financial aid for his academy but apparently did not return to Richmond.[33] The academy hall continued to be used as a theatre for many years.[34]

The Richmond Academy of Arts and Sciences apparently ceased to function in December 1786, and soon thereafter a new teacher, Mr. Capus, announced that he would open a dancing school at the house on Shockoe Hill, "lately occupied by Mr. Quesnay. . . ."

> Mr. Capus moreover will take Scholars to instruct in MUSIC, viz: harpsichord, forte piano, violin, German flute, guitar, and violoncello.[35]

A year later, Jeremiah Moriarty was teaching dancing and "the use of the GLOBES" in Mr. Quesnay's house.[36] Capus continued to teach in Richmond for several years, relocating his school from time to time.[37] The principal dancing teacher of the last decade of the eighteenth century was Louis Roussell, who moved to Richmond from Baltimore in 1790. Judging from his numerous newspaper advertisements, Roussell operated a flourishing business in and around Richmond to the end of the century.[38]

Among other musicians who advertised as teachers of music in Richmond during the late-eighteenth-century period were John Widewilt and Mr. Garnet. Widewilt is

---

32. *Ibid.*, November 22, 1786.
33. *The Virginia Gazette and Weekly Advertiser*, September 11, 1788. An article tells of a speech made by Quesnay while in England. For detailed accounts of Quesnay's Academy see: Mordecai, p. 200, and Richard Heyward Gaines, *Richmond's First Academy* (Richmond: Virginia Historical Collections, 1891).
34. See Appendix A—Theatre.
35. *The Virginia Gazette and Weekly Advertiser*, January 4, 1787.
36. *The Virginia Independent Chronicle*, February 13, 1788.
37. *Ibid.*, March 5, 1788, *et al. The Virginia Gazette and General Advertiser*, October 13, 1790, *et al.*
38. *The Virginia Gazette and General Advertiser*, September 8, 1790, *et al.*

mentioned by Mordecai as a German "whose trumpet called the troops to horse" and as the owner of an island in the James River.[39] Widewilt announced that he would teach "the VIOLIN and GERMAN FLUTE, or any other instrument required" during the winter of 1789.[40] Mr. Garnet, a member of the theatre orchestra of West and Bignall's company, proposed to "give lessons on the violin, tenor violin, violoncello, flute, and clarinet" during his stay in the city.[41] In addition to performing in the theatre and giving music instruction, Garnet also tuned harpsichords and pianos.

Richmond may have had a piano manufactory during the last decade of the eighteenth century. James Juhan, who had been in Boston during 1768–70, in Charleston in 1771, and had exhibited his "great North American Forte Piano" in Philadelphia during 1783,[42] announced that he hoped to "meet with some encouragement in Manufacturing . . . Grand Piano Fortes" in Richmond.[43] He proposed to repair "stringed instruments of all kinds," to sell instruments and parts, and to make harpsichords, spinets, and guitars "if bespoke."[44] David Dunnenberay from Philadelphia, possibly an associate of Juhan, advertised that he would repair and quill harpsichords and put spinets and guitars in order.[45]

During the last two decades of the eighteenth century, Richmond developed its potentiality as a center of music culture from a state of primitiveness through a period of growth that provided the beginnings of instructional facilities and merchantry indicative of optimistic future growth.

---

39. Mordecai, p. 25.
40. *The Virginia Gazette and Weekly Advertiser,* October 8, 1789.
41. *The Virginia Gazette and General Advertiser,* October 2, 1793.
42. *Groves Dictionary, American Supplement,* p. 8.
43. *The Virginia Gazette and General Advertiser,* Extraordinary, October 17, 1792.
44. *Ibid.*
45. *The Virginia Gazette and General Advertiser,* May 20, 1793.

The Theatre

Toward the end of the colonial period, theatrical companies were well established in America, and they played to audiences in the principal cities of the eastern part of the country. On October 4, 1774, the Continental Congress resolved that theatrical and other forms of amusements should be discouraged during the war, but the cities controlled by the English, New York and Baltimore in particular, continued to provide outlets for the thespians' talents of the British Army and Navy. These actors "plied their trade between Baltimore and New York without interference from either belligerent."[46] Orchestras for the British military theatres were composed of the best musicians from several British regimental bands stationed in America.[47]

After the Revolutionary War, opera and other theatrical entertainments were again offered to American audiences in the principal cities of the country. The post-revolutionary theatrical performances in Philadelphia still went under the guise of "lectures, moral and entertaining" when the theatre was reopened there in 1784, and it was only after some verbal sparring over theatrical terminology that a play was called a play in New York in 1785. In Boston as late as 1792, the theatre was called the "New Exhibition Room," and "lectures, moral and entertaining" were the fare for the patrons. After some harassment by law enforcement officers who threatened to halt the actors' activities by enforcing the Boston theatrical prohibition act of 1750, a company was allowed to produce plays in 1793 without having to disguise them as lectures and concerts. The law against permitting theatrical entertainments in Rhode Island was not repealed until 1793.

Virginia and other southern colonies offered no such

46. Sonneck, *Early Opera* . . . , p. 57.
47. *Ibid.*

stringent resistance to the theatre, plays having been produced during the early eighteenth century, and operas as well as plays were given during the later colonial period at Williamsburg and in other Virginia localities. It is not surprising, then, to find that a theatrical company played a season in Richmond during 1784, and soon thereafter the theatre became well established.

The principal American theatrical company of the decade immediately following the war was that of Hallam and Henry, whose lineage is traced back to the London Company that played in America beginning in the mid-eighteenth century. The partnership of Hallam and Henry was formed in November 1785, and for seven years their Old American Company "controlled the amusement field from New York to Annapolis."[48] The Old Americans produced plays and operas in Richmond during 1786, but afterwards, when they journeyed to Philadelphia, they found it necessary to disguise their operas and plays as concerts and lectures. Sonneck lists 50 different operas, musical farces, pantomimes, and ballets "performed 'with the original overture and accompaniment' (as the term went) " by the Old American Company during the six-year period immediately following the formation of the partnership of Hallam and Henry.[49]

During the last decade of the eighteenth century, Richmond, along with several other southern cities, became a part of the circuit of an English company under the management of West and Bignall, and these actors and musicians dominated the theatrical scene in Richmond and in the south into the nineteenth century. The theatrical productions of the Old American Company, as well as those of West and Bignall and other companies that performed in America during the eighteenth century, were representative of the English stage and musical reper-

48. *Ibid.*, p. 67.
49. *Ibid.*, Table A, p. 77.

tory. These English operas were essentially plays interspersed with music, patterned after the *Beggar's Opera*, which was first produced in 1728 in London and enjoyed an immediate popularity that lasted throughout the century. Italian opera was not given in the United States until well into the nineteenth century, but English operas such as *Love in a Village* and *Lionel and Clarissa* included Italian music by Italian opera composers. Therefore, eighteenth-century American audiences got a taste of Italian opera music but did not hear entire operas in the Italian language. French music and musicians were represented on the stage and in the pit of the American theatre during the short-lived French migration to America. The migration, which took place during the mid-1790s, was due to the French Revolution and its aftermath in the West Indies. Except for this brief interlude, French music, musicians, and actors were, like the Italian music, absorbed into the English music and stage repertory of the eighteenth-century American theatrical companies. German musicians began to join the theatrical groups as members of the orchestra during the last decade of the century, and by the end of the century theatre orchestras, especially in the north, were composed of superior musicians of all nationalities.

The rigors of travel and the lack of adequate communication did not deter the eighteenth-century theatrical companies' activity. Audiences in Charleston, Richmond, Boston, and many points between were offered plays, operas, pantomimes, and other forms of musical entertainment that had been presented to London audiences only a short time before.

Richmond's First Theatre

Mordecai, Richmond's patriarch and probably most quoted historian, states that "the very first dramatic performance in Richmond was, as I have heard, in a wooden house, large in that day, which stood in the rear of the old jail . . ." [near what is now Eighteenth and Main Streets].[50] The lower portion of a playbill advertising a performance in this (the first) theatre is owned by the Virginia State Library. The playbill offers the earliest documentary evidence of a formal musical performance in Richmond and is the earliest known specimen of a Richmond playbill. The preserved portion of the playbill announces "A Favorite Song by Mrs. Lewis. To which (by desire) will be added a FARCE, called the CHEATS of SCAPIN."[51] The last line of the playbill states that "Good MUSIC is engaged."[52] From a knowledge of the customs of the day, and from the following additional information found on the playbill, it is known that the performance was for the benefit of an actor named Smith.

> The Ladies and Gentlemen who are disposed to befriend Mr. Smith, may not be deterred from coming, they may be assured, that every precaution is taken for the safety of the house, and Peace Officers are appointed to keep good order outside.[53]

The journey to and from the theatre in those days must have been a perilous one. From evidence reported by Christian, Stanard, and Shockley, it is known that Lewis and Smith were members of a company of comedians managed by Dennis Ryan that performed in Richmond in 1784.[54] Shockley's research established the date of Ryan's company in Richmond as June through December 1784, whereas other historians had reported an erroneous date

---

50. Mordecai, p. 200.
51. Playbill held by the Virginia State Library.
52. *Ibid.*
53. *Ibid.*
54. Asbury Christian, *Richmond, Her Past and Present* (Richmond: L. H. Jenkins, 1912), p. 22. Mary Newton Stanard, *Richmond, Its People and Its Story* (J. B. Lippincott Co., 1923), p. 45. Martin Staples Shockley, "The Richmond Theatre, 1780–1790," *The Virginia Magazine,* LX (July 1952), 421–36.

of 1783 for Ryan's visit. The following account of the first theatrical company to perform in Richmond has been constructed with the information furnished by the earliest known Richmond playbills, the research of Shockley, and information provided by Sonneck.[55]

Dennis Ryan became manager of the theatre in Baltimore in February 1783, and his company played in Baltimore through April of the same year. From Baltimore they went to Annapolis, then to New York, and finally returned to Baltimore where the company played from December 1783 to February 1784. Sonneck states that Ryan's company disappeared temporarily from Maryland after having added theatrical amusement to the races at Annapolis.[56] Ryan's company was probably in Richmond from June through December of 1784, because the records of the Common Hall show that he obtained permission to put on performances in June 1784, and that in December the Mayor was ordered to demand an accounting of plays performed and a payment of the tax thereof.[57] Ryan's company spent the first half of the ensuing year in Charleston, South Carolina, and was back in Baltimore in September 1785.[58] Soon thereafter, Ryan died, and the company disbanded. Sonneck states that the *Beggar's Opera* and *Love in a Village* were among the operas performed in Baltimore by Ryan's company soon before they came to Richmond. The Richmond playbill lists only four of the actors, and these same persons were also in Baltimore and played in *Love in a Village*.[59] It is reasonable to assume, therefore, that the *Beggar's Opera* and *Love in a Village* were performed in Richmond in 1784. These two operas were popular in England and America, and both were in the standard repertory of the American theatrical

---

55. Sonneck, *Early Opera* . . . , p. 60.
56. *Ibid.*
57. Shockley, *Ibid.*
58. Sonneck, *Early Opera* . . . , p. 62.
59. *Ibid.*

companies that were capable of performing operas.

Since little is known about the performances, the performers, or the repertoire of Ryan's company in Richmond, no conclusion may be drawn concerning the quality of the music offered to Richmond's citizens at that time, but since the company was apparently in or around Richmond for six months or more before moving to Charleston, it may be assumed that they offered their patrons enough entertainment to encourage that rather long residence.

Richmond's first theatre may have fallen into disuse for a while after Ryan's company left, but it was used again in the fall of 1787 and once more in 1788. In both instances the entertainment may have been under the management of a man named Villiers about whom little is known. In Virginia he was an actor-manager and artist, and during the last years of the century, a singer and comic actor named Villiers was performing in New England.[60] A Richmond newspaper announced in the fall of 1787:

> We hear from Petersburg that the New-Emissioned COMPANY OF COMEDIANS, under the old Veteran V_____s, shortly intend to show new and old faces in a new style at the Old Theatre in this city. And however strange it may appear—'tis said they are chiefly from Old and New England, and e'n part of the Old and New American Company of Comedians.[61]

The reference to the Old American Company of Comedians must have meant Hallam and Henry's company that had played at the new theatre in Richmond in 1786, and the New American Company probably referred to Ryan's company that had used that name. A double *entente* probably also implied that the Old American Company had played in the new theatre and the New American

---

60. Sonneck, *Early Opera* . . . , p. 214.
61. *The Virginia Independent Chronicle* (Richmond), October 10, 1787, p. 2.

Company had played in the old theatre. The old theatre was used again during the subsequent fall season when the following announcement was published:

EIDOPHUSIKON, OF MOVEING PICTURES

The subscribers are requested to take notice, the exhibition proposed, will open at the old theatre in this city. . . . The theater is already decorated, and fitted up, for the above occasion.[62]

The announcement also stated that the artist had been indisposed and the showing consequently had been delayed. An announcement printed later told of another postponement because the "artist . . . R. Villiers . . . has the dumb ague and so does the machinest (or rather carpenter)."[63] No further references to the old theatre in Richmond were found.

Richmond's Second Theatre

The Academy Hall Theatre, erected in 1786 as a result of the efforts of the ambitious Frenchman, A. M. Quesnay, was intended to be only part of a larger plan to establish a foremost academy in America. The theatre, which was to be the first building of many, proved to be the only one. After losing its identity as an adjunct to the academy, the theatre continued to be the center for music and drama for more than a decade. Mordecai called it "the first regular theatre opened in the city. . . ."[64]

The records of many activities in Richmond's second theatre are preserved in eighteenth-century Richmond newspapers. The building, referred to as the theatre on Shockoe Hill, the Academy Theatre, and the New Theatre, stood near the site of Richmond's third theatre.[65]

---

62. *The Virginia Gazette and Weekly Advertiser*, August 21, 1788.
63. *Ibid.*, September 4, 1788.
64. Mordecai, p. 200.
65. See Appendix A—The Theatre.

The first newspaper announcement concerning the use of the new theatre by professional actors and musicians was written by Quesnay, and it stated that Hallam and Henry were to use the "Hall of the Academy . . . as a theatre."[66] The same newspaper printed a news item stating that "the Old American Company of Comedians (under the direction of Messrs. Hallam and Henry) . . . has obtained permission to perform in this city next October when a spacious theatre on Shackoe [sic] Hill will be built for their reception. . . ."[67] Apparently the enterprising Quesnay had convinced Hallam and Henry that there was no need to build another theatre, as long as the Academy was available. Sonneck states that the Old American Company "opened on October 10, 1786, with the *Poor Soldier,* but it is not known when the first season of this curious enterprise closed."[68]

The second fall season in the new theatre was prefaced by three news items in a Richmond newspaper concerning the activities of Hallam and Henry in Philadelphia and in Baltimore.[68] One of the news items indicates that the company was not well received during its first season (fall 1786) in Richmond but that the second season should present an improvement.

> . . . We hear that they . . . have much improved their theatrical apparatus, having procured new scenery and other decorations, to render their house respectable and worthy [of] . . . public encouragement. We hear that in October they intend to pay a visit to this city, and it is hoped they will meet with better encouragement than before.[69]

The Richmond newspaper advertisements indicate that

---

66. *The Virginia Gazette, or the American Advertiser,* August 30, 1786.
67. *Ibid.*
68. Sonneck, *Early Opera* . . . , p. 185.
68. *The Virginia Gazette and Weekly Advertiser,* July 19, 1787; September 6, 1787; and September 20, 1787.
69. *Ibid.,* September 6, 1787.

a theatrical company played in the new theatre during November and December 1787, but Sonneck states that the names of the members of the cast "make it clear that the Old Americans had no part in the exhibition."[70] The company, which did not advertise its name, if it had one, presented dramas and "Comic Songs, &c. as will be expressed in the bills of the day."[71] The last newspaper advertisement of the 1787 company's activities was the most informative.

By Permission.
And the last night but ONE, of the Company's
Performing in this CITY.
For the benefit of Mr. Bisset,
    At the New Theatre (Shockoe-Hill)
On Friday Evening, December the 7th, 1787.
    will be PRESENTED the
    B E G G A R ' S   O P E R A
The characters by Mr. Kidd, Mr. Lewis, Mr. Wells, Mr. Lake, Mr. Bisset, Mr. Parsons, Mr. Rankin (being his first appearance on this stage), Mrs. Giffard, Miss Gordon, Mrs. Smallwood, Mrs. Parsons, and Polly by Mrs. Rankin (late Mrs. Remington, being her first appearance on the stage of this city, these last two years).
Between the play and Farce SINGING by Mr. BISSET, and Mr. WELLES.
To which will be added (by particular desire)
    MACKLIN'S celebrate FARCE OF
    LOVE A-LA-MODE

.   .   .   .
The whole to conclude with the Comic Song of "Four-and-twenty fiddlers all in a Row," by Mr. Bisset. . . .[72]

The above advertisement indicates that the company included more than a dozen members, that there must have been musical accompaniments and possibly an orchestra,

70. Sonneck, *Early Opera* . . . , p. 185.
71. *The Virginia Gazette and Weekly Advertiser*, November 8, 1787. Other advertisements by the same company but of different presentations are also in the issues of November 15, 1787; November 29, 1787; and in *The Virginia Independent Chronicle*, November 21, 1787.
72. *The Virginia Gazette and Weekly Advertiser*, December 6, 1787.

and that one of the actresses was known from her appearances in the city two years previously (which indicates that there was theatrical activity in Richmond during 1785). From a previous newspaper advertisement it is known that Mrs. Giffard, Mr. Kidd, and Mr. Welles were singers.[73] Therefore, including Bisset, there were four persons in the cast that at one time or another were featured as singers on the stage in Richmond. With the exception of Mr. Lewis, who was in Ryan's company in Richmond in 1784 and later with West and Bignall, the rest of the names were not found among those of the other eighteenth-century casts in Richmond nor in the larger cities in America. These facts substantiate Sonneck's contention that the company was not that of the Old Americans in spite of the preliminary announcements of their intended visit.

After the fall season of 1787, and with the exception of news items concerning the use of the academy theatre in 1788 by the State Convention, which met to ratify the United States Constitution, no further notices of activities in the theatre were found until the fall of 1790. Whereas there were two theatres in Richmond during the three-year period from 1784 through 1787, and several different theatrical companies performed a season each without returning; beginning in 1790 the New Theatre apparently became the only one in use, and it was visited annually by the same company.

The West and Bignall Company

West and Bignall, whose Virginia Company of Comedians returned each year to present a season of music and drama to Richmond audiences, made their first appearance in America in 1790. One of their early American performances was described in a letter to the printer of a Richmond newspaper, which was allegedly written by a

---

73. *Ibid.*, November 29, 1787.

resident of Petersburg. The letter is quoted in its entirety because of its unique style and because of the description given of the theatre event: both depict late-eighteenth-century customs.

Petersburg, August 30, 1790.

Mr. Davis.

Sir,

By inserting the following you will hold merit up to view, and oblige a constant reader of your very useful paper.

Last night I was attracted by the novelty of a handbill, to attend the exhibition of a new species of Entertainment, called the "Evening Brush"—'tis replete with laughter, sentiment, and satire without illiberality, and was recited and sung in a most masterly manner by Messrs. West & Bignall (who I am informed are just arrived from England). . . . The song of "Gad a mercy the Devil's in me," was received with great applause; at the conclusion of which, an universal encore ensued; and it was the acknowledged opinion of every one present, that he [Bignall] is the best performer on the Continent.

Mr. West attracted the notice of the audience in all his songs, particularly "Date Obolum Bellisario." A profound silence reigned during the song, at the end of which the most flattering applause resounded from every part of the house. . . .

I am informed the above Gentlemen are now on a tour through part of Virginia. . . .

I am convinced Richmond will prove a proper field for the display of their Theatrical Talents. . . .

An Inhabitant of the Town.[74]

West and Bignall's Virginia Company began their long association with Richmond audiences on October 21, 1790, after having been forced to "protract . . . the opening till the theatre was in every way completed for the reception of the Audience."[75] Table 4 presents a list of musical performances given in Richmond by West and Bignall's Company from 1790 to 1800.

---

74. *The Virginia Gazette and General Advertiser,* September 18, 1790.
75. *Ibid.,* October 20, 1790.

Table 4

MUSICAL PERFORMANCES IN RICHMOND THEATRES
1790–1800

Newspaper Reference[a]	Types of Performance[b]	Title	Composer
Oct. 13, 1790	Song	A Hunting Song	c
	Comic Opera	The Farmer	Shield
Jan. 5, 1791	Song	To the Greenwood Gang With Me	c
	Song	Lud, Don't You Keep Teazing Me So	c
	Song	I Tremble At Twenty Two	c
	Song	The Grecian Fabulist	c
	Musical Farce	The Padlock	Dibdin
Jan. 12, 1791	Song	Lash'd to the Helm	c
Sept. 28 and Oct. 19, 1791	Musical Farce	Rosina	Shield
Oct. 26, 1791	Musical Entertainment	The Farmer	Shield
Nov. 16, 1791	Song	High Mettled Racer	Dibdin
	Comic Opera	Rosina	Shield
Dec. 21, 1791	Song	Lash'd to the Helm	c
	Musical Entertainment	The Romp, or, Love in a City	Shield
July 25, 1792	Song	Tar for all Weathers	c

Date	Type	Title	Composer
Aug. 29, 1792	Comic Opera	The Maid of the Mill	Arnold
Oct. 3, 1792	Musical Entertainment	The Romp, or, Love in a City	Shield
Dec. 5, 1792	Song	No Indeed Not I!	c
	Comic Opera	No Song, No Supper	Storace
Dec. 12, 1792	Song	Dish or all Sorts	c
	Song	Jack the Guinea Pig	c
	Comic Opera	No Song, No Supper	Storace
Nov. 27, 1793	Song	Date Obolum Bellisario	c
	Musical Farce	The Son-In-Law	Arnold
	Song	Water Parted from the Sea	Arne
Dec. 23, 1795	Comic Opera	The Maid of the Mill	Arnold
	A Grand Pantomime	American Independence, or, the Fourth of July, 1776	c
Jan. 6, 1796 [Argus]	Comic Opera	Lionel and Clarissa	Dibdin
	Musical Farce	The Farmer	Shield
Nov. 23, 1796	Song	Poor Old Woman of Eighty	Dibdin
Jan. 12, 1798	Opera	Lionel and Clarissa	Dibdin
Jan. 18, 1799	Musical Farce	The Quaker	Dibdin

a. References are from *The Virginia Gazette and General Advertiser* except for the one marked *Argus*.
b. Songs were performed between two major offerings such as farces, comedies, operas, and pantomimes.
c. Ballad Tune. Neither composers nor specific tunes are positively identifiable in most instances. However, various possibilities of tunes used may be found in the works of Chappell, Moffat, and O'Neill, cited in a previous footnote.

From the information given in Table 4 it is apparent that the principal composers known to have been represented on the stage in eighteenth-century Richmond were English. In the order of their listing in Table 4, these English composers were: William Shield (1748–1829), Charles Dibdin (1745–1814), Samuel Arnold (1710–1802), Stephen Storace (1763–1796), and Thomas Arne (1710–1778). The ballad opera in England, which was chiefly represented by the names of Dibdin, Shield, and Storace, was "the most typical dramatic product of the time."[76] Shield's best and most successful opera was *Rosina,* which was performed many times in Richmond.[77] His chief fame came from the songs composed for the large number of operas, farces, and pantomimes that he wrote, and he was the leading viola player in London. His opera, *Poor Soldier,* was probably the most popular in America during the first decade after the Revolution. Dibdin devoted himself entirely to stage pieces and songs, and spent his life in close association with the theatrical world. His "table entertainments," in which he was composer, author, singer, and accompanist, were heard all over England.

Dibdin's comic opera *The Padlock* was first performed in England in 1768 and was produced the next year in New York within eight months of its premiere performance. *The Padlock* retained its popularity for many years and was performed in Richmond in 1791. Other works of Dibdin performed in Richmond were *Lionel and Clarissa* and *The Quaker* (Table 4).

---

76. Ernest Walker, *A History of Music in England* (London: Oxford University Press, 1952), p. 267.

77. *Ibid.* There were apparently several different versions of the opera *Rosina,* and since the composer's name was frequently omitted in the announcement of the opera to be presented, there is no way of knowing whether the *Rosina* given was that of Shield or whether it was a potpourri of popular songs tied together by a thread of drama and given a name such as *Rosina, or Love in a Village,* or *Rosina, or Love in a Cottage*—both of which were advertised by West and Bignall in Richmond. A similar observation may be made concerning the other titles mentioned.

Arnold, the composer of *Maid of the Mill,* was said to be "one of the most versatile and indefatigable musicians of the time," and among other activities, he served as organist at Westminster Abbey.[78] His compositions other than the comic operas included 49 dramatic works, five oratorios, and many anthems and instrumental pieces. *Maid of the Mill* was first performed in America in 1769, and in Richmond in 1792 and again in 1795 (Table 4).

Storace was the son of an Italian double-bass player who had settled in London. He studied in Italy, traveled in Europe, and spent his last eight years in England, where he wrote music for the stage. The opera *No Song, No Supper* was performed in Richmond and Philadelphia only two years after it was written, and it was one of Storace's most noteworthy compositions.

Arne, who is represented in Table 4 not with an opera but with a song, was a contemporary of Handel and the best known of the English-born composers of his time. His opera, *Love in a Village,* and the air, "Water Parted from the Sea," (Table 4) were popular with colonial Americans as well as with post-revolutionary Americans.

American Independence (Table 4), the musical entertainment given in Richmond, was evidently an original work by members of West and Bignall's company, and it was not in the repertory of the northern theatrical companies. The songs listed in Table 4 were evidently the more popular songs of the day, because these were the few songs listed by name in advertisements, the usual procedure being to state that a song, comic song, Scotch reel, or hornpipe was to be performed. One advertisement stated that a fandango was to be danced in Richmond in 1796.[79] A drama, *School for Soldiers,* included "a Military Procession to the field of execution."

---

78. Walker, p. 265.
79. *The Virginia Gazette and General Advertiser,* November 30, 1796.

ORDER

Six Pioneers,
Drum Muffled, with Fife.
The Coffin. . . .
Regimental Band, play the Dead March.
. . . .[80]

That the theatrical companies utilized novelties and spectacular feats as well as the better music and drama of the English stage is illustrated by a statement given in a West and Bignall advertisement of a benefit performance for Mr. Hallam:

> The whole to conclude with an EPILOGUE, and a flying leap through a hogshead of BLAZING FIRE.
> By Mr. Hallam.[81]

Lofty tumbling, fireworks, and a sagacious dog were also among the attractions offered Richmond audiences of the eighteenth century. Therefore it may be stated that the theatrical offerings were varied in quality and were designed to satisfy diverse tastes, their criteria for excellence being the offerings of the London theatres.

Whether it was quality or spectacularism or both that West and Bignall offered the public, their company seemed to have found the key to audience contentment. Little competition was offered them in Richmond. During April 1791, Mr. Godwin "of the Old American Company (twenty-five years ago)" advertised that he had been "favored with the theatre for some nights," but no additional information was found concerning his activities in Richmond.[82] Godwin was "a dancing and fencing master by trade but actor by ambition," and, as he advertised,

---

80. *Ibid.*, November 23, 1796.
81. *Ibid.*, January 12, 1791, p. 2. Mr. Hallam with West and Bignall was apparently not the Hallam of the Old American Company.
82. *The Virginia Gazette and General Advertiser*, April 27, 1791.

had been a member of Douglass' American Company before the Revolution. He had become a manager of his
own company around 1786.[83] West and Bignall's longest
season in Richmond was during 1792, after which they
established their headquarters in Charleston but returned
yearly to offer music and drama to Richmonders.

Temporary Theatres

Richmond's second theatre was destroyed by fire on
January 23, 1798.[84] The eighteenth century ended and the
new century began with Richmond's theatrical entertainers in temporary quarters. In 1799, the "Musical Farce
of the Quaker" (Table 4) was given in the City Hall, and
the Virginia Company of Comedians advertised that they
would perform "for the race week at the EAGLE TAV-
ERN; to Commence on Monday evening, Oct. 14—With
a favorite Comedy, Farce, and Entertainments, as would
be expressed in the bills of the day."[85]

Concerts

The professional musician earned a living, such as it
was, by performing in either the theatre, the church, or
both, and he likely found it necessary to teach or find some
other way to supplement his income. One way for the
professional musician to add to his income was to play
or sing in concerts. The words "for the benefit" added
to an advertisement distinguished such concerts from those
given by amateurs. The custom of revealing the names
of professional musicians but never those of amateurs in
concert and theatre presentations continued through the
period of this study.

The eighteenth-century concerts in Richmond fell into

83. Sonneck, *Early Opera* . . . , p. 62.
84. See Appendix A—The Theatre.
85. *The Virginia Gazette and General Advertiser,* October 11, 1799.

three categories: (1) those given by amateurs, (2) those given as benefits by theatre performers, and (3) those given by itinerant entertainers. Sonneck suggests another category of concert performances when he states that the early concerts may have emanated from those musicians who performed their favorite songs for tavern patrons, remuneration being expected after the musical offering. Sonneck reasoned that it was but "a short and logical step" to proceed to the state wherein the fee was paid before the concert instead of afterward.

> If we remember that by far the majority of public concerts were still held at taverns at the end of the eighteenth century, it will not be considered a fantastic idea, I hope, to trace the sources of our public concert-life to the taverns and their fiddling parasites.[86]

The Eagle Tavern was the site of Richmond's eighteenth-century concerts.

Richmond's amateurs were invited to join the apparently flourishing amateur group in Fredericksburg, Virginia. The invitation was extended through an advertisement in a newspaper published in Richmond.

> To all Lovers of MUSIC, Vocal or Instrumental,
> In Virginia or Elsewhere.
> The Harmonic Society of the Town of Fredericksburg, present their affectionate good wishes, and that the true spirit of harmony and concord may ever glow from breast to breast, is their sincere and ardent desire.
> The Society earnestly require the attendance of all gentlemen in the country, who are performers on instruments, or who have valuable collections of music, at the Concert Room in the Market house, on the evening of the concert, which is held there the third Wednesday evening in each month. And as they have private meetings every Wednesday evening, they would also be extremely happy that such gentlemen as can possibly make it convenient to attend with their instruments

---

86. Sonneck, *Early Concert Life* . . . , p. 4.

and music, would favor them with their company. As the concert which is held on the third Wednesday evening in each month is peculiarly intended for benevolent purposes, the tickets for those who are neither Members nor Performers, will be one dollar each. The music of the evening . . . affords a grand entertainment of four hours.[87]

If any Richmond amateurs journeyed to Fredericksburg they were hardy souls; for a few weeks following the appearance of the Fredericksburg Harmonic Society's advertisement, overland travel was hazardous and not even the mail could go through. It was reported that "the Postman who rides to Fredericksburg, had arrived within six miles of the town, when he could get no further, owing to the vast quantities of water."[88]

Mordecai mentions an amateur musical society in Richmond that lasted from the early days until well into the nineteenth century, but he neglects giving any clue as to how early the group was organized.[89] Perhaps he was

describing the amateurs referred to in the following advertisement of 1893:

> On Friday 17th instant, in the Evening, at the EAGLE TAVERN, will be Presented,
> A CONCERT OF MUSIC,
> By Mr. JUNGBLUTH, a celebrated Bassoon-Player—He will perform several pieces on that Instrument, accompanied by the Amateurs of this city. The pieces to be performed will be expressed in bills of the day.[90]

The amateur musicians of Richmond had a regular meeting place. An advertisement by James and Thomas Warrell states that their dancing academy will be opened "at the yellow building . . . occupied by the musical society,

---

87. *The Virginia Gazette, or the American Advertiser,* January 10, 1784.
88. *Ibid.,* February 7, 1848.
89. Mordecai, p. 170.
90. *The Virginia Gazette and General Advertiser,* May 15, 1793.

who have kindly indulged them with the use of it until a permanent situation offers."[91]

The first formal public concert in Richmond may have been given by Mrs. Sully, a member of the theatre company visiting the city. She later became a permanent resident and continued to take part in the musical life of the city for 30 or more years. Her announcement of the forthcoming concert was given in verbose manner characteristic of theatrical advertisements of the day.

> Mrs. M. Sully, (*with the greatest respect.*)
> Begs leave to inform her numerous patrons in particular, and the public in general, her C O N C E R T ,
> Is preparing with the utmost assiduity, and will be ready for representation in the course of ONE FORTNIGHT, and flatters herself the subjects dictated by her sound experience, will be considered replete with elegance of taste, added to extraordinary execution; the completion of which, every effort will, on her part, be exerted.[92]

Perhaps Raynor Taylor's entertainment, which was given a week before Mrs. Sully's concert, could be considered the first public concert in Richmond. His advertisement rather completely described the presentation, and it is illustrative of a stage in the evolution of the concert diverging from the theatre.

> Musical Performance.
> Eagle Tavern, Richmond,
> This Present Evening,
> Being Wednesday the 12th of September, will be
> A NEW PERFORMANCE, in three parts,
> The whole of the Music composed by Mr. Taylor,
> Music Professor, lately arrived from London.
> Part 1*st.*
> *An Interlude called the*
> CONSTANT LASS, or, The
> Sailor's Frolic.

---

91. *Argus*, October 1, 1800. See Appendix A—Tanbark Hall.
92. *Ibid.*, September 5, 1792.

Consisting of dialogue, songs, duet, &c. which will be recited and sung by Mr. Taylor, and his pupil Miss Huntley, late of the Theatre Royal, Covent Garden.

Part II*d.*

A selection of comic and pastoral Songs, Dialogue, &c. by Mr. Taylor and Miss Huntley.

Part III*d.*

A Burletta, in one act called
THE QUACK, or The
Doctor in Petticoats.

The songs will be accompanied on the grand piano forte, by Mr. Taylor, with several pieces on that instrument.[93]

Another stage in the evolution of the concert, apparently more typical of the colonial period, was the ball that was preceded by a concert. Sonneck reports that Mrs. Sully and Mrs. Pick "of the theatrical company just then performing" in Richmond held a " 'grand' concert and ball" on July 2, 1795.[94]

Mrs. Sully together with Mr. and Mrs. Pick formed a concert team in 1797. All three sang, Mrs. Sully played the piano, and, in the phraseology of the day, was accompanied by Mr. Pick on the violin. Their program given at the Eagle Tavern was probably similar to the one given in Petersburg.[95] Two other concerts presumably given at the Eagle Tavern during that same year are cited by Sonneck; one by "poor little 'Miss Marianne D'Hemard,' only five years old, 8 months from Paris," and the other by R. Shaw, "of the orchestra belonging to Wignell and Reinagle's" theatrical company.[96] The performers were Messers. Bartlet, Robins, Shaw, and Mrs. Shaw—singers; Mr. Frobel—pianist; Mr. Shaw—German flutist; and an orchestra.[97]

---

93. *Ibid.,* September 12, 1792.
94. Sonneck, *Early Concert Life* . . . , p. 61.
95. *Ibid.,* p. 59. The Petersburg program noted by Sonneck is included in Appendix B.
96. *Ibid.,* pp. 57, 61.
97. Program—Appendix B.

By the end of the eighteenth century, Richmond's music enthusiasts had been offered a variety of concert entertainments by itinerant vocal and instrumental performers. Amateur musicians of Richmond had their own organization, had appeared on at least one public performance, and probably met regularly for private practice. Secular music that was performed publicly was closely associated with the music of the theatre.

Music of the Church

During the last decade of the eighteenth century, Richmond had no church building in regular use for religious services. The one church building in the city was the former Anglican church of Henrico Parish, known then as the Church on Indian—or Indian Town—Hill and after 1828 as St. John's (Episcopal) Church. The church had been built in 1741, was used for religious services throughout the colonial period, and continued in regular use for a short period after the American Revolution. However, "from 1789 to about 1814 it was used only for funeral rites and for Holy Communion three times a year."[98] The church is best known to Americans today as the meeting place of the colonial Virginia General Assembly in 1775. The delegates, at odds with Lord Dunmore, chose Richmond for their meeting place because it was a safe distance from the royalist governor in Williamsburg, and the church building was probably the only meeting place in the city large enough to accommodate them.

One building erected for religious worship before the turn of the century was a Quaker meetinghouse, and other small places for worship were built during the last year or two of the century by other religious denominations.

98. Ulrich Troubetzkoy, ed., *Richmond, City of Churches* (Richmond: Whittet & Shepperson, 1957), p. 1.

The Capitol was being used for religious services before its completion in 1792, and it was the principal meeting place of the Episcopalians and Presbyterians until about 1815. Catholics and Baptists made sporadic use of it as a meeting place. Otherwise, "the religious denominations had occasional places of worship only, for occasional preachers—mere barns, where no regular weekly service was performed."[99]

The Episcopal and Presbyterian Church

The Church of England was well established in Virginia early in the seventeenth century, and with the exception of its suppression during the decade of the commonwealth in England, it continued to be the principal church in Virginia until the Revolution. The Protestant Episcopal Church of Virginia was incorporated in 1784,[100] and the Protestant Episcopal Church of the United States of America was organized in 1786. Ellinwood states that music in the Episcopal Church "differed little from that in the Puritan congregations of New England. The Clerk gave out the metrical Psalms from his desk, supported in some of the larger churches by a gallery choir" and an organ.[101] The records of St. John's Church give no accounts of music activities during the eighteenth century until 1790.[102] Burton indicates that the church had an organ that had been sold prior to 1790. The proceeds from the sale and from a concert were to be used for buying a new instrument, "but probably because the fund did not increase sufficiently for this purpose, the money was in 1794 loaned out to the minister."[103] Nevertheless, St. John's Church

99. Mordecai, p. 157.

100. Troubetzkoy, p. 1.

101. Leonard Ellinwood, *The History of American Church Music* (New York: Morehouse-Gorham Co., 1953), p. 41.

102. "The Vestry Book of Henrico Parish" (1730–1773) and "The Record Book of St. John's Parish" (1785–1887).

103. Lewis W. Burton, *Annals of Henrico Parish, Diocese of Virginia, and Especially of St. John's Church* (Richmond: Williams Printing Co., 1904), p. 28.

was the first church in Richmond to have an organ, for if one dismisses the above inconclusive evidence, the organ that was installed during 1816–17 preceded other church organ installations in the city.[104]

St. John's Church building was used only three times a year from 1789 to 1814, but the Rev. John Buchanan conducted Episcopal services during that time in the hall of the House of Delegates in the Capitol. On alternate Sundays the Rev. John D. Blair, a Presbyterian clergyman, conducted a service in the same hall, the congregations consisting of a large portion of the same individuals every Sabbath.[105] Presumably, the music changed little from week to week, and no real distinction may be made between music of the two denominations in Richmond during this period. Those who led the singing probably used Watts' *Hymns and Spiritual Songs,* or Andrew Law's *Rudiments of Music* (1783), or both. The former has been called the first hymnal of American Presbyterianism,[106] and the latter contains the first American adaptation of the Anglican chant.[107] That Laws' music books were sold in Richmond is evidenced by the following advertisements:

FOR SALE, on reasonable terms, at the Subscriber's store, A Collection of the Rudiments of CHURCH MUSIC, & MUSICAL MAGAZINES, By the Rev. Andrew Law, A.M.
ROBERT GAMBLE[108]

ROBERT GAMBLE, Has just received . . . Law's Church Music, and a constant supply of Flour, Butter, Whisky, and Venison Hams. . . .[109]

Andrew Law (1748–1821) was born and died in Connecti-

---

104. See Chapter 3.
105. Mordecai, pp. 158–59.
106. Arthur Stevenson, *The Story of Southern Hymnology* (Roanoke, Va.: The Stone Printing and Manufacturing Co., 1931), p. 16.
107. Ellinwood, p. 50.
108. *The Virginia Gazette and General Advertiser,* March 27, 1793. The fourth edition of Law's *Rudiments of Music* was published in 1792.
109. *Ibid.,* July 15, 1795.

cut. He was a man of good education and one of America's first writers of music. Law's two innovations were (1) setting the melody in the soprano rather than in the tenor, and (2) the substitution of character notes or shaped notes for more conventional symbols.

Watts' hymns may have been more popular than Law's in Virginia. Samuel Davies was an ardent advocate of Watts, and beginning with his work in the middle of the century, "the use of Watts's hymns and psalms spread rapidly . . . until by 1800, Watts completely dominated the hymnody in most churches."[110] The earliest advertisement of church music for sale in Richmond may have been for one of Watts's books.

JUST PUBLISHED, And for Sale at this Office, A collection of HYMNS and SPIRITUAL SONGS, On various subjects: Selected from different and approved Authors. Adapted to public and social Worship.[111]

Baptist Churches

Early Baptist hymn writers in Virginia included Eleazer Clay, Andrew Broadus, and Richard Broadus. *Hymns and Spiritual Songs, Selected from Several Approved Authors by Eleazer Clay; Recommended by the Baptist General Committee of Virginia to Be of Public Utility to the Community at Large and to the Church of Christ in Particular* was printed by John Dixon at Richmond in 1793. "Its author lived in Chesterfield County, Virginia (1744–1836). . . . He was the wealthiest Baptist minister in the United States in his day. . . ."[112] Andrew and Richard Broadus wrote a *Collection of Sacred Ballads,* which has

110. Howard, p. 16.

111. *The Virginia Gazette and General Advertiser,* June 1, 1791. This may have been an advertisement of a Baptist publication, which, in turn may have been taken from Watts' book.

112. Stevenson, p. 1. Eleazer Clay's book is in the collection of old hymnals owned by the Virginia Baptist Historical Association at the University of Richmond.

a preface dated January 1, 1790, Caroline County. Andrew
Broadus was born in Caroline County, Virginia in 1770,
preached between Richmond and Fredericksburg, and for
a short time was assistant to John Courtney, another hymn
writer, at the First Baptist Church in Richmond.[113] *A Selection of Hymns and Spiritual Songs from the Best Authors, by ANDREW BROADDUS* [sic], *V.D.M.* was frequently advertised for sale in a Richmond newspaper.[114]

An examination of the early hymn books cited above
gives no clue as to the music used in the eighteenth-century church service. The books contained only words and
occasionally an indication of the meter to be used. The
leader of the singing apparently "raised the tune" that
struck his fancy at the time. Baptist church historians do
not identify the tunes, and the earliest Baptist church activities in Richmond are summarized by White as follows:

> Beyond the statement that in June, 1780, a Baptist church
> was constituted by Joshua Morris, with a charter membership
> of fourteen, and that the organization meeting was held "in
> the home of one, Franklin," we have little authentic infor-
> mation concerning the initial decade in the life of the First
> Baptist Church in Richmond. The minutes of the church
> for the first forty-five years were not preserved.[115]

The Methodist Church

Richmond was an appointment on a circuit for some
years before a pastoral charge was formed in 1798, and the
Methodist circuit rider was a familiar sight to residents of
the city. The Methodists built a small house of worship
in 1799, but before this they had worshiped in the Henrico County courthouse until the privilege of using the
building was withdrawn "on complaint of the people re-

---

113. See Chapter 3. Many of Broadus' hymn books are in the Virginia
Baptist Historical Association collection.
114. *Argus*, January 18, 1799, *et al.*
115. Blanche Sydnor White, compiler, *First Baptist Church, Richmond,
1780–1955* (Richmond: Whittet & Shepperson, 1955), p. 7.

siding in the vicinity that the loud singing and shouting
. . . was a serious disturbance of their peace."[116] John
Wesley's collection of hymns published in England in 1780
is said to have had a large influence on Methodism, and
Robert Spence's *Pocket Hymn Book* gained wide accep-
tance in America, having its eighteenth edition published
in 1793.[117] These books may have been used in Richmond,
but the tunes used are not identifiable.

Other Religious Groups

No record of Catholic or Hebrew music performances
in eighteenth-century Richmond was found, but it may be
assumed that those people, with their exceptional musical
heritage, must have made use of their liturgy, chants, and
traditional songs in their respective services. The Roman
Catholics held services in the Capitol in 1791, and in 1798
Father Tonnant C. Mongrand became the first regularly
stationed priest to serve Richmond Catholics.[118] The sixth
oldest Hebrew congregation in the United States was organized in 1789 in Richmond.[119] They worshiped in private residences during the remainder of the eighteenth
century.

At the close of the eighteenth century, the people of
Richmond had divided themselves into a number of different religious groups in accordance with their own wishes.
The majority of the church members were of Anglican
Church lineage and probably practiced variations developed from their ancestors' English church music. Minority
groups represented other European countries, their reli-
gion, and music.

---

116. Edward Leigh Pell, ed., *A Hundred Years of Richmond Methodism* (Richmond: The Idea Publishing Company, 1899), p. 271.
117. Stevenson, p. 16.
118. Troubetzkoy, p. 1.
119. *Ibid.*, p. 6.

Chapter 3

Richmond as a Center for Music: The Early Years, 1800-1825

The population of the city of Richmond increased rapidly after the American Revolution. By 1800 there were just over five thousand residents and a decade later almost ten thousand persons lived there. Caucasians outnumbered Negroes only by a small majority in each instance. Virginia, with slightly over one million inhabitants in 1820, was the second most populous state of the United States, New York ranking first. Compared with present-day population figures, Richmond was indeed a small city during the first quarter of the nineteenth century, but it was the political capital city, a focal point for commerce, and possibly the principal center of music activity in Virginia.

There were two major periods of music activity during the first quarter of the nineteenth century, and a tragic theatre fire in 1811 separated them. In both the activity apparently centered around the theatre, for the periods of concentrated music activity were concurrent with the periods of successful theatre ventures, and the principal participants in music programs were generally theatre performers. During both periods music instruction and musical entertainment flourished. During the second period there was an increase in concert activity by theatre performers as well as by groups of Richmond amateurs. Especially indicative of musical progress on the local level were the concerts given in churches near the end of the latter period.

Music on Public and Social Occasions

Hay Market Garden was a popular pleasure resort in Richmond during the first decade of the eighteenth century.[1] The announcement of its opening for the summer season in 1801 states that "balls, ice-cream and tea parties will be prepared on notice—Best of liquors served."

> N. B. Liberal encouragement will be given to good Vocal, Violin, Clarinet, Horn and Bassoon performers; a good set of Players; Rope and Wire Dancers, or Equestrian Performers.[2]

The opening announcement for the ensuing year states that the organ has arrived and that the proprietor plans to have vocal and instrumental musicians "to accompany the organ occasionally."[3] Only "Amateurs by invitation" were permitted to enter the orchestra section of the music gallery. Music for dancing was provided on Wednesday evenings, and "Divine music" was performed on Sunday afternoons by "such Ladies or Gentlemen who wished to join the choir."[4]

The fourth of July was celebrated with fireworks and dancing at the Haymarket Garden in 1803,[5] and after the

---

1. See Appendix A—Hay Market Garden.
2. *The Virginia Gazette and General Advertiser*, May 19, 1801.
3. *Ibid.*, May 1, 1802.
4. *Ibid.*
5. *Ibid.*, June 29, 1803.

summer season was over, the proprietor proposed to offer "musical entertainments . . . to commence with such performances on the organ, grand piano forte, and other instruments, with songs, accompaniments, &c. as . . . will be highly pleasing."[6] The entertainments apparently met with some measure of success, for similar offerings were advertised during the ensuing years with the "particulars expressed in bills" of the day.[7] The garden was reported to be "in a high state of accommodation for entertainments" in 1804, "being provided with excellent Musicians and a Fireworker of great celebrity . . . to amuse visitors during the races."[8] Visitors to the garden were to be entertained with "concerts, balls, fireworks and illuminations, in the most splendid style—The musical arrangements directed by Monsieur Folly."[9]

As it had been in the previous century, dancing continued to be a popular social pastime in the first decade of the new century. Balls, cotillions, and dancing schools were held at the Hay Market Garden Ball Room in 1807 by Thomas Seawell.[10] Prior to that time James and Thomas Warrell gave dancing lessons in Richmond.[11] From 1808 to 1813 John Lataste was Richmond's principal dancing teacher and also a performer on the viola.[12] Cotillions written by Lataste and set to dance music arranged by A. Peticola, a Richmond musician, are to be found in *The Visitor*, a Richmond magazine published in 1809–1810.[13]

Entertainments, balls, and circuses were given in Hay Market Gardens throughout the first decade of the nineteenth century, but afterwards the gardens apparently fell into disuse. Few amusements of any kind were advertised

---

6. *Ibid.*, October 12, 1803.
7. *Ibid.*, August 1, 1804; July 31, 1805; and October 8, 1806.
8. *Ibid.*, October 3, 1804.
9. *Ibid.*
10. *Ibid.*, May 2, 1807.
11. *Ibid.*, December 9, 1800; December 5, 1804; *et passim.*
12. *Argus*, October 14, 1808; April 19, 1813; *et passim.*
13. *The Visitor*, II, No. 8 (March 1810), 36.

in the newspapers for several years after the theatre fire
of 1811. The dancing school of John Lataste survived
longer than most music and music-related activities of the
early part of the second decade.

A. E. Guigon was Richmond's principal dancing teacher
of the latter second decade period, and his advertisements
appeared in the newspapers until 1822.[14] "Guigon, A. E.—
Dancing School" and "Petticola—Musician" are listed in
Richmond's first city directory, which was published in
1819.[15] The announcement that no gentleman would be
permitted to appear in boots at one of the "cotillion
parties" held in 1818 may include the beginning of an
era of social sophistication.[16]

During the summer months of 1819 through 1821 two
pleasure gardens in Richmond, Vauxhall on Mayo's Island
and Jackson's on Shockoe Hill, advertised "illumination,"
fire works, flights of "air balloons," and bands of music to
play for patrons.[17] The Eagle Hotel Yard offered bands,
fireworks, balloons, and circus performers during the winter months.[18] At Washington's "Birth Night" ball sponsored by the Richmond Light Infantry Blues in 1822,
almost 700 persons danced to the music of two bands, one
in each of two rooms, at the Eagle Hotel.[19] In 1824, when
LaFayette visited the city, the Eagle Hotel Yard was converted into a ballroom with a wooden floor and a canvas
canopy so as to accommodate one thousand persons attending the ball in honor of the hero.[20]

Exhibits of curious objects, animals, mechanism, and
feats of activity frequently offered music performances as

14. *Enquirer*, February 15, 1817; *Compiler*, March 3, 1819; September
20, 1821; *et passim*.
15. *The Richmond Directory, Register and Almanac, for the Year 1819*
(Richmond: John Maddox, 1819).
16. *Compiler*, December 16, 1818.
17. *Compiler*, May 27, 1819; June 28, 1821; *et passim*.
18. *Ibid.*, January 25, 1821 and December 10, 1821.
19. *Ibid.*, February 25, 1822.
20. Mordecai, 288–89.

an extra inducement to prospective purchasers of admission tickets. "Music on an elegant organ" was given with a showing of a collection of wax figures at Mr. Hallam's Washington Tavern in 1804.[21] A similar exhibition given the following year at the Bell Tavern provided entertainment "by a choice band of Music, with several Italian pieces" performed at intervals during the day.[22] Exhibited along with "A Live Cassowary" was a mechanical organ playing "several favorite tunes, . . . [with] a number of figures as natural as life, dancing to the music, while several artillerists discharge their pieces, &c."[23] More wax figures shown in 1810 were presented with "good music on an organ," in one instance, and "elegant pieces . . . performed by a masterly hand on the violin," in another.[24] When Richmond opened its first museum, the proprietors had an organ "fitted up in their Gallery of Paintings," and in addition to music on the organ, the patrons of the museum were informed that "a Band of Music, of Amateurs who have politely offered their services, will conduce to render the evening's amusement agreeable."[25] A band of music was in attendance at the museum on several occasions during the next few years.[26] An organ provided music later when wax figures were exhibited at the museum.[27]

The amateur musicians performing at the museum were probably those depicted by Mordecai, who gives a description of William Henry Fitzwhyllson, successively a school teacher, book and music store proprietor, and mayor of the city.

Mr. Fitzwhyllson was a patron of the fine arts, and more

21. *The Virginia Gazette and General Advertiser,* December 1, 1804.
22. *Ibid.,* November 6, 1805.
23. *Argus,* September 6, 1808.
24. *Ibid.,* February 2, 1810, and July 10, 1810.
25. *Enquirer,* January 1, 1818. See Appendix A—Virginia Museum.
26. *Compiler,* December 9, 1818; March 27, 1819; February 9, 1820; and October 17, 1820.
27. *Ibid.,* July 16, 1823.

especially of music. He was one of the founders of the *Musical Society* that held its regular concerts at *Tanbark Hall,* and on these occasions, it may be truly said,

"With nose and chin he figured in;"

for those features were in him exceedingly prominent, and as, like most short men, he held his head exceedingly high, he could not be otherwise than conspicuous among the harmonious band, as was his bass-viol, even taller than himself. This society contained several other members in strong contrast to each other, whose faces and figures, and ecstatic gestures, would have furnished a group worthy of the pencil of Hogarth.

. . . .

He literally *shone* in every station that he occupied; his capacious bald head reflecting the light in all directions, like a *halo.* He died, full of years and full of honors, in the year 1837.[28]

The writing and the singing of ballad songs continued to interest the people of Richmond through the first quarter of the century. Poems were published periodically in the Richmond newspaper, and many identified the tune that was to be sung with the poetry. "The British Grenadier," "Yankee Doodle," and "Derry Down" had apparently retained their popularity won in the eighteenth century. Patriotic ballads recounting deeds of valor were popular during the War of 1812.[29] Tunes used in ballad writing during the first quarter of the eighteenth century that are well known today are "Anacreon in Heaven," "Hail Columbia," "Marseillaise Hymn," "Auld Lang Syne," "Drink to Me Only With Thine Eyes," and "Robin Adair." The above tunes were named with 46 other tunes and folk songs in a Richmond publication:

---

28. Mordecai, pp. 170–72.
29. Popular ballad songs of the day may be heard on the recording: *War of 1812 Sung by Wallace House* (Folkways Record Album No. FP 48-3, 48-4, FP 5002. Copyright 1954 by Folkways Records and Service Corp., 117 W. 46th Street, New York City).

The Vocal Standard or The Star Spangled Banner, **Being** the latest and best selection ever offered to the public, particularly of American Patriotic Songs; as well as Sentimental Humorous and Comic Songs, Duetts, Glees, &c. many of which are original and not to be found in any other collection.[30]

The book's Preface states that the selection of the ballads included in the publication was made by a "committee of taste, consisting of Ladies and Gentlemen of this city," but no persons are named. Besides indicating the favorite ballads of the day enjoyed by citizens of Richmond, the contents of the book intimate that at social gatherings there was singing, and within the groups that gathered there probably were persons who could lead and others who could follow the singing of a repertory consisting of 50 or more tunes.

One song in *The Vocal Standard, or the Star Spangled Banner,* the poetry to which was possibly written in Richmond, the topic probably concerning Richmond, is as follows:

HARD TIMES—*Tune—Robin Adair.*

What's this dull town to me?
No cash is here!
Things that we used to see,
Now don't appear.
Where's all those Plattsburgh bills
Silver dollars, cents and mills?
Oh! we must check our wills,
No cash is here.

What made the city shine?
Money was here.
What makes the lads repine?
No cash is here.

30. Published by J. H. Nash, 1824; the quotation is from the title page. The book is held by the Virginia State Library.

What makes the farmers sad,
Factors crazy, merchants mad?
Oh! times are very bad—
    No cash is here.

. . . . [31]

Music Merchantry and Instruction

William Prichard, probably the principal music merchant in Richmond during the last decade of the eighteenth
century, continued to keep a supply of music and instruments in his bookstore after the turn of the century. His
last newspaper advertisement, printed in 1807, offered
music, musical instruments, and a church organ for sale.[32]
The next business firm to sell music and instruments over
an extended period of time was the bookstore of Fitzwhylsonn [*sic*] and Potter, which began advertising violin
bows, bow hair, strings, music, and music books for sale
in 1810.[33] By 1815 they apparently offered a complete line
of music supplies and instruments, including "Broad-
wood's Piano Fortes."[34] The store was under the sole
proprietorship of William H. Fitzwhylsonn from *ca.* 1818
to 1829.[35]
In 1816 the bookstore of Mayo and Frayser advertised
"a handsome assortment of musical instruments," including "plain and ivory mounted" clarinets, flutes and flageolets, and "a handsome assortment of music" that included:

> *The Gentleman's Amusement.* A select collection of songs,
> marches, hornpipes, &c. &c. properly adapted for the flute,
> violin and patent flageolet, which they will sell low.[36]

Frayser's name was dropped in 1818, and during that year

31. *The Vocal Standard* . . . , pp. 225–56.
32. *The Virginia Gazette and General Advertiser,* March 21, 1807.
33. *Argus,* June 8, 1810.
34. *Ibid.,* November 8, 1815.
35. *Compiler,* December 2, 1818; *Whig,* April 1, 1829; *et passim.*
36. *Enquirer,* August 21, 1816.

and the next, Frederick A. Mayo continued to advertise music merchandise for sale.

Beginning in 1817 and continuing into the next decade, Thomas White and Company, George Hendree, L. Convent, William Stodart, Joseph Hicky, W. C. and G. Clarke, E. T. Robb, J. H. Nash, and others advertised pianos and other music merchandise for sale in Richmond.[37] By the end of the second decade of the century, music merchants were well supplied with instruments and music, and from that time on, advertisements of pianos and other music merchandise were seen regularly in Richmond newspapers.

Several instrument repairmen and tuners were in Richmond at the end of the second and beginning of the third decades. Francis Niclot, E. T. Robb, and T. H. Taylor advertised their services as instrument makers, repairers, and tuners.[38] Men performing similar services had advertised at the beginning of the century. J. Widewilt, who had taught music in the eighteenth century in Richmond, advertised that he would tune piano fortes during the summer of 1804.[39] O. Shutze and Thomas Henley also tuned pianos in 1804.[40] Henley apparently also made instruments in Richmond during the first decade of the century, for among his many notices published in the newspaper is:

> Thomas Henley, Music Instrument maker, returns his thanks to the citizens of Richmond and hopes by his assiduity and attention to merit a continuance of their custom,[41]

Tuning pianos was apparently a means of extra income for many musician-teachers of the period. Music teachers who tuned pianos avocationally in Richmond during this

37. *Enquirer*, February 14, 1817; June 19, 1818; *Compiler*, August 3, 1818; May 22, 1821; July 6, 1820; December 2, 1820; August 12, 1823; May 21, 1823.
38. *Compiler*, September 4, 1819; December 30, 1819; and June 8, 1821.
39. *The Virginia Gazette and General Advertiser*, July 18, 1804.
40. *Ibid.*, February 8, 1804, and July 18, 1804.
41. *Ibid.*, March 15, 1806.

period included Mr. Vogel, Monsieur Folly, and Mr. Dyke. They were probably organists at the Hay Market Garden, and each advertised that he would give instruction in piano playing and would tune pianos.[42] Vogel also proposed to teach harp and composition, and to repair musical instruments "of every description."[43] Folly offered to teach violin or clarinet in addition to giving piano instruction and tuning pianos.[44] Since the names of the three men are not mentioned in other records, it is assumed that each left Richmond after playing one or more seasons at the Hay Market Garden.

An indentured servant-musician at the Hay Market Garden was advertised, probably by his master, as follows:

Any person in want of a MUSICIAN who is regularly indentured and has about fourteen months to serve may be accommodated on application at the Hay-Market in this City. The qualifications of this man for teaching & tuning the Piano Forte, Violin, Violoncello, Clarinet, Trumpet and French Horn can be ascertained on applying as above.[45]

Long-term Richmond resident musicians who taught music beginning in the first decade of the century were P. A. Peticolas, August Peticolas, Charles Southgate, and John J. Abercrombie. An advertisement by P. A. Peticolas states that he and his son, August, "intend to teach music on the piano forte or harpsichord," and that Peticolas senior "tunes instruments."[46] An advertisement published in 1808 states that John J. Abercrombie,

Having returned from his tour to the Northward, begs leave to acquaint his friends and the public, that he still continues teaching in this city, on the Piano, Violin, and Guittar. He

42. *Ibid.*, July 30, 1803; August 1, 1804; and May 23, 1807.
43. *Ibid.*, July 30, 1803.
44. *Ibid.*, August 1, 1804.
45. *Ibid.*, October 1, 1806.
46. *Enquirer*, December 4, 1804.

likewise tunes instruments as formerly, and respectfully solicits the favor of their patronage.[47]

Charles Southgate notified the citizens of Richmond in 1806 that he had relinquished his day school and would turn his attention entirely to music.[48] He proposed to teach vocal music to children in groups of ten, to tune pianos, and to copy and arrange music. Southgate probably continued with his music vocation through the year 1814 after which he went into the dry goods business.[49] In the interim he was musical editor of *The Visitor* and included some of his own compositions in that publication; he was a clerk in the Episcopal Church wherein he led the singing; and he performed as a cellist and singer in the theatre and on concerts. Southgate's *Harmonia Sacra,* published posthumously, consists of anthems and hymns, some his own compositions.[50]

Only two teachers of this decade proposed to give music instruction without also offering to tune instruments: Mrs. Blagrove, who announced that she would "teach young ladies the Piano Forte" in 1803, and A. Baker, who "fixed his permanent residence at the Virginia Inn, for the purpose of teaching Music on the Piano Forte" in 1810.[51]

The middle years of the second decade were notably lacking in musical activities, including instruction, but advertisements concerning music instruction and other musical activities are seen again in the Richmond newspapers toward the latter part. Elisha Purrington stated that he would "open a singing school in the Baptist Meeting House" in 1818.[52] Purrington's singing school antedates the movement that became popular in Richmond two

47. *Argus,* December 23, 1803.
48. *Enquirer,* September 30, 1806.
49. *Ibid.,* December 8, 1814.
50. References and further information concerning Charles Southgate's career are given in other parts of this chapter.
51. *The Virginia Gazette and General Advertiser,* December 14, 1803; and *The Visitor,* II, No. 18 (June 1810), 57.
52. *Compiler,* November 23, 1818.

decades later. Southgate had proposed a similar project earlier, but prior to that, Purrington had conducted Psalmody in Richmond during the latter eighteenth-century period.[53]

J. S. Richardson, P. De Bihl, S. Milon, A. Passage, and J. H. Hoffman were transient musicians who offered to give music lessons in Richmond during 1818 and 1819. Richardson came from London by way of Philadelphia to lead the circus band and give concerts in Richmond. In addition, he gave instruction in playing harp, piano, flute, violin, guitar, flageolet, and in singing.[54] Being an opportunist, he sold music "from London and Philadelphia"—some his own compositions—and offered to tune pianos. He brought waltzes and the flageolet to Richmond, and both became more popular as a result of his performances. De Bihl, a theatre orchestra performer, proposed to give lessons on the violin as "taught in the Conservatory of France."[55] Milon gave piano, guitar, and voice lessons, "being himself an Italian and a pupil of the celebrated Conservatory of Naples."[56] A. Passage, from Paris, advertised instruction in fencing, "music in general and the wind instruments in particular, as the Flute, Clarionet, Flageolet, Trumpet, Trombone, and Bassoon."[57] Hoffman's announcement stated that he was from Europe and New York and that he would teach group instrumental lessons. His teaching procedures were far ahead of his times, for he proposed to teach his pupils to play 20 favorite airs in one month's time on the condition that if the student did not learn to play the instrument of his choice he would not be obligated to pay for the lessons. Hoffman's prospectus states:

53. Burton, p. 28.
54. *Compiler*, November 21, 1818; December 28, 1818; and January 6, 1819.
55. *Ibid.*, June 26, 1819.
56. *Ibid.*, August 21, 1819.
57. *Ibid.*, October 7, 1819.

Military Bands complete, [are] taught accurately, on a correct scale with appropriate music composed for the same.

.   .   .   .

Can there be a more rational and pleasing recreation after the toils of the day, a more powerful external incentive to youth to shun the haunts of nocturnal dissipation, to the witching harmony of sweet sounds?[58]

C. Stephan's announcement in 1819 that he "has resumed the profession of music . . . having declined the confectionary business" may be an indication that musicians were able to remain solvent at that time."[59] In the announcement, Stephan offers to tune pianos. P. A. Peticolas' advertisement in 1823 states that he "continues to give lessons the pianoforte and to tune the instrument."[60] No advertisements by Peticolas are seen in Richmond newspapers published between 1804 and 1823, but his arrangement of dance music was printed in *The Visitor* in 1810 and he is listed in the city directory of 1819 as a musician. These facts point to the possibility that he and other teachers may have been active professionally yet saw no need to publish public advertisements. It is possible that Peticolas' advertisement indicates that the economic depression was affecting his teaching income. However, only one other music teacher advertised his services during the first half of the third decade: J. Wintersteiner, who had performed on the violin, English and German flute, and Spanish guitar in Europe, offered to teach in Richmond.[61] Wintersteiner's announcement is also of interest because it is the first reference to the Spanish guitar, which was then surpassing the English guitar in popularity.

Schools for young ladies taught music and dancing as subjects of comparable importance to English, French, writing, and arithmetic. The ability of a young lady to

58. *Ibid.*, December 9, 1819, and January 13, 1820.
59. *Ibid.*, October 2, 1819.
60. *Ibid.*, July 31, 1823.
61. *Ibid.*, January 25, 1821.

perform on the piano, guitar, harp, or as a singer constituted a social grace revered by society throughout the
period of this study. From the first of the nineteenth century, advertisements of schools for young ladies are seen
in Richmond newspapers with regularity, and nearly all
indicate that music is to be taught by approved masters
of music.

Ward and charity schools were established in Richmond
in 1802 for those children whose parents could not afford
the private schools of the city.[62] Ward schools were supported by neighborhood contributions and the children
lived at home. Charity schools were usually for orphans
and often included boarding. Richmond's first tax supported school offering free tuition was established in 1816,
and the corner stone was laid "amidst an immense con-
course of Citizens, accompanied by the Free Masons, and
a fine band of music."[63] Music instruction was evidently
offered only in the private schools, academies, and semi-
naries attended principally by girls.

Music of the Theatre

During the first quarter of the nineteenth century,
Richmond had two theatre buildings, several places used
for temporary theatres, and several circuses. Taverns and
other public buildings were utilized at the beginning of
the century for the presentation of entertainment when
no theatre was available and were later used occasionally
in competition with theatre resident companies. The first
of the nineteenth-century theatres was built in 1806, and
its burning, in 1811, was one of the major disasters in the
history of the city.[64] The second theatre building, completed in 1819, continued as the principal theatre in Rich-

62. *The Richmond News Leader,* August 29, 1958.
63. *Enquirer,* June 29, 1816.
64. See Appendix A—The Theatre.

mond to the Civil War period.[65] About one year prior to
the completion of this second theatre, a temporary building called the Richmond Circus was erected, and equestrian, dramatic, and musical performances were given
there. The Bell Tavern, the Eagle Tavern, the Old City
Tavern, and the Mason's Hall were advertised as places
wherein theatrical entertainments were given.[66]

The construction of the first "New Theatre" was
financed by subscription and was begun in 1804.[67] Completed and occupied by the company of West and Bignall
in January 1806, it was financially successful until the
night of December 26, 1811, when disaster struck. The
story of that disaster has been written many times. The
following excerpts are taken from a Richmond newspaper
of the period.

> The fire grew with rapidity, almost beyond example. Within
> ten minutes after it caught the whole house was wrapt in
> flames. . . . A few who had escaped, plunged again into the
> flames to save some dear object of their regard—and then
> perished!: The Governor perhaps shared this melancholy
> fate. . . . Almost the whole town rushed to the fatal spot.
>
> There could not have been less than 600 in the house. . . .
> Sixty-one persons were devoured by that most terrific element.
>
> Most if not all who were in the pit escaped. Mr. Taylor the
> last of the musicians who quitted the orchestra finding his
> retreat by the back way cut off leapt into the pit. . . . He
> was the last that escaped from the pit.
>
> From Friday morning [December 27] until this day, by
> universal consent, almost every house in the place has re-
> mained shut, the dejected inhabitants have suspended their
> usual occupations, an awful gloom has pervaded the coun-

65. See Appendix A—Richmond Theatre.
66. *The Virginia Gazette and General Advertiser,* July 20, 1803; July
30, 1806; August 12, 1808; *Argus,* August 9, 1810 and May 14, 1814.
67. *Argus,* March 24, 1804.

tenances of all, and the only thing thought of, or spoken of, is the melancholy story of all our griefs.[68]

The City Council passed an ordinance on December 27, 1811, including the stipulation that for four months no person would be permitted to "exhibit any public show or spectacle, or open any public dancing Assembly within this city."[69]

More than two years elapsed before advertisements concerning entertainments were seen in the newspapers.[70] Readings and Recitations were given in 1816, and an announcement was printed that same year that a new theatre was being proposed.[71] "New Circus" advertisements began in July 1818, and were numerous thereafter until June 11, 1819, when the new theatre opened.[72] Despite "the unprecedented depression of business and scarcity of money," the first season of the new theatre was financially successful.[73] The theatre was operated for five years under the management of Charles Gilfert. The outstanding theatrical event in 1821 was the American debut of Lucius Junius Booth, who appeared as Richard III on July 6th, and the Gilfert company was particularly strong thereafter for two years: "It was perhaps the best company in America at that time."[74]

Over a five-year period from its opening, the theatre was not a financial success, however, and by the end of the first quarter of the century it was closed. Shockley gives the two most important reasons for the financial

68. *Argus,* December 30, 1811.
69. *Ibid.*
70. The first advertisement noted was in the *Argus,* May 14, 1814. The program, a concert by two itinerant musicians, is reported later in this chapter.
71. *Enquirer,* May 22, 1816, and May 18, 1816.
72. *Compiler.*
73. *Ibid.,* June 12, 1819.
74. Martin Staples Shockley, "A History of the Theatre in Richmond, Virginia, 1819–1839" (unpublished Ph.D. dissertation, Department of English, University of North Carolina, 1938).

losses sustained by the theatre as: "generally unfavorable economic conditions and the constant drain on the box office receipts through the use of free passes by the shareholders."[75]

The Audience

Theatre audience mannerisms were much the same throughout America during the early nineteenth century. Hewitt summarizes the audiences' behavior, beginning with the most offensive members—those in the gallery.

> Although constables were stationed in the gallery to keep order, they did not do so. The gallery gods whistled, shouted, hissed, and groaned. They showered spectators in the pit with apples, nuts, and gingerbread. They demanded a bow from the candle snuffer. The spectators in the boxes were not so noisy, but for them too, play-going was a social occasion. The belles simpered and coquetted. The beaux studiously wielded their glasses and ostentatiously ignored the play. The men in the pit suffered drip from the chandelier and barrages from the gallery, but their own behavior was not of the best; they stood on the benches before the curtain went up like spectators at a football game before the opening kick-off.[76]

Shockley surmised that, in contrast to some other theatres of the time, the Richmond Theatre audience "seems to have been, with the possible exception of the gallery, unusually well-behaved."[77] A newspaper writer objected to the "loud and frequent cheers" and admonished the audience to "wait until the song is finished before they commence their cheers."[78] Although the audience did not hesitate to voice their disdain for a poor performance, the better performances commanded their attention, and when

75. Shockley, pp. 2–3.
76. Barnard Hewitt, *Theatre U.S.A. 1668 to 1957* (New York: McGraw-Hill Book Company, 1959), p. 61.
77. Shockley, p. 67.
78. *Mercantile Advertiser*, June 14, 1822.

Junius Brutus Booth played in the theatre in 1821 "on several occasions a pin might have been heard to fall."[79]

The Orchestra

Washington Irving published a series of letters under the name of Jonathan January. Among them is an account of a visit to the Park Theatre, New York, in 1802, wherein he describes having heard the orchestra play the overture.

> What I heard of the music, I liked very well; (though I was told by one of my neighbours, that the same pieces have been played every night for these three years;) but it was often overpowered by the gentry in the gallery, who vociferated loudly for *Moll in the Wad, Tally Ho the Grinders,* and several other *airs* more suited to their tastes.[80]

Evidence that Richmond Theatre orchestras suffered similar abuse is offered in many advertisements published at the beginning of the century that concluded with: "The music as well as the business of the stage being selected for the evening, it is presumed no particular tunes will be called for during the performance."[81] After the theatre burned and the circus was the principal theatrical attraction, the advertisements concluded with, "Mr. West hopes that no Gentleman will enter the ring, during the performance."[82]

The audience paid an additional discourtesy to the orchestra of the new theatre that opened in 1819, and were thereby censured in a newspaper item for their "bad habit of visiting the bar-room" while the orchestra was playing.[83] There were other members of the audience who had a taste for music, however, and the Richmond Theatre or-

---

79. *Ibid.,* July 10, 1821.
80. Quoted in Hewitt, p. 60.
81. *The Virginia Gazette and General Advertiser,* January 22, 1806, *et al.*
82. *Compiler,* November 21, 1818 *et passim.*
83. *Mercantile Advertiser,* June 14, 1822.

chestra was reported to have been excellent. They apparently lacked quality and variety in their selections, as did other theatre orchestras of the day.

> If it is one of the best orchestras in America they are shamefully indifferent to their selection and performance, for in place of the divine airs of Handel, Haydn, Mozart, &c. I have heard nothing better than a few Waltzes, Marches, Scotch Airs, &c. and the same ones repeated night after night. . . .[84]

Performances

Vocal music by the actors and instrumental music by the orchestra comprised an integral part of nearly all theatre performances. Occasionally instrumentalists appeared on the stage. Advertisements of the dramatic presentations frequently stated that songs and novelties such as hornpipes and other dances would be presented between the acts or between the drama and the farce. "Steali, or, the Lady of the Goal, A melodrama in one act," printed in the *Visitor* in 1809, includes directions for singing and for orchestral background music during the dramatic presentation. Apparently the choosing of appropriate melodies was entrusted to the actor-singer. The practice of playwrights supplying words to be sung during a dramatic presentation was not new. Shakespeare utilized the device. Popular songs of the day were not only sung between acts and between the main presentation and the afterpiece; they were often inserted in the drama.

Apparently the designation of a performance as an opera, a comic opera, a musical entertainment, or a musical farce signified that the audience could expect to hear more songs than if the performance were designated as a drama, comedy, or farce. The dramatic plots were flexible and were altered to suit the talents of the cast. When the star

---

84. *Virginia Patriot,* November 26, 1819.

performer was a singer, a drama could become a musical
drama by the insertion of a few popular songs. Olios, consisting of singing, dancing, and dialogue with little or no
dramatic plot, were given occasionally.

Table 5 lists musical performances that were advertised
in a Richmond newspaper during 1804. The offerings
were typical of those given throughout the first quarter of
the century. Table 6 lists performances advertised for the
year 1819 by the "Richmond Circus," and Table 7 illustrates that the "New Theatre" offered entertainment similar to that offered by the circus. Perennial favorites listed
in the three tables are *Sprigs of Laurel, No Song, No Supper, Rosina,* and *The Agreeable Surprise. The Poor Soldier,* a popular eighteenth-century title, remained in the
permanent repertory. It is listed in Table 7 but not in
Table 5 or Table 6.

Table 5

MUSICAL PERFORMANCES IN RICHMOND THEATRES
1804

References from the Virginia Gazette and General Advertiser *1804*	*Type of Performance*	*Title*
January 11	Musical Entertainment	Sprigs of Laurel; or, Rival Soldiers
January 18	Musical Entertainment	The Sixty-third Letter
January 21	Opera	Inkle and Yarico; or, The American Heroine
February 25	Musical Farce	Flitch of Bacon
March 3	Musical Entertainment	No Song, No Supper
March 7	A Comic Song	What is Woman Like?

March 24	Song	The Sweet Little Girl that I Love
	A Comic Song In the course of the evening, several new pieces of music will be introduced.	
March 31	Musical Entertainment	Children in the Wood
April 4	Song	The Moments Were Sad When My Love and I Parted
	Musical Farce	The Padlock
May 2	Musical Farce	No Song, No Supper
July 4	Musical Entertainment	Sprigs of Laurel . . .
July 17	Musical Entertainment	The Shipwreck; or, The Sailor Boy
July 19	Comic Opera	Rosina
August 4	Musical Farce	The Flitch of Bacon
August 8	Comic Opera	The Highland Reel
August 11	An Olio: To consist of Recitations, Songs, and Dances	
August 18	Grand Military Music, On the Stage, assisted by Amateurs—consisting of Clarinets, Flutes, Bassoon, French-horn, Tambonr [sic] de Bass and Drum.	
	Musical Farce	The Agreeable Surprise
September 1	Pantomimical Ballet	The Scheming Milliners
	Comic Opera	The Shipwreck
December 8	Comic Opera	Inkle and Yarico
December 26	Ballet Pantomime	Christmas Gambols

Table 6

MUSICAL PERFORMANCE OF THE RICHMOND CIRCUS
1819

References from the Richmond Compiler, *1819*	Type of Performance	Title
January 11	Song with flute accompaniment	Echo Song
	Song	Tea Table Talk, or, Scan Mag
January 14	Musical Farce	Turn Out
January 16	Operatic Farce	No Song, No Supper
January 18	Musical Farce	The Benevolent Tar, or, The Purse
January 19	Flute Solo	The Tyrolese Song of Liberty with variations
January 20	Opera	Rosina, or, the Reapers
January 21	Musical Farce	The Turnpike Gate
January 22	Musical Farce	Of Age Tomorrow
January 25	Tragedy	Macbeth, (with all the original music by Handel, Purcel and Dr. Arne. Scots music between the acts.)
January 26	Ballet	The Soldiers Return

Table 7

MUSICAL PERFORMANCES IN THE "NEW RICHMOND
THEATRE"
1819

References from the Richmond Compiler, *1819*	*Type of Performance*	*Title*
July 14	Musical Farce	Sprigs of Laurel
June 15	Musical Farce	Agreeable Surprise
June 19	Musical Farce	The Grandmother
June 21	Musical Farce	The Purse, or, the Benevolent Tar
June 25	Musical Drama	Rob Roy, or, Auld Long Syne
	Musical Farce	Lock & Key
June 26	Musical Farce	Rosina
June 29	Musical Farce	Love Laughs at Locksmiths
July 5	Opera	The Mountaineers
July 13	Musical Farce	Highland Reel
July 26	Grand Operatic Romance	Devil's Bridge
	Musical Farce	Turn Out
July 29	Musical Farce	Poor Soldier
August 2	Musical Farce	The Prize
October 11	Musical Afterpiece	The Poor Soldier
October 12	Musical Farce	My Grandmother
October 14	Musical Afterpiece	The Prize
October 19	Musical Farce	The Romp
October 22	Musical Afterpiece	Of Age Tomorrow

October 26	Musical Afterpiece	Lock & Key
November 5	Musical Afterpiece	Love Laughs at Locksmiths
November 6	Musical Farce	The Spoil'd Child
November 8	Musical Farce	Turn Out
November 9	Musical Farce	No Song, No Supper
November 13	Musical Afterpiece	Rosina, or, The Reapers
November 15	Musical Farce	The Prize
November 18	Musical Farce	Agreeable Surprise
November 20	Musical Afterpiece	The Review
November 22	Musical Afterpiece	Of Age Tomorrow
November 25	Musical Afterpiece	No Song, No Supper
November 30	Musical Afterpiece	The Agreeable Surprise
December 13	Musical Farce	Highland Reel
December 15	Musical Afterpiece	Lock & Key
December 16	Musical Drama	Paul & Virginia

Performers

Actor-singers in the theatre before the fire of 1811 were Comer, Green, Hopkins, Fox, Smalley, Spear, Story, Sully, West, and Wilmot. Actress-singers were Mrs. Green, Mrs. Hopkins, Mrs. West, and Mrs. Wilmot. Story sang in the temporary theatre of 1804, taking the leading role in *Inkle and Yarico,* and on another occasion he sang "Sweet Little Girl that I Love."[85] Comer, Spear, Fox, and Twaits were featured as singers in the new theatre from 1806

85. *Virginia Gazette,* January 21 and March 24, 1804. (See Table 5.) The Library of Congress has a copy of "Sweet Little Girl that I Love" by James Hook.

through 1811.[86] Sully, who, with his wife and children, had probably quit the theatre and settled in Richmond, sang several novelty and comic songs in the theatre in 1809.[87] Wilmot sang a duet with Charles Southgate in 1807, and on the same program, Southgate played in an instrumental quartet.[88] The other members of the instrumental group with Southgate were Decker, playing flute, Widemeyer, playing violin, and Lataste, playing viola. The selection was advertised as "A favorite quartett of Pleyels." Decker was probably a professional actor, having taken a benefit performance in 1804.[89] Widemeyer may have been a professional musician, but his name is seen only once again, appearing in a later concert. John Lataste was the previously mentioned dancing master.[90]

Two other musicians and associates of Southgate during this early nineteenth-century period were John Bray and A. Baker. Southgate, as an editor of the *Visitor,* published Bray's "Maid of the Mill," "Nancy of the Hill," and "The Unquenchable Flame." He also wrote the words that were published with the latter tune.[91] Southgate's own compositions appearing in *The Visitor* are "President Madison's March," written for two cornos, two clarinets, and a basso, and "A New Song" for voice with piano accompaniment.[92] A. Baker advertised in *The Visitor* as a teacher of piano in Richmond in 1809, and a composition by A.B., "The Canary Bird," is published in the same maga-

86. *Virginia Gazette,* January 29, 1806; February 4 and June 13, 1807; December 15, 1809; August 15 and November 4, 1811; and *Argus,* November 7, 1809.

87. *Argus,* November 7, 10, and 17; December 5, 1809; and *Gazette,* December 15, 1809.

88. *Gazette,* February 7, 1807.

89. *Gazette,* March 26, 1804.

90. *Gazette,* October 14, 1808 *et passim.*

91. *The Visitor,* I, No. 20 (November 1809) , 160; I, No. 22 (December, 1809) , 176; I, No. 24 (January 1810) , 198.

92. *Ibid.,* I, No. 12 (July 1809) , 96, and I, No. 23 (December 1809) , 192.

zine.[93] Since Baker's advertisement was the only one of its kind in *The Visitor,* A.B. the only unidentified composer, and Southgate the music editor of *The Visitor,* it is assumed that Baker and A.B. were the same person.

Mr. and Mrs. West and Mr. and Mrs. Green are the only theatre singers whose names appear in theatrical advertisements both before and after the theatre fire of 1811. The Wests had been active in southern theatres since 1790. Both appeared in the circus in 1818 with Mr. West apparently as manager.[94] Mr. Green, who had been brought to America by Wignall in 1794, was one of the managers of the theatre when it burned in 1811. He also played a season in the new theatre during 1819–20.[95]

Musicians performing with the circus preceding the opening of the new theatre in 1819 were Mr. and Mrs. Richardson and Messers. Boyle, Hunter, Stuchbury, Williams, Stamp, and Norton. Richardson led the band and was featured as a double flageolet and piano player.[96] Mrs. Richardson and Boyle sang duets and also solos.[97] Hunter, Stuchbury, Williams, and Stamp were featured as singers,[98] Norton as a flutist.[99]

The manager of the "New Theatre," which opened in 1819, was Charles Gilfert, a talented musician who later managed the Bowery Street Theatre in New York. An advertisement of the performance of "The Ethiope" stated that the music was by Gilfert.[100] "Bed of Roses," sung by Moreland in the theatre, was written by Gilfert.[101] Moreland later sang a comic song, "Irish Promotion, or, Paddy

93. *Ibid.,* II, No. 6 (March 1810) , 28.
94. *Compiler,* December 7, 1818.
95. Shockley, p. 85.
96. *Compiler,* December 2, 1818 *et al.*
97. *Ibid.*
98. *Ibid.,* July 23, December 1, 1818, and January 11, 1819.
99. *Ibid.,* January 7, 1819.
100. *Compiler,* October 16, 1821.
101. *Ibid.,* July 24, 1822.

Carey's Fortune," with a Kent Bugle obligato by Mr. Nevoty.[102] Among his offerings on the Kent Bugle, Nevoty included Gilfert's "Bed of Roses."[103]

> When Nicolas of the Theatre orchestra gave a concert at the Eagle Hotel, he was assisted by Mrs. Waring, Green, Hilson, and Howard of the acting company; and Gilbert not only closed the Theatre for the occasion but himself performed on the Piano Forte for the first time in Richmond.[104]

Two other musicians who shared in the apparent conviviality under the management of Gilfert were Keene and Philipps, both of whom also gave concerts outside of the theatre. Keene was featured as a singer from September through October 1821.[105] Thomas Philipps was introduced to the Richmond audience as a vocalist and actor who had been successful in Boston, New York, Philadelphia, Baltimore, Charleston, and Savannah.[106] One critic considered him the best singer ever heard this side of the Atlantic.[107] An excerpt from a newspaper advertisement illustrates a typical playbill format with the individual songs listed.

·   ·   ·   ·   ·   ·   ·   ·   ·   ·   ·   ·   ·

Romantic Opera of the Devil's Bridge
Count Belino   Mr. Philipps
Who in the course of the Opera, will sing the following Songs, composed by Braham.
  "Behold in his soft expressive face."
  "Tho' Love is warm awhile."
  "Is there a Heart that never Loved?"
    'TIS BUT FANCY'S SKETCH,
      (The celebrated Picture Song.)

102. *Ibid.*, September 6, 1823.
103. *Ibid.*, September 25, 1823.
104. Shockley, p. 88.
105. *Ibid.*, p. 91.
106. *Mercantile Advertiser,* June 10, 1822.
107. Shockley, p. 130.

And will introduce the Grand Cantata of
  WILLIAM TELL, THE SWISS PATRIOT
. . . .[108]

Concerts

As it had been in the last decade of the eighteenth century, the Eagle Tavern, later called the Eagle Hotel, continued to be the principal gathering place for concert
audiences during the first quarter of the nineteenth century. Other public buildings—the Hay Market Garden, the
museum, the Union Hotel, and the Capitol—were also
used for concert presentations. Theatre entertainers and
orchestra musicians were the principal performers, the
concert being a means of supplementing their earnings.
There were some concerts or musical entertainments by
itinerant musicians not associated with theatrical troupes,
but the touring artist or virtuoso of the concert field who
was not associated with theatrical entertainment was rarely
seen in Richmond until after the first quarter of the
century.

Mrs. Sully, who announced her first concert in Richmond in 1792 and gave others during the last few years
of the century, advertised a proposed concert in 1803
while she and her husband were performing in a circus
held on the grounds of Hay Market Gardens.

> Mrs. SULLY
> Respectfully informs the Ladies and Gentlemen of Richmond
>   and Manchester, that she proposes having
>   A CONCERT
> (Assisted by several Gentlemen Amateurs of Richmond) of
>   Vocal & Instrumental Music,
> At Hay-Market Gardens, on Thursday, September 15th, the
> particulars of which will be announced in the bills of the
> day.[109]

---

108. *Compiler,* June 14, 1822.
109. *The Virginia Gazette and General Advertiser,* September 17, 1803.

Mr. Folly, organist at Hay Market Gardens and music teacher in Richmond, gave a concert of vocal and instrumental music at the Gardens "with the assistance of Mr. Hopkins and others."[110] Hopkins was a theatre performer and the "others" may have been both theatre musicians and some of the amateurs who had appeared with Mrs. Sully.

The last concert given by theatre performers before the calamitous theatre fire of 1811 suggests that Lefolle, Ribes, Taylor, Gallaher, and Southgate were members of the theatre orchestra. Miss Thomas, Mr. Twaits, and Mrs. Green were actor and actress-singers of the theatre troupe. However, neither Southgate, a cellist as well as a singer, nor Gallaher, clarinetist, has been positively identified as regular members of the theatre orchestra.

Grand Vocal and Instrumental CONCERT
Messers. Lefolle & Taylor, of the Richmond Theatre, respectfully inform the lovers of harmony, that with the approbation and at the request of many Amateurs of Musick, they intend giving a Concert at the Eagle Tavern, on the 26th inst. to consist of the following

FIRST PART

Grand Overture, Full Orchestra   Pleyel
    Song, Awake ye dull Sluggards
        By Miss Thomas,
    Air, with variations on the Violin
        By Mr. Lefolle   Kreutzer
    Song, When Edward left his native plain,
        By Mrs. Green   Hook
    Concerto, On the Clarinet
        By Mr. Gallaher   Michel
    Finale   Pleyel

SECOND PART

Grand Symphony Concertante, Violins Principal
    Messers. Lafolle and Ribes   Kreutzer
    Song, By Mr. Twaits

110. *Enquirer,* December 29, 1804.

Concerto, on the Flute,
          By Mr. Taylor   Devienne
Glee,   By Miss Thomas, Mr. Twaits,
          and Mr. Southgate   Ebdon
Concerto, on the Violin,
          By Mr. Lefolle   Kreutzer
Favorite Pollaca. Now Love and Joy
          By Miss Thomas   Condell
Finale   Pleyel[111]

Soon after the termination of the city ordinance that prohibited entertainment for four months following the theatre fire, two itinerant Italian musicians proposed a "grand" concert of vocal and instrumental music. They were Signor Pucci and L. Brucherie, who sang and played instrumental accompaniments and instrumental duets. Pucci played a "grand" overture and a "Sonneto," Brucherie performed an "Extempore Sonata" and a "Concerto Piano," and together they played "grand" duets and variations. Their vocal presentations consisted of both Italian airs and English songs.[112] A final program of that visit was given two weeks later.[113] The concerts by Pucci and Brucherie were unique in that theatrical personalities and presentations found no place on them, and the musicians themselves were not associated with a theatrical troupe. Brucherie's allied vocation was that of musical instrument repairman advertising himself as "being competent and highly recommended."[114] Pucci's allied vocation was that of demonstrating, selling, and teaching the harp, an instrument popular among lady amateurs. Pucci returned to Richmond four years after his first visit.

SIGNOR PUCCI
GRAND CONCERT
of Vocal and Instrumental MUSIC, in the Long Room, at

111. *Argus*, November 25, 1811.
112. *Ibid.*, May 14, 1812.
113. *Ibid.*, May 30, 1812. Program—Appendix B.
114. *Ibid.*, May 12, 1812.

the Bell-Tavern. By request of several Ladies and Gentlemen of Richmond, Signor Pucci . . . will exhibit a performance on the much admired King David's PEDAL HARP.[115]

Pucci returned to Richmond once again during 1819 to perform on the pedal harp "for his own benefit" at the museum.[116]

Theatre performers gave a concert in 1814 under the leadership of Gallaher, the clarinetist who had performed on previous concerts. Other instrumentalists were Stephan, violinist; Weidemeyer, flutist; and Southgate, cellist. Singers were West and Maher.[117]

When the circus and the newly built theatre were giving regular performances in 1819, the performers from both places gave several concerts. Richardson, the orchestra leader of the circus, gave a concert at the museum, in which he played the "Grand Piano Forte, Pedal Harp, Flute, Violin, and double Flageolet."[118] Vocal performers were Boyle, Hunter, and Mrs. Richardson; and "the admired Band of Amateurs" assisted Richardson in the performance of military airs, marches, and patriotic songs given at intervals during the program. Twibill, of the circus, gave two concerts at the Eagle Hotel. He was the only singer on those programs and was accompanied by a band of music on the first.[119]

Mrs. French gave several ballad concerts at the Eagle Hotel in Richmond during January 1819. Her piano accompanist was Mrs. Sully, whose daughter also appeared on a program for her first Richmond performance. Miss Sully played harp accompaniments for Mrs. French and also played duets with the piano.[120] Later in the year the *Compiler* reprinted from a Boston newspaper a review

---

115. *Enquirer*, January 23, 1816.
116. *Compiler*, December 21, 1819.
117. *Argus*, April 9, 1814. Program—Appendix B.
118. *Compiler*, January 7, 1819.
119. *Compiler*, March 30 and April 2, 1819. Program—Appendix B.
120. *Ibid.*, January 18 and 20, 1819.

in which Mrs. French was given the highest praise for her appearance in Boston.[121] Mrs. French returned to Richmond in 1821, giving a concert "accompanied on different instruments."[122] Returning the next year, she gave several concerts accompanied by Mrs. Sully.[123]

"The whole orchestra of the theatre," under the direction of Nichols, accompanied theatre performers in two concerts at the Eagle Hotel, one in June and the other in August, 1819.[124] The first concert featured Mr. P. De Bihl, "lately from Europe, and pupil to the celebrated Lafont, first violin of the Conservatory of France."[125] The second concert was given "for the benefit of Mrs. Green," who was assisted by Mrs. Sully and "several Musical Gentlemen" of Richmond along with the theatre orchestra. Mrs. Green and Mr. Nichols sang; Mrs. Sully played the piano accompanied by De Bihl, probably the concert master of the orchestra. De Bihl also played two violin solos, and the theatre orchestra supplemented by amateurs played a "simphony" [sic] and an overture by Mozart.[126]

Mr. M'Cleary, "from Dublin, Montreal, New-York, and Philadelphia theatres," gave several entertainments consisting of songs and recitations at the Union Hotel and the museum.[127] For his final concert he announced that "the Band is engaged for this evening and will perform several patriotic and fashionable airs."[128]

Philipps, the popular ballad song writer and theatre performer from Dublin, gave a concert at the Eagle Hotel while he was in Richmond appearing in the theatre. He was assisted by his pupil, Miss Davis, from Dublin.[129]

121. *Ibid.*, June 4, 1819.
122. *Ibid.*, January 6, 1821.
123. *Ibid.*, February 19 and 25, 1822. Program—Appendix B.
124. *Ibid.*, June 21 and August 9, 1819.
125. *Ibid.*, June 21, 1819.
126. *Ibid.*, August 9, 1819. Program—Appendix B.
127. *Ibid.*, April 30, May 3, 15, and 16, 1822.
128. *Ibid.*, May 16, 1822.
129. *Ibid.*, June 20, 1822. Program—Appendix B.

Keene, also of the theatre, gave a series of ballad concerts before leaving Richmond.[130] Apparently the theatre orchestra accompanied him, and in addition to the sentimental and comic songs by Keene, several waltzes arranged by Mr. Berg were played. The waltz had recently been introduced in America and had not yet found general approval as a proper dance in polite society.[131]

During the latter part of the first quarter of the nineteenth century, touring musical entertainers independent of the theatre began to appear more frequently, giving their programs one or more times at each stop on their itinerary. The Lilliputian Songsters from Boston sang in Richmond at the Eagle Hotel in 1821.[132] The Songsters were apparently two midgets, Miss Caroline and Master Edward Clark.[133] The Lewis family, the first of a long succession of family groups to perform in Richmond, gave concerts in 1821 at the Eagle Hotel.[134] Mr. P. Lewis with four of his children played the piano, harp, violin, and cello at the beginning of the year; and on his return visit at the end of the year, the youngest member of the family had also been added to the act.[135]

Other itinerant entertainers giving concerts were Miss Victoire Boudet, Patrick Connelly, Mr. Denny, Mr. Stanhope, and Mr. Smith. Boudet sang and played the harp at the Eagle Hotel.[136] Connelly gave a "concert of music, comprising the Irish Bag-Pipes, Flute and Violin . . . at the room lately occupied as the Intelligence Office."[137] Denny advertised as the "celebrated performer on the

130. *Ibid.*, January 25, 28, and 31, 1823.
131. Program—Appendix B. Objections to dancing the waltz are cited in Chapter 4.
132. *Compiler*, January 2, 1821.
133. *Ibid.*
134. *Ibid.*, January 15, 1821, and December 4, 1821.
135. *Ibid.*
136. *Ibid.*, August 14, 1822.
137. *Ibid.*, April 21, 1819.

Pipes" and proposed to give "a concert on the Violin and
Patent Union Pipes at the Union Hotel."

> He will perform on both instruments, at the same time, a
> number of Scotch and Irish Airs, &c. together with some
> fashionable Waltzes, and also imitate with the pipe the
> human voice.[138]

Stanhope offered a "novel exhibition by performing . . .
popular airs on that melodious combination, called the
CELESTENA, or HARMONICAL GLASSES, at the Virginia Museum."[139] Smith also played a set of music glasses, which
he called a Harmonicon and which could be purchased
from Smith at Fitzwhylsonn's store for $50. His perfor-
mances were given several times in the Hall of the House
of Delegates and finally in the theatre.[140]

Compared to the artistically inferior offerings of visiting
performers during this first quarter of the century, the
resident Richmond musicians apparently produced some
programs of relatively good taste. Under the leadership
of Mrs. Sully a concert was given in 1823 at the Eagle
Hotel that included instrumental works of Haydn, Rossini,
and Mozart, but concessions were made to the public's
taste, and many popular airs of the day were also performed. The performers were Mrs. Sully, piano; Mr.
Milon, guitar and violin; Mr. Berg, violin; Miss Sully,
harp; and Mr. Sully, flute.[141] The Sully family had offered
musical leadership in Richmond throughout the early
period of Richmond's concert life. The other concerts
of relatively high merit by Richmond residents were given
in churches.

---

138. *Ibid.*, December 19, 1822.
139. *Ibid.*, April 27, 1819.
140. *Ibid.*, December 17 and 24, 1824.
141. *Ibid.*, May 21, 1823. Program—Appendix B.

Music of the Church

The Protestant, Roman Catholic, and Jewish faiths were represented among the organized religious groups in Richmond during the latter part of the eighteenth century. The organizations were predominantly Protestant Christian groups, and all continued their activities into the nineteenth century. During the first quarter of the nineteenth century, religious groups experienced both progress in building places of worship and growth in numbers, and among the Protestant denominations, musical practices were established that were to persist until after the Civil War. The Protestant Episcopal Church, which traced its ancestry to the Anglican Church, was probably the strongest of the organizations, and the music activities of the Episcopalians apparently exceeded those of other churches in both quality and quantity.

Whether or not the surge in denominational growth and church building that took place in the second decade of the nineteenth century was incited principally by the theatre fire of 1811 is conjectural, but the fact that the disaster was cited by ministers in Richmond and in other cities as an evil omen possibly added impetus to the developing religious fervor of the period. The Monumental Church, still in use today, was built on the site of the theatre fire, and was first used for public worship in 1814. Members of all denominations subscribed funds to build the church in memory of those who lost their lives in the fire. It was determined by vote that the Protestant Episcopal Church would be entrusted with the duties of Divine worship in the building. The Episcopal portion of the Capitol congregation, which had been meeting with Presbyterians, moved into the new church, and the Presbyterians of that congregation continued to worship in the Capitol until their own church was completed in 1821.

There was much additional organizational and building activity by church groups during the first quarter of the century. A group of Presbyterians apart from the Capitol congregation organized in 1812 and built the First Presbyterian Church in 1816. Regular services at St. John's Church (Episcopal) were resumed in 1814. The First Baptists had built a new church by 1802, and the Second Baptist Church had been organized by the beginning of the third decade of the century. The Methodists in Richmond were a small but growing denomination. The Catholics were renting a chapel in 1815, and in 1820 the state of Virginia became a diocese with its see at Richmond. The Hebrews built places of worship in 1811 and again in 1822.

It is apparent that it would have been feasible for churches to utilize organs of some type if they had wanted them, since several early nineteenth-century entertainments in Richmond included organ music, and there was an organ in Hay Market Garden by 1802. However, by the end of the first quarter of the nineteenth century, there were apparently only two organs in use in Richmond, both in Episcopal churches. Other Protestant denominations, the Presbyterians possibly excepted, evidently preferred singing without the aid of instrumental music. They also preferred to have a song leader with a reasonably accurate ear and a strong voice than to have a choir to lead the singing.

Music of the Episcopal Church
The earliest reference to specific music used in a church service in Richmond was found in *The Visitor*. A letter to the editor of *The Visitor* comments on the lack of taste for music used in church worship at the Capitol.[142] The writer who identifies himself as Mentor, considered the

142. See 143.

"84th, Old Hundred, Wells, Windle, &c," excellent but thought "Sherburne & Easter Anthem" to be trash."[143] The next issue of *The Visitor* contained an answer to Mentor, signed by Senex, who was also a member of the Capitol congregation. Senex wrote that "Sherburne" and "Easter Anthem" were his favorites, and his letter indicates that congregational singing had recently been introduced or had recently become fashionable. He wrote that formerly he had been satisfied with listening to others sing and play, but now he must give in to the new way—"nothing will do, it seems, unless every man is to sing and join in the 'noise of a numerous Congregation,' whether he is acquainted with the music or not."[144] The Capitol congregation was supported in its singing by a choir "composed of some ladies and gentlemen of the city," among whom were Mrs. George Fisher and Mrs. Charles J. Macmurdo, Senior, and during services "Mr. Patrick Gibson performed very sweetly on the flute."[145] After the Episcopalians moved from the Capitol to the Monumental Church they "had pretty much the same choir which had

143. *The Visitor*, I, No. 6 (April 1809), 42. The "84th" may have referred to the setting of the 84th Psalm, which is included in Charles Southgate's *Harmonia Sacra* (New York: Edward Riley, n.d. [1820]). "Old Hundred" was included in the *Bay Psalm Book* and is known best today as the "Doxology." "Wells," an Anglican Church tune, may be found in Erik Routley, *The Music of Christian Hymnody* (London: Independent Press Limited, 1957), p. 276. "Sherburne" was probably a fuging tune written by Daniel Read (1757–1836) and published in his *The Columbian Harmonist* (1793—fourth edition in 1810). "Easter Anthem" probably referred to a fuging tune written by William Billings and first printed in his *Suffolk Harmony* (Supplement) published in Boston (1786). Read's "Sherburn" and Billing's "Easter Anthem" were included in later compilations used in singing schools. One of these was *The Lexington Cabinet, and Repository of Sacred Music . . .*, compiled by Robert Willis (Lewisville [*sic*]: Norwood & Palmer, 1831). The Virginia Baptist Historical Association, University of Richmond, has a copy of the latter publication.

144. *Ibid.*

145. George D. Fisher, *History and Reminiscences of the Monumental Church, Richmond, Virginia, from 1814 to 1878* (Richmond: Whittet & Shepperson, 1880), p. 174. Fisher is quoting a letter written by Thomas H. Drew.

been accustomed to sing in the hall of the house of delegates."[146]

The first conclusive evidence concerning the use of church organs in Richmond begins with the events recorded in 1816, when Mr. Hart was authorized by the vestry committee of St. John's Church "to treat for and purchase, for the use of this Church . . . an organ valued at . . . $1,000" by its New York builder.[147] In December of the following year the committee discussed means of raising money to pay for the organ and "other fixtures for the church."[148] The names of the organists were not given in the existing records until 1823, but it is recorded that a committee was appointed to employ an organist in 1820, "the term of the late organist having expired."[149] In 1823, Mr. Evans was appointed organist with the stipulation that he would receive a fixed percentage of the Sabbath collections for his duties, a minimum guarantee being $100 per year.[150] The record book shows that Mr. Evans asked the Vestry to make up the deficiency when his alloted percentage of the collection had amounted to $34 less than the guaranteed minimum.[151] Mr. Evans was to be asked in June 1825 to serve as organist and clerk, and the last payment was made on the organ that year.[152]

The organist at St. John's Church, James Evans, was also the first person to play the organ for a service in the Monumental Episcopal Church. The Monumental Church organ was imported from London "and put up under the direction of Mr. Charles Southgate, assisted by carpenters, from minute and specific directions of Bevington, the

146. *Ibid.*, p. 181.
147. "Record Book of St. John's Parish," 1785–1887, May 17, 1816 (no pagination).
148. *Ibid.*, December 16, 1817.
149. *Ibid.*, July 15, 1820.
150. *Ibid.*, July 15, 1823.
151. *Ibid.*, November 15, 1824.
152. *Ibid.*, June 29, 1825.

organ builder,"[153] James Evans described the events leading to and following the first service in which the organ
at Monumental Church was used.

> When the organ was up, and partially tuned, public notice
> was given that it would be used the following Sunday, and
> a sermon preached by Bishop Moore prepared for the oc-
> casion. It was arranged that Mrs. Sully was to play the organ
> on the occasion, and I on the following Sunday. On the
> morning of Sunday, before service, Mrs. Sully informed the
> Bishop she would not be able to play, as she had no oppor-
> tunity to try the organ. The bishop sent for me, and said,
> "James, you must play the organ to-day, as Mrs. Sully is not
> prepared, and will not be here." I remarked that I was in
> the same situation; had not tried the organ, or practised
> with the choir. That good old gentleman replied that . . .
> I must play. I did so, going through with the choir, the full
> Episcopal service. The following Sunday Mrs. Sully played.
> During the week I was waited on by two of the vestry, in-
> forming me that I had been elected organist. Having under-
> stood that Mrs. Sully had a large and dependent family, and
> music her profession, and only means of support, and the
> organist's salary would much aid her, I respectfully declined
> accepting the situation. Where-upon Mrs. Sully was elected,
> and appointed, and held the situation of organist for a num-
> ber of years. Mr. Southgate died while Mrs. Sully was organist.
> There was but one church in the city that had an organ, and
> that was the "Old Church," now "St. John's." Miss Sally
> Sully was organist for several years.[154]

From data concerning the dates of Southgate's death
and the installation of the new organ at St. John's Church,
the conclusion is drawn that the organ at the Monumental
Church was installed in 1817 or 1818. However, the organ
is not mentioned in the following notice of a concert, the
first of its kind in Richmond, presented in the Monumental Church:

    The Oratorio.

153. George D. Fisher, pp. 187–88, quoting a letter written by James
Evans.
154. *Ibid.*

The Music Teachers Room in Colonial Williamsburg, Virginia, exemplifies the living-working atmosphere of Cuthbert Ogle, Francis Russworm, and many others who taught music in eighteenth-century Virginia. Popular instruments for instruction included recorders, harpsichord, violin, French horn, and guitar. Today, visitors can hear eighteenth-century music played on these instruments during a visit to the one-room Music Teacher's Shop. (Photo: Colonial Williamsburg, Inc.)

Carter's Grove Plantation near Williamsburg was a principal center of culture in colonial America. Philip Fithian was employed as tutor to the Carter children during 1773 and 1774. Fithian's copious journal and letters tell us a great deal about the musical lives of colonial Virginians. (Photo: Colonial Williamsburg, Inc.)

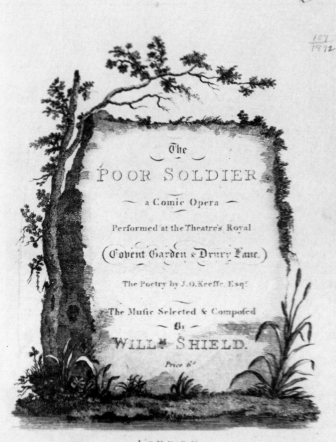

The Poor Soldier, *with music selected and compiled by William Shield (1748–1829), followed the format established by John Pepusch (1667–1752) in the* Beggar's Opera, *first performed in 1728. These musical entertainments were known as "ballad operas." The libretto was about common man rather than the aristocracy of traditional operas. The melodies were selected from well-known tunes of the day, and performers often substituted their own words and choice of tunes. The Poor Soldier was a favorite musical entertainment of eighteenth-century theatre patrons. The complete score is available at the Library of Congress. (Photo: from a Library of Congress microfilm)*

Bruton Parish Church, Colonial Williamsburg, has been in continuous use since it was built in 1711–15 to replace the first Bruton Parish Church that had become too small. Peter Pelham was instrumental in the installation of the organ in 1755 and served as organist for almost 50 years thereafter. He also worked as a clerk, jailer, and musician in Williamsburg. (Photo: Colonial Williamsburg, Inc.)

A FAVOURITE SONG by Mrs. LEWIS.

To which [by desire] will be added a FARCE, called

The CHEATS of SCAPIN.

SCAPIN,	BY	Mr. WALL;
GRIPE,		Mr. LEWIS;
LEANDER,	BY	Mr. SMITH;
CLARA,	BY	Mrs. SMITH.

End of the Farce a much admired Epilogue, in Character

of an Old Woman.

N. B. TICKETS may be had at Mr. FORMICOLA's TAVERN, Mr. ANDERSON's TAVERN, and at Mr. SMITH's lodgings, at the BIRD in HAND TAVERN, at ONE DOLLAR each, and no distinction of price.

*** Those Ladies and Gentlemen who are disposed to befriend Mr. Smith, may not be deterred from coming, they may be assured, that every precaution is taken for the safety of the house, and Peace Officers are appointed to keep good order outside.

Good MUSIC is engaged.

A portion of the earliest known playbill of a Richmond Theatre is held by the Virginia State Library. Lewis and Smith were members of a company of comedians managed by Dennis Ryan. The company played in Baltimore, Annapolis, New York, Richmond, and Charleston during 1783–1784. (Photo: Virginia State Library)

The Virginia State Capitol, Richmond, shown in this earliest known drawing of the building illustrates how it may have appeared at its completion in 1792. From before its completion to 1815, church services were conducted by Episcopalian and Presbyterian ministers on alternate Sundays. The congregations and hymn singing probably changed little from week to week. The building was also used for various social occasions including dancing at celebration balls. (Photo: Virginia State Library)

Disaster struck on December 26, 1811 when the Richmond theatre burned. The theatre had been completed and occupied in 1806. The city mourned the event and built a church on the site of the tragedy in memory of those who died in the fire. (Photo: Virginia State Library)

Monumental Episcopal Church, Richmond, is depicted in an old drawing. The church was built on the site of a tragic theatre fire as a memorial. Members of all denominations subscribed funds to build it. The building stands today and is utilized by the Medical College of Virginia. (Photo: Virginia State Library)

The First Baptist Church in Richmond, with additions made to the small building occupied in 1802, became cruciform and was the largest auditorium in Richmond at the time. It had a colorful history both as a religious place of worship and as an auditorium for political, civic, and musical events. In 1841 the Negro members organized as the First African Baptist Church and took possession of the building, and from that date it was known as the African Church. Ole Bull, Adelina Patti, Paul Julien and numerous other musical artists performed there. (Photo: Courtesy the First Baptist Church, Richmond, and the Virginia State Library)

Metropolitan Hall, Richmond (foreground), was formerly the First Presbyterian Church. It opened in 1853 and soon became the leading place of variety, minstrel, and concert entertainment in the city. (Photo: Courtesy of Whittet & Shepperson, publishers, Richmond, and the Virginia State Library)

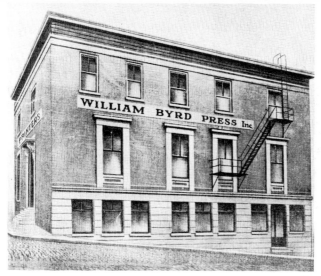

The Odd Fellow's Hall, Richmond, became one of the three principal places in the city, in addition to the theatre, offering musical entertainment to audiences during the 1840s. Called the Odeon, it may be considered the first vaudeville theatre in Richmond. (Photo: Virginia State Library)

The Exchange Hotel, Richmond, was one of the finest hotels in the city prior to the Civil War. Its concert room was a popular place for more elite musical performances, balls, and dancing academies. In 1848, for example, the opera troupe then appearing at the theatre also gave concerts at the hotel. Theodore Thomas, who contributed much to the founding of our American symphony orchestras, performed there at the age of 15. (Photo: Virginia State Library)

The Richmond Female Institute offered instruction in music. Voice, piano, and harp were proper media for ladies of that day, and no lady was considered properly educated until she had developed some musical skills. (Photo: Virginia State Library)

Louis Antoine Jullien, an Englishman, visited Richmond in 1855 with his orchestra. He brought good music and high quality performances, but with these he mixed showmanship and novelty arrangements. The performance pleased the public, and a newspaper reported that "we have little doubt the echoes of it will be heard in Metropolitan Hall for twelve months to come." P. T. Barnum was Jullien's manager for the visit. (Photo: Virginia State Library)

The Citizens of Richmond and its vicinity are respectfully
informed that the proposed ORATORIO will be performed
in the Monumental Church, on TUESDAY Evening next at
½ past 6 o'clock—the net proceeds of which will be devoted
entirely to charitable purposes.[155]

ORATORIO; or Concert of Sacred Music,
    (For Charitable purposes)
At the Monumental Church, THIS EVENING, December 3,
1818.

FIRST PART

1. Old Hundredth Psalm, by   M. Luther.
2. Anthem—"Blessed be thou Lord God,"   Kent.
3. Trio and Chorus—"Sound the Loud Timbrel," Avison.
4. Solo and Chorus—"Strike the Cymbal,"   Pucitta.
5. Trio and Chorus—'Welcome, Welcome, Mighty King,"
                                         Handel's Saul.
6. Duett and Chorus—"Hosanna,"   Greger.

PART SECOND

1. Recitative, Duett and Chorus—"Sweet was the Song,"
                                              Original.
2. Air—"Must I Leave Thee Paradise,"   M. P. King.
3. Chorus—"O Sing unto the Lord a New Song," Clarke.
4. Recitative Air, Duett & Chorus: "Sweet as the
      Shepherd's Tuneful Reed,"   J. F. Hering.
5. Grand Hallelujah Chorus,   Handel's Messiah.[156]

Five years after the first concert was given, a similar concert was held in the Monumental Church but with "an
introductory piece on the organ" given at the beginning of
each half of the program.[157]

Charles Southgate, Richmond's first resident composer
whose works are preserved, also composed and compiled
music of the Episcopal Church. His most ambitious works
were advertised posthumously in the *Compiler*.

155. *Compiler*, November 28, 1818.
156. *Compiler*, December 3, 1818.
157. *Compiler*, December 20, 1823. The program is included in Appendix B.

HARMONIA SACRA

Southgate's Sacred Music, containing
a collection of Original and Choice
Psalm & Hymn Tunes, with An Ode to
Harmony, Two Gloria Patria's, one
Collect, six Anthems—and
A TE DEUM
Composed and Harmonized
by the late
Charles Southgate, of Richmond, Va.[158]

The preceding advertisement establishes an approximate date of Southgate's death. The printing, first advertised to be completed in 1818, was not completed until 1820 when an advertisement stated that the subscribers were "invited to pay the subscription and receive the work after 15th March at the store of Mary Southgate."[159] Two copies of Southgate's *Harmonia Sacra* are known to exist—one in the Henry E. Huntington Library, San Marino, California, and the other in the University of Pennsylvania Library. Seven of the compositions in the collection are by Southgate: "Sabbath Morning," "The Spacious Firmament on High," "Warminister," "Supremely Great Eternal Cause," "Give Ear O Heavens," "Funeral Anthem," "The Lord My Pasture Shall Prepare."

Music in the Presbyterian Church

No distinction can be made between the music of the Episcopal Church and that of the Presbyterian Church in Richmond during more than a decade at the beginning of the nineteenth century because the congregations worshiped together at the Capitol. From the middle of the second decade of the century the Presbyterians of the Capitol congregation held their services without the Epis-

---

158. *Compiler*, November 24, 1818.
159. *Ibid.*, March 7, 1820.

copalians, and they continued to worship at the Capitol until they built a church in 1821, which was the beginning of today's Grace Covenant Presbyterian Church.

That the First Presbyterian Church membership apparently did not object to the use of musical instruments in the church is shown by a concert given there in 1824. The program printed in the *Whig* stated: "N.B. The above pieces will be accompanied with a variety of Musical Instruments which have been judiciously selected for the occasion."[160] The program is similar to those given in the Episcopal Church of that period, but it is one of the few examples of this kind given during this first half of the century.

Records concerning other music used by Richmond Presbyterians during the first quarter of the century are obscure or lost. Foote states that "the book most widely used among the more conservative Congregationalists and the Presbyterians was . . . commonly called Dwight's Watts."[161]

Music in the Baptist Church

John Courtney, Senior's *The Christian Pocket Companion*: "Being a collection of the newest and most admired SPIRITUAL SONGS, Now made use of amongst the United Baptists of Virginia" was sold in Richmond in 1802.[162] Courtney's "Collection of Hymns & Spiritual Songs" was advertised in 1804 and in 1805.[163] Courtney was pastor of the First Baptist Church in Richmond during most of the first quarter of the nineteenth cen-

---

160. *Whig*, May 11, 1824. See the program in Appendix B.
161. Henry Wilder Foote, *Three Centuries of American Hymnody* (Cambridge: Harvard University Press, 1940), pp. 187–88.
162. *The Virginia Gazette and General Advertiser* (Richmond), July 24, 1802.
163. *The Virginia Argus* (Richmond), March 28, 1804, and *The Virginia Gazette and General Advertiser* (Richmond), May 29, 1805. The book was frequently advertised in other issues of these papers during those years.

tury, and "although he loved the great hymns of Christianity, . . . he preferred to 'line out' the hymns of his congregation, resisting the desire of some members of his congregation to use hymn books in the worship service."[164] Courtney's *Christian Pocket Companion . . .* , published in Richmond in 1805, includes hymns by Watts, Wesley, and other hymn writers of the day as well as a collection of spiritual songs unidentified by author. Tunes are not specified, but the meter is indicated for some of the hymns. It is clearly indicated in the preface that the book was intended to be used in singing, but the tunes that were used in Richmond when these hymns were sung were not recorded.

Music in the Methodist Church

The Methodists, who had been denied the privilege of using the Henrico County courthouse because their enthusiasm for singing and shouting disturbed the peace of the neighborhood, had, at the beginning of the nineteenth century, "a small but comfortable church, built of brick, in which they held services morning and evening on Sundays, and night services during the week."[165] The principal Methodist hymn books of the period were Wesley's book, published in England in 1780 and in Baltimore in 1814, and Robert Spence's *Pocket Hymn Book,* which included 320 hymns in the 1802 revision. Later, Daniel Hitt's supplement was bound with Spence's book and became known as the Double Hymn Book. With revisions and supplements, Wesley's book was used until mid-nineteenth century.[166] One of the best known Methodist hymn books in Virginia was Stith Mead's *A General Selection of the Newest and Most Admired HYMNS and Spir-*

164. White, p. 37. The minutes of the First Baptist Church in Richmond through 1825 have not been preserved, but White has assembled some information concerning activities of the church.
165. George D. Fisher, p. 174.
166. Stevenson, p. 16.

itual Songs Now in Use. . . . It was first printed in Richmond in 1807, and the second edition, printed in Lynchburg in 1811, was "published by permission of the Virginia Conference held at Raleigh," North Carolina.[167] The 1807 edition contains 151 hymns—words only—and no indication is given concerning meter or tunes. The words of several of the hymns included in the book have a camp-meeting flavor. Mead was appointed to a pastorate in Richmond in 1805, and he was "one of the most effective of the Virginia camp-meeting organizers."[168] The Mead *Journal* and other documents that Mead had collected were destroyed in the Richmond evacuation fire in 1865.[169]

The camp meeting, universally recognized as primarily a Methodist institution, was never officially so. The Methodist historian, Pell, gives an evaluation of the movement.

> The social and revival meetings of early Methodism possessed no greater influence over the popular mind than the hearty singing of the spiritual songs of that day. Nor has Methodism suffered anywhere a greater loss than in the substitution of the over-cooked and dessicated productions of so-called musical science, rendered, alas! too often, by unwashed lips, for the spontaneous, simple, heart-stirring worship of an entire congregation.[170]

The camp-meeting, spiritual, and hymn tunes produced during the first quarter of the nineteenth century comprise a unique segment of our developing American music. They have added little if anything to our present-day music literature, but they undoubtedly left their mark on later developments in our musical heritage.

---

167. Quotation is from the title page. Both editions are in the Virginia State Library, Richmond, Virginia.

168. William Warren Sweet, *Virginia Methodism, A History* (Richmond: Whittet & Shepperson, 1955), pp. 163–64.

169. *Ibid.,* p. 169.

170. Pell, p. 222.

Chapter 4

A New Generation:
Twenty Years of Musical
Development, 1826-1845

Steam-powered boats and trains were gradually coming into use and replacing sailboats and stagecoaches during the second quarter of the nineteenth century. The steam engine had brought about the first major change in modes of travel since the early days of recorded history. Formerly, man had depended upon animals and the forces of nature for means of locomotion, but the new generation was utilizing a machine to carry itself about. Unlimited possibilities in a new mechanical and scientific age were foreseen.

The period was so engrossed in natural wonders, so eager for prodigies of all kinds, so responsive to the extraordinary and the outlandish, so consumed with credulous curiosity, that if it were necessary to select among its exponents the most typical figure of the age one would be tempted to name [Phineas Taylor] Barnum who more than any other personage of his day, understood these national characteristics and made haste to exploit them.[1]

1. Meade Minnigerode, *The Fabulous Forties, 1840–1850* (New York: G. P. Putnam's Sons, 1924), p. 222.

Barnum's circus enterprises and charlatanry have over-shadowed more worthy undertakings such as his management of the American tours of Ole Bull and Jenny Lind.

The people of Richmond were fascinated with panoramas, circuses, daguerreotypes, and balloon ascensions, and any performance that could be seen or heard in amazement was assured an audience. Musical counterparts to the extraordinary developments of the era were the minstrel, Swiss bell ringers, Ole Bull, Fanny Elssler, the polka, and the quadrille. But in addition to catering to the multitude's preoccupation with shallow and spectacular entertainments, Richmond's visiting and resident musicians provided performances and leadership toward the development of refined musical tastes.

Music on Social and Public Occasions

"Bands of Music" were present at balloon ascensions, circuses, and exhibits. "Feats on a gymnastic principle" and the swallowing of six swords were accompanied by a band of music in the museum.[2] An advertisement of a panorama presented at the museum states that "the pictorial display will comprise 3000 square feet of canvas: the whole accompanied on the violin by Mr. Parnell."[3] Music given later with the panorama comprised "a fantasia on the violin by Mr. Parnell, and a variety of songs by Mrs. Conduit, Miss S. Buckley, and Mr. Franklin."[4] The performers were otherwise associated with the theatre.

Maelzel's exhibitions were presented three times in Richmond: in 1829, 1834, and in 1836—the music was "automatic."[5] The mechanical "base fiddler," the "automaton trumpeter," and the "melodium" were among the

2. *Whig*, August 15, 1833, and January 4, 1834.
3. *Whig*, October 31, 1834.
4. *Ibid.*, November 21, 1834.
5. *Whig*, February 26, 1829; September 16, 1834; and March 4, 1838.

exhibits brought to Richmond by Maelzel.[6] "Daguerre's magical pictures from Paris" were shown in the Exchange Hotel Concert Room, and it was announced that "Madame Lonati, from the Royal *Conservatoire* at Paris, will execute on the Piano Forte, at intervals of the Pictures, several favorite airs."[7] A steam engine "attached to an organ" performed "a great variety of pieces for the entertainment of the visitors" at a fair sponsored by the Second Baptist Church in 1843.[8] A temperance festival featured a choir singing "Touch Not the Cup," and "a real Clay Whig Concert" featured "a variety of Whig Songs set to the most popular airs" during 1843 and 1844.[9] Such was the nature of musical offerings heard by Richmond residents as they attended public events during the second quarter of the nineteenth century.

Dancing continued to be a popular social pastime, and many dancing teachers made Richmond their permanent or temporary home between 1826 and 1845. They taught dances that were popular in the north, for by that time merchandise and social fads from the city of New York were considered the epitome of fashion. Mr. Boissieux, a dancing teacher from New York, arrived in Richmond in 1829. He built and occupied a new dance hall, which was opened with a "Grand National Ball" at the close of 1830.[10] It was stated that Boissieux's building, called Terpsichore Hall, would accommodate 800 to 1000 persons, and that an orchestra of 12 musicians would play marches between the cotillions.[11] Other dancing schools

6. The melodium may have been one of Maelzel's Panharmonicons, which consisted of flutes, trumpets, drums, cymbals, triangles, strings struck with hammers, clarinets, violins, and cellos. An early model played music by Haydn, Mozart, and Crescenti. Later, Beethoven composed music for one of Maelzel's "automations." (*Groves Dictionary*, V, 500–01).

7. *Whig*, March 22, 1842.

8. *Ibid.*, February 24, 1843.

9. *Ibid.*, October 26, 1843, and April 3, 1844.

10. *Whig*, December 29, 1830.

11. *Ibid.* See Appendix A—Terpsichore Hall.

were held in Tanbark Hall, the Union Hotel, and in residences. Among the persons offering dancing instruction in Richmond between 1828 and 1842 were Mr. Guigon, T. W. Vaughan, Auguste Tatin, Mr. Blondel, E. C. Breeden, Casmire Grodzinski, and Madame Hazard.[12]

Dancing classes and balls found opposition from some Richmond citizens, their objections stemming from religious tenets of the day. An unsigned article published in a Richmond newspaper listed "ten reasons why ladies ought not to waltz."[13] In spite of opposition and setbacks confronting dancing masters, balls and dancing schools were apparently popular throughout the fourth decade of the century. However, during the fifth decade dancing possibly lost the public favor for a short period. From 1843 through 1845 no dancing school notices nor references to dancing being taught in the young ladies' academies are to be seen in the newspapers of Richmond. The burning of Terpsichore Hall in 1843 and the severe economic depression of 1844 may have been relative to the cause of the apparent temporary cessation of dancing activities. However, dancing was again popular from 1846 through the Civil War.

Music Merchantry and Instruction

Richmond's music merchants carried substantially complete stocks of music supplies and were able to offer adequate services for tuning and repairing instruments throughout the second quarter of the century. William N. Fitzwhylsonn, who had been one of the leading music merchants in Richmond for ten years or more, was succeeded by R. D. Sanxay when he apparently closed his music and bookstore (*ca.* 1830).[14] Sanxay advertised:

---

12. *Ibid.,* November 24, 1828; January 4, 1842; *et passim.*
13. *Ibid.,* March 12, 1832.
14. *Whig,* August 31, 1830. Sanxay advertised his business as successor to Fitzwhylsonn.

Blake's, Cramer's, Clementi's and Challoner's Preceptors for the Forte Piano; also preceptors for the Flute, Violin, Flageolet, Guitar, Hautboy with marches, cotillions, waltzes, airs, Rondos attached to them, Cadences and scales of major and minor keys. . . .[15]

A later advertisement by Sanxay was typical of those published by music merchants of the day.

Music for the Piano, of every variety and the latest and most fashionable, is received from the northern publishers every few days, which renders the assortment very extensive.[16]

J. H. Nash, bookseller and stationer who had sold musical instruments since 1824, offered violins, guitars, flutes, clarinets, flageolets, fifes, tambourines, and "every other article in the music line," including instruction books and other music scores.[17] Of the numerous merchants advertising in the newspapers of the day, Collins and Company, succeeded by R. I. Smith; Smith and Palmer; Smith, Drinker and Morris; and Drinker and Morris, respectively, were among the principal names seen.[18] P. H. Taylor, flutist and probably Richmond's leading musician, opened a music store in 1836, and soon became the leading music merchant in the city.[19] His was the principal music shop of Richmond throughout the mid-century period.[20] W. J. Davis and J. W. Randolph, both Civil War era publishers of music, were music merchants beginning respectively in the fourth and fifth decades of the century.[21] All well-known piano

15. *Ibid.*, November 3, 1830.
16. *Ibid.*, January 4, 1834.
17. *Ibid.*, September 26, 1829.
18. *Ibid.*, January 30, 1829; February 23, 1844; *et passim*.
19. *Whig*, January 28, 1836, *et al.*
20. *Ibid.* and *Dispatch*, March 25, 1861, *et passim*. The latter article is an obituary giving some details of Taylor's career.
21. *Whig*, October 7, 1833, and October 25, 1842.

manufacturers of the day were represented by Richmond merchants, and at least two persons, F. R. Burkhart and William Kearsing, advertised pianos that were made in Richmond.[22] Kearsing was also a local piano tuner and repairman for a number of years.[23]

Other music merchandise advertisements selected from newspapers issued during the period give further indications of the musical trends of the day. The first accordions and seraphine were sold in Richmond by C. Hall in 1836.[24] The same year, P. H. Taylor first advertised unichord pianos containing "only one string for each note (supposed not to get out of tune so easily) ."[25] Advertisements of Taylor's merchandise indicate that his store was well stocked with music merchandise, and repair and tuning services were provided. Innovations of the fifth decade of the century are indicated in the advertisements of quadrilles,[26] Ethiopian operas tunes,[27] Henry Russell's songs,[28] "the Manual of the Boston Academy of Music for instruction in the elements of vocal music in the system of Pestalozzi,"[29] *The Music Library*,[30] and the polka.[31] A

22. *Ibid.*, October 10, 1829, and November 13, 1838.
23. *Ibid.*, January 30, 1838; November 1, 1844; *et al.*
24. *Whig*, February 23, 1836. The accordion was invented in Vienna by Danian in 1829 (*Groves Dictionary*, I, 29) . A precursor of the harmonium, the seraphine was a keyboard-operated, wind-blown reed instrument with a harsh and rasping tone (*Groves Dictionary*, VII, 705) .
25. *Whig*, July 6, 1836.
26. *Ibid.*, April 15, 1841. P. H. Taylor, merchant.
27. *Ibid.*, January 28, 1843. Smith, Drinker and Morris, merchants.
28. *Ibid.*, October 31, 1843. J. W. Randolph, merchant.
29. *Ibid.*, November 29, 1843. Drinker and Morris, merchants. The advertisement possibly refers to Lowell Mason's: *The Manual for Instruction of the Boston Academy in the Elements of Vocal Music*, 1834 (*Groves Dictionary, American Supplement*, p. 286) .
30. *Whig*, February 27, 1844. Rufus Morse, merchant. A series of English publications of 1834–1836, the *Musical Library* "proposed to publish a collection of music, both vocal and instrumental, by the best of masters, ancient and modern. . . ." [*Musical Library*, London: Charles Knight, I (April 1834) , preface]. Copies of the *Musical Library* are held by the Virginia State Library.
31. *Whig*, October 17, 1844. P. H. Taylor, merchant.

wide variety of instruments and music scores were available in the music stores of Richmond from the fifth decade of the century to the Civil War period.

The musical merchandise was made available, partially if not to a great extent, for instructional purposes. Instruction in music was offered to the citizens of Richmond by theatre performers, concert artists, church school or singing school music teachers, and teachers in the young ladies' schools. The purposes of music study were apparently varied and included: (1) acquiring a social grace fashionable among young ladies, (2) learning to play an instrument or to sing for pleasure, (3) developing necessary skills needed to participate in church services and amateur sacred music groups, and (4) preparation for a theatrical, concert, or teaching career. Neither the academies for young men nor the public schools included music instruction in their curricula, and students in these schools studied music privately if they were interested and could afford to take lessons. Also, they could avail themselves of less expensive group instruction in sacred music given from time to time in Richmond's churches.[32]

Advertisements of the young ladies' schools generally stated that music and dancing were taught by the best masters available but usually did not identify the teachers. Exceptions to the general practice were announcements stating that Miss A. Hudson would teach music at Mr. and Mrs. Reynolds' Female Seminary in 1828, Mr. M. B. Poitiaux would teach music at Miss Mackenzie's female seminary, and Miss Ford would teach piano at Mrs. Jarvis and Miss Liscomb's school in 1840.[33] Teachers who offered to give private music instruction and who may have taught in the young ladies' schools include Mr. Pena, Mrs. Giles Hallam, Miss Frank, Miss Frances E. Nelson, Rufus Morse,

32. The topic is developed further in this chapter under *Music of the Church.*
33. *Whig,* August 27, 1828; October 18, 1830; and November 2, 1840.

Mr. M. Messersmith, and Mrs. M. A. Clark. Pena moved to Richmond from Williamsburg in 1830 and offered his services as a teacher of piano, guitar, singing, and composition through the columns of the *Whig*.[34] Mrs. Hallam announced that she would teach young ladies to play the piano.[35] Miss Frank advertised that she had studied in New York and would teach singing in Richmond in 1839.[36] That same year, Miss Nelson offered instruction in piano playing.[37] Morse advertised in 1840 that he would "resume teaching piano, singing, and classes in vocal music."[38] Morse was also a music merchant. Messersmith announced that he would continue to give lessons on the guitar, trombone, key trumpet, French horn, flute, and violin and that he had a German brass band available for engagements.[39] Mrs. Clark stated that she would resume giving instruction on the Piano Forte in 1843.[40] Other persons who taught music in Richmond during the years 1826 through 1845 were theatre performers, concert artists, or teachers of sacred music, and they are presented in the sections that follow.

Music of the Theatre

During the second quarter of the nineteenth century, the Richmond Theatre was probably not as strong in music and drama as it had been from 1819 to 1823. Three reasons for its inability to reestablish a strong position in the next two decades were (1) the unsettled economic conditions of the times, (2) the star system that dominated the American and English stage at that time resulting in

---

34. *Whig*, September 11, 1830.
35. *Ibid.*, October 3, 1833.
36. *Ibid.*, January 29, 1829.
37. *Ibid.*, September 27, 1839.
38. *Ibid.*, October 9, 1840.
39. *Ibid.*, April 13, 1841.
40. *Ibid.*, September 19, 1843.

strong leading roles but weak supporting casts, and (3) increasing competition, at first from circuses and later from other forms of theatrical entertainment—minstrels, concert artists, and other traveling entertainers. Gilfert, the manager of the theatre from 1819 to 1823, left Richmond in October 1823. From that time until November 1827, the theatre was idle except for a short season in 1824 given by James H. Caldwell's company from Petersburg. From 1827 to 1834 the theatre was operated periodically by several managers. In 1829, there were three companies playing in close succession, each under different managership, and in that year more performances were given than in any other year during the period 1826–1845. The State Constitutional Convention that was held in Richmond in 1829 was probably largely responsible for the series of successful seasons that year. On October 3, 1829, it was announced that the theatre had been repaired and decorated "equal in splendor to the Northern Theatres" and the best orchestra and stage departments of the United States had been procured.[41] The attractions leaned heavily toward vaudeville presentations, and the management announced that prices were up "to meet the heavy expenses incurred by engaging STARS."[42] After the successful year at the end of the third decade of the century, the Richmond Theatre again fell into disuse except for about one month of each year until 1838, when the building was sold, renovated, and reopened under the name of Marshall Theatre.[43] Dramas and musicals were offered in the Marshall Theatre for several seasons, but by 1844 the management resorted to reducing prices because of the depression; thus the theatre fare for the next two years consisted of novelties and minstrels rather than any attempt to produce more refined musical stagings.

41. *Compiler.*
42. *Compiler,* October 9, 1829.
43. *Whig,* November 20, 1838. See Appendix A—the Richmond Theatre.

There were a number of circuses that played in Richmond from 1826 to 1845. Many of them were given in the Amphitheatre, which was a large wooden building on Fourteenth Street near Main Street. Dramatic pieces were given regularly and often were combined with equestrian performances. The Amphitheatre was erected in the fall of 1829 during the Theatre's biggest year; and, while the financial panic caused the Theatre to be closed possibly for the entire year of 1835, the Amphitheatre opened in April of that year with "a stud of 30 horses, a splendid band of music," and theatrical entertainment.[44]

> The Amphitheatre with its clowns and jugglers, its spectacular horsemanship, and its inferior presentations of broad farces and high melodramas, was the Theatre's most serious competitor for the popular favor of the Richmond audience.[45]

The third decade of the nineteenth century saw the entrenchment of a form of theatrical entertainment born in the theatre but later destined to coexist with its parent as a separate entity. The new medium began in the theatre as a short burlesque sketch of serious drama and opera. It emerged in its permanent form as an Ethiopian opera later known as a minstrel show, an American form of entertainment destined to capture the fancy of audiences from all walks of life in the United States and to some extent in Europe.

Performances

The custom of presenting a major piece such as a tragedy, melodrama, comedy, or musical followed by a shorter afterpiece, usually a farce, continued through the second-quarter century period, as did the custom of filling in the intervals between the two pieces with singing and dancing

---

44. *Compiler,* April 22, 1835.
45. Shockley, p. 56.

by members of the acting company or the visiting stars. Throughout the period the specialties between the dramatic pieces became more numerous, but Shakespeare's dramas retained their popularity. "In spite of the large number and the great popularity of farces and operettas, and in spite of the tendency of this period toward sentiment and spectacle," Shakespearean plays were more numerous than those of any other playwright, Cibber's *Richard III* being the most popular offering.[46] A comparison shows that there was a close relationship between the Richmond Theatre, other American theatres, and the contemporary English theatre.

In one instance the specialty presentation completely overshadowed the drama. Soon after Fanny Elssler toured America as a danseuse and a theatrical star, the Richmond Theatre postponed its dramatic engagements "for the purpose of presenting the accomplished French *artistes* of her Troupe."[47] Ordinarily, however, drama continued to be offered when the theatre was open, and in 1845 a series of melodramas and the Shakespearean repertory with Edwin Booth were given.

Musical plays continued to follow the pattern established during the first quarter of the century. "Evidently both composers and singers felt free to use whatever material they desired regardless of where it might be found."[48] No operatic company played in Richmond until 1848, but operas were given periodically by the dramatic companies augmented by visiting stars, the music being altered and arranged to suit the talents of the company.

---

46. Shockley, p. 171.
47. *Whig*, January 5, 1841. Fanny Elssler, pioneer performer of the abbreviated costume and free motion of the limbs school, brought in $24,000 in 15 New York performances in 1840, and was welcomed to Richmond with the firing of cannon and tolling of bells (Minnigerode, pp. 48–49).
48. Shockley, pp. 151–52. Shockley presents detailed citations that illustrate the freedom enjoyed by stars who inserted their favorite songs in various stage productions.

The operas must have been remarkably uneven in quality, for the casts contained all degrees of musical talent; but audiences accustomed to the star system undoubtedly expected and accepted uneven productions.[49]

The theatre advertised a performance of *The Marriage of Figaro* in 1829 in which Susanna was played by Madame Feron,

> who will introduce besides the music of the opera, the following songs:—"I pray thee now list to me," "though from thee I now depart," Italian variations composed for Madame Feron called "Confuso a l'amore," and by desire, "The Soldier tired of War's alarms." At the end of the opera Madame Feron will sing a new Italian song called "A Compir Gia," accompanied on the violin by Mr. Parnell. And a new and highly popular Ballad called "The Milk Maid," will be sung in character by Madame Feron. Mr. Dickson will sing an entirely new Song, called "Tree-Hill Races."[50]

In 1841 the Theatre advertised the presentation of the opera *"Barber of Seville* with all of the original music" by Rossini, followed by a "favorite Scotch Ballad," "My Boy Tammie," sung by Miss Inverarty, and the evening's entertainment was to conclude with a comedy.[51]

During the fall of that same year (1841) a series of operas were given, each followed by the inevitable afterpiece. The dates of performances, the operas, and the composers are as follows:

November 22, 1841	La Sonnambula	Bellini
November 23, 1841	Cinderella	Rossini
November 24, 1841	The Elixir of Love	Donizetti
November 25, 1841	Fra Diavolo	Auber
November 27, 1841	Cinderella	Rossini
November 30, 1841	Fra Diavolo	Auber[52]

49. *Ibid.*, p. 155.
50. *Whig,* October 22, 1829.
51. *Ibid.*, March 29, 1841.
52. *Ibid.*

The capstone to this first English opera series given in Richmond was a concert presentation of the first act of both *Cinderella* and *Fra Diavolo* followed by a farce.[53]

Orchestras and Bands

The Theatre orchestra supplied overtures, accompaniments for singing and dancing, and background music for the drama. For the most part, theirs was a secondary or supporting role. However, in one instance the "Leader of the orchestra, Mr. Willis" was placed at the top of the playbill.[54] In another instance the orchestra was featured with Master Burke, who not only played the leading dramatic roles of the evening, but was also scheduled to "lead the orchestra in the overture of Tancredi," and "play a Fantasia, on a violin with only one string."[55] When the Marshall Theatre opened the orchestra was featured and sometimes played three overtures during an evening's performance.[56] Advertisements for the first season of the Marshall Theatre announced the following overtures to be played by the orchestra:

Overture to *Tancredi*
Overture to *Fra Diavolo*
The "New Overture"
"Overture Elise et Edward"
Overture to *Massaneillo*
The Overture to the *Bronze Horse*
The Overture to *William Tell*
The "National Airs" Overture
"Lodoiska" Overture
The Overture to *Il Barbiere de Seveglia*[57]

53. *Ibid.*, December 1, 1841. Ballad operas and musical dramas had been performed periodically from the beginning of the Theatre in Richmond, but not in series nor by an opera company.
54. *Whig*, April 25, 1829.
55. *Ibid.*, January 3, 1833.
56. *Whig*, December 21 and 25, 1838, and January 22, 1839.
57. *Ibid.*, November 30, 23, 27, 20; December 7, 11, 14, 18, 21, 25, 1838; January 1, 4, 22, 1839; and March 30, 1839.

Most of these overtures were repeated at subsequent performances, and the above list formed the core of the orchestra's overture repertory. Nine musicians including the orchestra leader were named in an advertisement of the opening of the fall season in 1840.[58] This number of musicians, which may be assumed to be the usual complement of the Richmond theatre orchestra of the day, would hardly be expected to perform from the original scores. Their overtures were probably arranged to suit the musicians on hand as well as to suit the taste of the audience.

Bands and orchestras performed with the circuses. The circus offered melodrama, horsemanship, vaulting, dancing, singing, and performances by trained animals, advertising that "the splendid Band of Music will accompany the performers, and play several favorite overtures."[59] Palmer's New Amphitheatre advertised that the orchestra will, "as usual, perform a number of pleasing airs and Operatical pieces."[60] Waring, Raymond & Co.'s "Mamoth Menagerie & Museum" brought to Richmond the "Washington Military Band from Philadelphia, whose science and taste in music there are none to surpass and but few to equal in the United States."[61]

The band of the Richmond Light Infantry Blues performed in the theatre on two occasions in 1829: once on the stage during the presentation of a play, and again at a later date between a play and the afterpiece.[62] "The whole Military Band of the Blues" was engaged to play in the theatre with circus acts in 1837, and the next year the same band "volunteered their services" for a benefit performance.[63]

---

58. *Ibid.*, September 29, 1840.
59. *Ibid.*, May 1, 1835.
60. *Ibid.*, April 26, 1836.
61. *Ibid.*, June 9, 1837.
62. *Ibid.*, February 16, 1829; and *Compiler*, June 8, 1829.
63. *Whig*, April 28, 1837; and February 9, 1838.

Beginnings of the Minstrel

The first Ethiopian opera in Richmond was given as an afterpiece to a circus performance in 1834. The performance was advertised to conclude with

> The Ethiopian Opera of O HUSH!!! Or, the Long Island Cupids. In the course of the opera, the following Glees, Duets, Trios, Songs &c. will be sung:—Glee, "Come all you Virginny Gals"—Glee, "Down in Old Virginny"—Glee, "Sam Johnson," &c.—Song, "Long Tail Blue"—Duett, "Lubly Rosa." The whole to conclude with a dance by the characters.[64]

Given along with an exhibition of gymnastic feats in Terpsichore Hall was an Ethiopian Concert by Sanford in 1836. It was announced that "Mr. Sweeny, whose performances on the Banjo are so highly appreciated in Richmond, will accompany Mr. Sanford."[65] Two months later Sweeny and Sanford were a part of the theatre cast, Sweeny playing "a real Banjo, made by himself."[66]

Apparently little notice was taken of the "Negro Delineator" entertainment, and when Thomas Dartmouth Rice, "The original Jim Crow," performed in the Richmond Theatre in 1838, the newspaper praised the dramatic presentation but did not mention Rice.[67] The minstrel show began to take the nation by storm in the early 1840s. Perhaps it was not coincidental that the first minstrel was introduced to Richmond audiences in the guise of a lecture, a method similar to that used in the eighteenth century when plays were first introduced as lectures or readings.

Lectures on Music, &c.
At the Concert Room, Exchange Hotel.

64. *Ibid.,* July 4, 1834.
65. *Ibid.,* December 9, 1836.
66. *Ibid.,* February 18, 1837.
67. *Ibid.,* January 16 and 18, 1838.

Messrs. German, Harrington, Stanwood and Pelham . . .
propose giving a Series of Lectures on Music and Phren-
ology, commencing on FRIDAY NIGHT, November 3d., at
the Concert Room in the Exchange Hotel.

The citizens may rest assured that there is nothing in the
Lectures, either in word or action, to offend the most fas-
tidious. . . .[68]

Within a week the lecturers were assured of success and
popularity as they moved into the theatre.

The Ethiopian Serenaders have created quite a sensation
amongst our Concert Room Visitors, and they have politically
determined to extend it throughout all classes by taking the
Theatre for three nights, and reducing their prices to such
rates as to afford all persons the power of witnessing an Entertainment which has been invariably extolled by all who
have attended their performances. The surprising talent of
the Ethiopians, on their Peculiar Musical Instruments, is too
well known in Richmond, to require eulogium, and their
liberality in reducing their prices of admission to twenty-five
cents for Boxes and half that sum for the Pit, is certain to
ensure them delighted and crowded audiences.[69]

The same group returned to the theatre the next spring
and presented

entertainments varying nightly, and consisting of Songs,
Glees, Trios, Quartetts, Overtures, Quicksteps, Waltzes,
Comic Lectures, Conundrums, &c., accompanied with Ac-
cordeon, Banjo, Congo, Tambo, and Bone Castinetts.[70]

In 1845 the Ole Bull Band of Serenaders, whose instrumentation was "Violin, Triangle, Jaw-Bone, Tamborine,
and Banjo," gave a "concert" in the theatre.[71] The Ethiopian Serenaders and Joe Sweeney both returned to the theatre as specialty performers between dramatic offerings.[72]

68. *Ibid.,* November 2, 1843.
69. *Whig,* November 2, 1843.
70. *Ibid.,* March 26, 1844.
71. *Ibid.,* February 3, 1845.
72. *Ibid.,* October 20 and December 1, 1845.

Performers

Actor-singers featured in the theatre during the period 1826–1845 included Keene, Cargill, Philipps, Ferrell, Garner, Stickney, Dixson or Dickson, Pennington, Heyle, Sloman, Cowell, Young Cowell, Kenny, Hadaway, Collett, Sanford, Cooper, Meer, Master Meer, Foster, Knight, Horn, Garner, Braham, Brough, Chapman, Reynolds, and Robinson.[73] For the most part, few contemporary accounts of their activities are available other than the advertisements indicating that they were to sing in the theatre. Several of the performers also gave concerts.

Some of the actress-singers during the same period were Mrs. Belcour, Mrs. Collins, Mrs. Osborne, Mrs. Stickney, Mrs. Flynn, Mrs. Jefferson, Mrs. Cooper, and Mrs. Robinson.[74] Other actress-singers who were given more notice in the press were Miss Clara Fisher, Miss Kelly, Miss Rock, Madame Feron, Mrs. Knight, Miss Horton, Mrs. Martyn, and Miss Inverarity. Miss Clara Fisher was regarded as a 17-year-old wonder by newspaper writers.[75] Miss Kelly and Miss Rock played roles comparable to Miss Fisher's, all three actresses receiving praise for their singing and acting in musical dramas.[76] Miss Rock also played the harp, and on one occasion she sang "The Dashing White Sergeant" and "Oh! I ne'er shall Forget" while accompanying herself on the harp.[77] Madame Feron played in Richmond less than a year after she had made her debut in New York. Her four-night theatre engagement followed by a benefit and a concert at the Capitol "attracted the most fashion-

73. Shockley, pp. 100–10; *Whig,* April 22, October 10, 13, 23, 1829; February 4, 1833; December 16, 1836; January 6, March 3, June 24, December 12, 1837; January 19, 1838; March 23, December 3, 1841; October 15, November 10, 1845; *et al.*

74. *Ibid.*

75. *Whig,* February 16, 1828.

76. *Whig,* October 6, 27, 1828; November 2, 1829. *Compiler,* November 7, 1828.

77. *Whig,* January 7, 1829.

able house" of the season.[78] Mrs. Knight, who appeared
with her husband as piano accompanist, had been "the
reigning vocal favorite" in New York before coming to
Richmond.[79] Besides playing in the theatre, Mr. and Mrs.
Knight taught and gave concerts in Richmond from 1829
to 1831.[80] Miss Horton, pupil and later the wife of C. E.
Horn, co-starred with Horn in the theatre and in concerts
during 1838.[81] Mrs. Martyn and Miss Inverarity were the
only theatre performers giving benefit and farewell concerts in the theatre rather than in some other public hall.[82]

Theatre orchestra leaders during the 1826–1845 period
were Parnell, Willis, Barrett, Rogers, J. K. Opl, and Arth.
Parnell took an active part in Richmond's concert life
while he was associated with the theatre. He had been the
orchestra leader in 1828, co-manager of the theatre and
orchestra leader in 1829–30, and apparently the manager
during the short seasons in 1830–32.[83] Willis, "celebrated
as a leader and composer" from Philadelphia, led the orchestra and played the violin for a theatre company apparently unrelated to Parnell's.[84] Barrett led the orchestra
with Barber, the pianist, in 1837.[85] Barber remained in
Richmond and took an active part in Richmond's musical
life as teacher, organist, and as accompanist in concerts.
J. K. Opl, who also took an active part in Richmond's
musical life outside of the theatre, was introduced as
"Leader of Operas" in the theatre orchestra of 1840, and
the same orchestra had a "Dramatic Leader," Mr. Arth.[86]

---

78. *Compiler,* November 6, 1820.
79. George O'Dell, *Annals of the New York Stage* (New York: Columbia University Press), III, 239–40.
80. *Compiler,* April 14, 1831, *et al.*
81. *Whig,* January 19, 1838.
82. *Whig,* April 8, 12, 1841.
83. Shockley, pp. 101–03.
84. *Whig,* April 15 and 29, 1829.
85. *Whig,* October 3, 1837.
86. *Ibid.,* September 29, 1840.

The other musicians of the orchestra were F. A. Opl, J. Laing, Kenneberg, W. B. Cook, Murano, Wagner, and Rauk, but they were not listed among musicians on concert programs in Richmond.[87] Rogers was billed as "the celebrated Equestrian Leader" of the orchestra for Howes' "Great Olympic Circus," which played in the theatre in 1844.[88]

Instrumental entertainers in the Richmond Theatre were Peterson, Master Burke, Mr. and Mrs. St. Luke, and Joe Sweeney. Peterson was featured as pianist with the orchestra directed by Parnell giving "The Grand Turkish Overture to the Caliph of Bagdad" between two melodramas.[89] Master Burke led the orchestra in the same overture as an added attraction to his playing the lead in Richard III.[90] Master St. Luke and Mr. St. Luke had a "trial on Violins" during a "Grand Musical Pot Pourri" presented between Shakespeare's *Tempest* and a "comic extravaganza."[91]

Joe Sweeney was probably the only Virginia-born musician who rose to fame as a theatre entertainer before 1865. His performances were well received in Richmond, but he won his fame touring and performing in other American cities. On his return to Richmond in 1845 Sweeney was presented in a specialty number between dramatic offerings in the theatre and was advertised as "Old Joe Sweeney the great original banjo player having returned from a successful tour through England, Ireland, and Scotland."[92] Much of Sweeney's career is shrouded in legend. He is said to have made and played on the first banjo of the type that later became standardized—the banjo with

87. *Ibid.*
88. *Ibid.,* January 16, 1844.
89. *Ibid.,* November 28, 1828.
90. *Ibid.,* December 27, 1832.
91. *Ibid.,* October 16, 1840.
92. *Ibid.,* December 1, 1845.

a circular resonator box.[93] He was born in 1810 or 1813 in Buckingham County, Virginia, and died in Washington in 1860.[94]

Concerts

A gradual refinement of musical tastes is noted in the concert presentations to Richmond audiences through the third, fourth, and into the fifth decades of the nineteenth century. Throughout this period the greater portion of the musical programs called concerts were similar to the special music performances given between dramatic offerings in the theatre but were removed from the theatre and given in the concert hall. Since the theatre served as a nucleus for most music activities, it established the mode for audience taste, and the entertainers and artists independent of the theatre adjusted their offerings to some extent to please the audience.

Concerts during the period from 1826 to 1845 are presented under three general classifications, but the delineations are not explicit. They are: (1) concerts by theatre performers—actor-singers or orchestra musicians active in the theatrical profession, (2) concerts by music artists or entertainers whose vocation was principally that of giving concerts, and (3) concerts in one of the above classifications but of special interest because Richmond musicians performed in them. Several musicians who had toured with theatre and concert troupes made Richmond their permanent residence and consequently contributed to activities designed to raise the standard of musical taste in the city.

Concerts by Theatre Performers
Parnell, orchestra leader in the theatre, appeared with

93. *Times-Dispatch* (Richmond), September 11, 1955.
94. *Ibid.*

members of the orchestra in several concerts at the Eagle Hotel during the spring of 1829. Miss George, daughter of G. George who later taught and performed music in Richmond for several years, gave two concerts assisted by Parnell, Mrs. Gill, Mr. Andre, Mr. Harman, Mr. Sully, and some other instrumentalists.[95] Miss George and Mrs. Gill were vocalists, Parnell arranged the music and played the violin, Mr. Andre played the guitar, Harman is listed as clarinetist on the first program, and Sully is listed on the second program as flutist. That same month, Parnell assisted Mr. and Mrs. Pearman in a concert followed soon thereafter by another concert in which the Pearmans assisted Parnell.[96] Before leaving Richmond, Parnell assisted in another program in 1829—a "Harp concert" given by Mr. Francis. The music, arranged by Francis and Parnell, included "The Blue Bells of Scotland," "Yankee Doodle," "The German Hymn," "The Grand Russian March," and for the finale Francis proposed to play "Extempore Variations on any appropriate theme that may be handed him."[97]

Four other concerts were given during that busy theatrical year of 1829. Mr. and Mrs. Pearman with Mr. Francis gave two or more concerts at the Eagle Hotel in May, the final program being given with the assistance of "several distinguished Amateurs."[98] In March, Mr. Lee, "late of the orchestra of the Richmond Theatre," proposed a concert in which he would be assisted by "the members of the Richmond Blues Band and several gentlemen amateurs."[99] Madame Feron, star theatre performer, gave her benefit concert at the Capitol in the fall of 1829 with the assistance of Mr. and Mrs. Plumer.[100]

---

95. *Whig*, March 6 and 12, 1829. The first program (March 6, 1829) is given in Appendix B.
96. *Ibid.*, March 31 and April 4, 1829.
97. *Ibid.*, April 25, 1829.
98. *Ibid.*, May 9 and 18, 1829.
99. *Ibid.*, March 17, 1829.
100. *Ibid.*, November 4, 1829.

Parnell returned to the theatre in 1831 and led the orchestra for Mr. and Mrs. Knight's concert in the Capitol that year.[101] His successors as theatre orchestra musicians and as associates of the Knights on concert programs were W. and S. Cunnington. Mrs. Knight gave two "ballad concerts" in 1832 at Terpsichore Hall assisted by Mr. Knight, pianist; W. Cunnington, French hornist; S. Cunnington, cellist; and on the last concert, Berg, violinist.[102] Some of Knight's compositions were included on the programs, and instrumental music by Bishop, Mozart, and Rossini was also performed.

Other theatre performers who gave concerts in Terpsichore Hall were Mrs. Gibbs, Master and Mr. St. Luke with amateurs,[103] Horn and Horton,[104] and the Masters Hughes.[105] In the four concerts given by Horn and Horton in 1838, the theatre orchestra's pianist, E. B. Barber, assisted, and in the last three concerts, the theatre orchestra's flutist, P. H. Taylor, performed. Both Barber and Taylor became long-term residents of Richmond and were leaders in musical affairs of the city. The final program by Horn, Horton, Barber, and Taylor is given in Appendix B. The program is typical of others given by Horn at that time, but while sentimentality and comedy comprise a good portion of the program, there are some selections included that are aimed at an audience with more refined musical tastes.

---

101. *Ibid.*, February 19, 1831.
102. *Ibid.*, January 20 and February 13, 1832. The last concert is given in Appendix B. See also Terpsichore Hall—Appendix A.
103. *Ibid.*, November 10, 1837.
104. *Ibid.*, November 25, 1834, and January 2, 1835. Horn gave piano concerts while he was a teacher and piano merchant in Richmond. *Whig*, January 5, 9, 16 and March 6, 1838. Horn and Horton gave "Soiree Musicales" in addition to appearing as stars in the theatre. Horn also conducted an "Oratorio" in the Monumental Church—see *Music of the Church* in this chapter. See also: Richard A. Montague, "Charles Edward Horn: His Life and Works" (unpublished Ed.D. dissertation, School of Music, the Florida State University, 1959).
105. *Whig*, March 20, 1841.

In the spring of 1841, when Mrs. Martyn and Miss Inverarity were star actress-singers in the theatre, they gave their benefit performances as concerts in the theatre —a novel procedure since it was customary for theatre benefits to comprise drama, specialties, and farces, but for benefit concerts to be held elsewhere than in the theatre.[106] The theatre orchestra directed by Opl provided the overtures and accompaniments for the concerts by Martyn and Inverarity. The vocal numbers, solos and duets from various theatre presentations, included English opera selections, ballads, and comic songs.[107]

John Braham, the popular English songwriter-entertainer, was the next and possibly the last theatre performer to give benefit concerts in Terpsichore Hall.[108] He was assisted by Mr. and Mrs. Watson, and the three performers sang sentimental, comic, and Scotch ballad songs accompanied at the piano by Mr. Watson.

Concerts by Itinerant Entertainers and Artists
Independent of the Theatre

The Lilliputian Songsters, who had visited the city in 1821, returned to Richmond to give concerts at the Union Hotel in 1827.[109] Three other performers gave a "grand vocal concert" at the Eagle Hotel in 1827. The opening selection, a "grand overture—'Zauberflute,' for two performers on the piano forte"—was followed by popular songs and ballads sung by the Misses Guillinghams and Mr. Paddon.[110] Francis H. Smith returned to the Hall of the House of Delegates in 1829 to give exhibitions of the "grand harmonicon or musical glasses," allegedly his own

---

106. *Ibid.*, April 8 and 12, 1841.
107. Mrs. Martyn's benefit program is given in Appendix B. Mr. Pearson also sang, and at the conclusion of the concert a "comedietta" and a farce were played.
108. *Ibid.*, May 29 and 31, 1841. The first program is given in Appendix B.
109. *Ibid.*, January 23, 1827.
110. *Ibid.*, February 20, 1827. The program is given in Appendix B.

invention that "only needs to be more generally known to become a fashionable appendage to the parlor."[111] All other concerts between 1825 and 1835 were apparently given by theatre performers.

During the fourth decade of the century, few itinerant concert artists who were independent of the theatre advertised concerts in Richmond newspapers. The earliest noted was a "grand concert" given at Mr. Blondell's Large Ball Room on Main Street by Mr. Schmidt and a "young lady."[112] Schmidt combined virtuosity and showmanship, performing songs, variations *"a la* Paganini," and numerous imitations of non-musical sounds on the violin—all given with piano accompaniments by the young lady.[113] The first Richmond concert to be identified as a "soiree musicale" was given at Terpsichore Hall in 1837 by Mrs. Morley, "Primo Mezzo Soprano, from London, New York, Boston, Philadelphia and New Orleans Concerts," together with Mr. Morley, "Primo Basso Vocalist from the Theatre Royal, Covent Garden, London and the National Theatre, New York."[114] Two selections on the program were from Italian operas and were possibly sung with the original text. The other songs were English adaptations from Italian operas, comic songs, and ballads. The Morleys were assisted by C. W. Taylor, theatre singer; P. H. Taylor, flutist; and E. B. Barber, pianist.

Henry Russell, popular English songwriter and pioneer ballad concert singer, performed twice in Richmond in 1838, singing his own songs interspersed with recitations.[115] His first program was printed in the *Whig,* as was an article announcing the concert.

111. *Ibid.,* October 15 and 16, 1829.
112. *Ibid.,* January 2, 1835. Blondell's ballroom may have been Tanbark Hall.
113. The program is given in Appendix B.
114. *Whig,* November 14, 1837. Program—Appendix B.
115. The ballad concert was "a special kind of concert flourishing in London from the late 19th century . . . and now happily extinct." (*Groves Dictionary,* I, 375).

The lovers of Music, of whom this City numbers many, will not forget that Mr. Russell gives his Concert at Terpsichore Hall this evening. The Northern papers speak well of Mr. R's. vocal powers—and our friends at Washington, who are fully capable of appreciating merit in this respect, assure us that his skill to charm the ear and awaken the sensibilities of the heart, is unsurpassed. Despite the weather, we trust he will have a full attendance of the fair and the fashionable.[116]

Russell gave a second concert at Terpsichore Hall the following week and returned to give a concert five years later at the Exchange Hotel.[117]

As the fourth decade of the century drew to a close, concerts in Richmond by performers independent of the theatre became more numerous. Whereas the American theatre continued to develop along the lines of its English heritage, but with indigenous outcroppings such as the minstrel plus some foreign importations such as English actors and Italian opera singers, the American concert stage began to play host to artists from various European countries, gradually at first, but increasingly to the extent that by mid-century the concert artists from across the Atlantic dominated America's concert life. The first concerts with a substantial number of Italian songs on the programs were given by Madame Brengeri and Signor Fabj, opera singers, accompanied by Richmond's pianist, E. B. Barber.[118] After playing a few nights in the theatre, Fabj "volunteered his services," as did Barber, to assist Madame Dussek O'Connor in a concert given at Terpsichore Hall.[119] They presented operatic selections in Italian and English along with English and Irish ballads.

The spring of 1840 brought three novel concert entertainments to Richmond. Mr. White, advertised as "author

---

116. *Whig,* February 2, 1838. Program—Appendix B.
117. *Ibid.,* February 9, 1838, and November 1, 1843.
118. *Ibid.,* March 12 and 15, 1839. The first program is given in Appendix B. Madame Brengeri offered music instruction to Richmond residents. (*Whig,* March 26, 1839).
119. *Ibid.,* April 2, 1839. Program—Appendix B.

of the 'Boudoir Melodies,' &c.," held a "conversazione musicale with illustrations."[120] Mr. Wall, the blind Irish harper, was "aided by the Artillery Band" in a concert.[121] Miss S. G. Shore, "the Albino Lady," and Mr. J. O'Clancy, "the Irish giant," gave a concert "assisted by Mr. Tank, musician," who accompanied them on the Spanish guitar and on "another new and rare instrument, called the setter."[122]

The year 1843 was eventful for concert audiences in Richmond. In the first part, Taylor and Barber, leading Richmond musicians who had performed with many visiting artists, sponsored their own concerts for the first time.[123] They also performed as assistants to visiting musicians that year: H. S. Beavers, "the celebrated Blind Vocalist"; Signor Nagel, "first violin to the King of Sweeden, and pupil of Paganini"; and Mr. Dempster, "the celebrated vocalist and composer," all of whom gave concerts at the Exchange Hotel Concert Room.[124] In the fall of 1843 the Herren Arnold gave "musical soirees" at the Exchange Hotel. The *Whig* reported that "their manner of executing vocal quartettos, without being sustained by accompaniment, is eminently pleasing and novel to the musical public," and their music is "wide apart from tinsel and trickery of any kind."[125] The article begins as follows:

> The vocal and instrumental Concert given on Tuesday Evening, at the Exchange Hotel, we consider to have been the greatest musical treat within our memory. The entertainments were in the highest degree pleasing and scientific—so

---

120. *Ibid.*, March 21, 1840.
121. *Ibid.*, April 17, 1840.
122. *Ibid.*, May 5, 1840. The setter may have been a citole or a cittern, both respective predecessors of the English guitar—popular ladies' instruments of the eighteenth and early nineteenth centuries, which was gradually replaced by the Spanish guitar during the first third of the nineteenth century.
123. *Whig*, January 12 and February 27, 1848.
124. *Ibid.*, January 31, March 20 and 30, 1843.
125. *Whig*, November 16, 1843.

much so as to put our musical connoisseurs in perfect raptures. Though not over numerous, the audience was highly fashionable and select, and throughout the evening gave vent to the utmost enthusiasm.[126]

The Herren Arnold was followed in a week by W. V. Wallace, pianist and violinist, performing with Mrs. Bailey, a singer. They gave several concerts with Wallace performing "grand fantasias, brilliant variations, and grand variations" on both the piano and the violin and with Bailey offering a variety of songs from operas, Scotch ballads, and Irish airs.[127] A *Whig* article concerning their first concert stated that "Mr. Wallace and Mrs. Bailey are both eminent in their profession. Their united powers will constitute an attraction rarely met with."[128] Richmond's pianist E. B. Barber played accompaniments for Bailey and Wallace on the second and third concerts, and on the final program Wallace performed "the celebrated solo on one string by Paganini, by desire."[129]

The year 1843 ended with a flourish when Ole Bull, Mrs. Bailey, and an orchestra of 16 musicians from Washington directed by Signor La Manno gave a concert at the theatre while on the same night a concert was given at the Exchange Hotel by Madame Cinti Damoreau, "prima donna," and Monsieur J. Artot, violinist.[130] The *Whig* probably devoted more space in reporting the events than had ever been given by a Richmond newspaper to the reporting of musical events.

The musical mania, which follows exactly the old track of the cholera in 1832, has at length reached this city, and is prevailing to an extent of which former epidemics afford no example. We will venture to say, that since Richmond was a city, the same number of persons, or anything approaching

---

126. *Ibid.*
127. *Ibid.*, November 22, 24 and 27, 1843.
128. *Ibid.*, November 22, 1843.
129. *Ibid.*, November 27, 1843.
130. *Ibid.*, December 28, 1843.

to it, never went, in any one night, to indulge in the luxury
of listening to music, that attended the two exhibitions of
Mad. Damoreau at the Exchange, and Ole Bull at the
theatre. . . .

We cannot boast of a highly cultivated musical taste, and it
is probable, therefore, that much of Ole Bull's performance
was lost upon us. But it required very little cultivation, to
enable us to perceive, at once, that he was a wonderful
master of the Divine Art. Such extraordinary tones, so sweet,
so rich, and so soft, we could have not believed it possible,
to proceed from a merely mortal instrument, touched by a
merely human hand. . . . If anything could have heightened
the effect of the extraordinary performance, it would have
been found in the modest demeanor and prepossessing ex-
terior of the performer. He did not tug, labor and puff, like
a galley-slave at the oar—he neither shrugged his shoulder
nor distorted his face with grimaces. His countenance was
calm, self-possessed, and modest; his features seemed to enjoy
entire repose; and he alone, of all the crowd, appeared to be
utterly unconscious of the powerful effect he was producing.
. . .[131]

The Ole Bull troupe gave a second performance a few
nights after the first concert.[132] It was one of only two programs noted in 1844, a year of extremely unsettled economic conditions in Richmond. The second program of
the year was an "entertainment of vocal and instrumental
music" given in the fall by Theodore H. Vandenburg,
"Professor of Music from Europe," who also announced
that he was making Richmond "his place of residence"
and that he would teach music.[133] The program was given
in the Exchange Hotel and consisted "chiefly of the newest and most popular songs and ballads of Mr. Henry
Russell."[134]

By 1845 the economic and musical depression had eased

---

131. *Ibid.,* January 2, 1844.
132. *Ibid.*
133. *Ibid.,* September 24, 1844.
134. *Ibid.* One of the original printed programs for this concert is
held by the Virginia Historical Society.

considerably, but the visiting performers that year lacked the quality of musicianship that Richmond had heard in 1843. The Orphean Family visited the city twice, giving several performances; two child prodigies, Josephine Bramson and her sister, gave a series of three piano programs, followed by three more programs on which Opl and Vandenburg appeared; and during the Bramson sisters' stay in Richmond, another pair of sisters, the Misses Macomber, gave a concert of national, sentimental, and temperance songs, "one playing violin and one playing violoncello accompanying their own voices."[135] Possibly the first complete formal band concert in Richmond was one given in 1845 by the band of the Fourth Regiment of Artillery, directed by Mr. W. L. Bloomfield.[136] Bands had often appeared in the theatre and in concerts but always in the capacity of assisting others, and Bloomfield's band gave its program without the assistance of non-band member performers. All of the concerts given during 1845 took place in the Exchange Hotel.

Concerts by Richmond Musicians

E. B. Barber and P. H. Taylor, who had once been itinerant theatre musicians, made their homes in Richmond beginning in the fourth decade of the century. As has been noted, visiting artists frequently called upon Barber and Taylor to assist them in concerts in Richmond, and therefore these two were probably well known and held in high esteem by traveling artists as well as by Richmond residents. Two other musicians, Berg and Opl, have been mentioned in connection with music activities in Richmond. Also, Vandenburg, as previously noted, settled in Richmond in 1844, and other apparently excellent musicians who chose Richmond for their home during the

135. *Ibid.*, March 27, June 20, 1845, *et passim*.
136. *Ibid.*, October 20, 1845. Program—Appendix **B**.

early 1840s were Dunderdale, George, Rosier, Ulmo, and Rosen. Their names are seen frequently thereafter as teachers and performers. With such superior musicians in Richmond, the concerts offered by them and the concerts by visiting performers who utilized their services as musicians were probably the better programs given in Richmond in 1845.

The series of apparently superior programs given from 1842 through 1845 by, or with the assistance of, Richmond musicians came after the Richmond men had had several years experience in assisting visiting artists. Both Taylor and Barber had performed with Mr. and Mrs. Morley in 1837 and with Horn and Horton in 1838. Barber had accompanied Madame Brengeri, Signor Fabj, Madame O'Connor, Mrs. Bailey, and W. V. Wallace during 1838 and 1839. In 1841, Barber and Taylor assisted Madame Pardi Marras, singer and harpist, and C. Bassini, violinist, in a concert at Terpsichore Hall.[137] Bassini returned the next year and procured the services of Barber and Taylor to give a "soiree musicale" at the Exchange Hotel.[138] Bassini may have remained in Richmond to teach or play in the theatre orchestra, for in January 1843, P. H. Taylor gave his first "soiree musicale," in which Bassini played the violin and two arrangements by Bassini were performed.[139] The other performers in this, Taylor's first concert, were Barber, piano; Berg, viola; Ulmo, cello; and an amateur, clarinet. The program was unusual for that day in that it consisted entirely of instrumental music, and besides ensemble selections, Taylor, Bassini, and Barber played solos on the flute, violin, and piano respectively. A month later, Barber gave a "soiree musicale" offering similar selections by the same instrumental performers

137. *Ibid.*, May 10, 1841. Program—Appendix B.
138. *Ibid.*, November 18, 1842. Program—Appendix B.
139. *Ibid.*, January 12, 1843. Program—Appendix B.

that had appeared on Taylor's program with the exception of Berg.[140] Two weeks later, Madame De Goni, guitarist, and George Knoop, cellist, gave a "grand vocal and instrumental concert" assisted by Barber.[141] The following week, De Goni and Knoop gave a concert assisted by both Barber and Taylor.[142] Taylor and Knoop apparently formed a friendship that led to similar concerts some years afterwards.

By 1845 Barber had been replaced in Taylor's group of musicians by John Dunderdale, whose multiplicity of talents saw him as singer, pianist, organist, and possibly flutist. Dunderdale first performed in Richmond in 1841 with Mr. Damer and Signor George, the three men singing trios, duets, and solos with piano accompaniments by Dunderdale.[143] Signor George also made his home in Richmond some years later, where he taught, composed music, and performed on programs in the city.

When Taylor gave a "musical soiree" in 1845, Dunderdale played the piano and sang; F. W. Rosier, cellist and guitarist, made his first appearance in Richmond where he was to teach and perform for many years; H. A. Knecht, pianist, made his only recorded public appearance in Richmond; the amateur clarinetist who had played on former concerts given by Taylor also performed; and Dempster, ballad singer from the theatre, sang on the program.[144] The following month, Rosier gave a "soiree musicale" on which Taylor played flute, Dunderdale sang and played the piano, "several gentlemen amateurs" sang, and Rosier played the cello.[145]

Prior to the concerts by Taylor and Rosier, T. H. Vandenburg announced his second "vocal and instrumental

---

140. *Ibid.*, February 27, 1843. Program—Appendix B.
141. *Ibid.*, March 11, 1843.
142. *Ibid.*, March 17, 1843.
143. *Ibid.*, January 2, 1841.
144. *Ibid.*, March 17, 1845. Program—Appendix B.
145. *Ibid.*, April 14, 1845. Program—Appendix B.

concert," in which he would sing "the newest and most popular songs of Mr. Henry Russell."[146] Later in the spring Vandenburg formed an alliance with J. K. Opl, the theatre orchestra leader, and Charles Rosen, for many years teacher of singing and guitar in Richmond. The three musicians gave a concert assisted by a "gentleman amateur" who played "several solos on the Cornopian."[147]

Two other concerts by visiting artists in 1845 were given with the cooperation of Richmond musicians. Signor and Madame Marano, "from Italy," gave a concert in April at the Exchange Concert Room "assisted by several other Professors of Music of this City."[148] In November, Mr. Barton, flutist, was accompanied by Dunderdale at the piano.[149]

Throughout the period from 1826 through 1845, the concerts given in Richmond increasingly offered more quality in performance and in performers. Midway through the period, domination of the concert field by theatre performers was seriously challenged for the first time by independent concert artists and entertainers, and by the end of the period the touring concert artists had established the trend that was to further delineate the contrast between a musical entertainment and a performance of art music. The appearance of several European concert artists in Richmond had set the stage for the large number of foreign musicians that were touring America with Richmond on their itinerary in the next 15 years. The city had acquired its own group of excellent musicians who had established a precedent for future musical developments by presenting programs of increasingly improved quality to its audiences.

---

146. *Ibid.*, January 17, 1845.
147. *Ibid.*, April 11, 1845. The cornopian was an early form of the cornet with piston valves.
148. *Ibid.*, April 25, 1845.
149. *Ibid.*, November 18, 1845.

Music of the Church

Religious organizations increased in size and number, new places of worship were built, and an effort was made to improve the quality of church music, especially in congregational singing, during the period of progress in Richmond from 1826 through 1845. Two new Episcopal congregations built churches—St. James' (1835) and St. Paul's (1843). Two new congregations, Second and Third Presbyterian, began their building programs. The First Baptist Church building, with additions made to the small building first occupied in 1802, became cruciform and was the largest auditorium in Richmond at the time. It had a colorful history both as a religious place of worship and as an auditorium for political, civic, and musical events. The Negro members of the First Baptist Church, having organized as the First African Baptist Church in 1841, had taken possession of the building, and from that date the structure was known as the African Church. The white members of the First Baptist Church moved into a new building, which is now at Tenth and Broad Streets and is used today by the Medical College of Virginia. The Second and Third Baptists and the Second African Baptists also developed churches during the period. In 1828 the Methodists built a church called Trinity on Franklin Street between Fourteenth and Fifteenth Streets. That building also had an unusual history. It burned in 1835, was rebuilt the next year, and was eventually used as a theatre after the Methodist congregations split and built two additional churches—Trinity and Broad Street. There were two other Methodist churches during this period—Shockoe, which became Centenary, and Union Station, whose congregation formed from Trinity. Other religious activities included the building of St. Peter's (Catholic) Church in 1834, the organizing of a German Catholic Church (St. Mary's), the division of the Hebrew congregation (Beth Ahabah was formed out of the older Beth Shalome), and the establishment of the first Protestant German congregation in Richmond (St. John's Evangelical and Reformed Church). Some of the outstanding musical events held in these churches along with the attempts to improve congregational singing are given in the following section.

Organs in Episcopal Churches

In 1829, the vestry of St. John's Church was again having difficulty in paying the organist.[150] In June 1835, Miss Sarah Sully was appointed an organist at a salary of $100 a year.[151] Whether to replace or repair the organ at St. John's was debated in 1840, and the decision was made to repair the old organ.[152] E. E. Ulmo was elected organist by the vestry of St. John's Church in 1842, and F. W. Rosier was elected organist in 1844.[153]

At the consecration of St. Paul's Church in November 1845, "the music of the choir was remarkably good and the rich full tone of the fine organ was fully developed by Mr. Dunderdale. . . ."[154] The organ was said to be "among the largest built on this continent. . . . It contained 33 stops and 1,319 pipes. . . ."[155] A writer for the *Enquirer* describes an afternoon concert, giving comments on audience mannerisms and reactions to the performance of the organ.

. . . We were delighted with its rich tones, at one moment swelling into notes of thunder, and then fading away like the "Sweet South" breeze. The gentle quality of my delicate ears, contended that it was impossible to appreciate the softer stops—as the *beaux would* whisper to their fair companions, and little children *would tune* their treble pipes. But on

---

150. "Record Book, St. John's Parish," p. 152.
151. *Ibid.*, p. 209.
152. *Ibid.*, p. 272.
153. *Ibid.*, p. 228.
154. *Enquirer*, November 12, 1845.
155. *Ibid.*

approaching very near the end of the performance we heard all the stops perfectly. We were particularly struck with the brilliant effect of the "Night Horn," "Clarionet" and "Trumpet" solo stops. . . . As soon as the organist shall form a complete acquaintance with its various parts, details, and the powers of the instrument, it will be a great pleasure to hear its eloquent breathings. This organ will cost $4,000.[156]

Music in the Baptist Churches

The musical activities of the Baptists present a stark contrast to those of the Episcopalians and Presbyterians. The Episcopal Churches sponsored concerts and had choirs and organs; the Presbyterians were active in singing schools as well as in the amateur choral organization, the Richmond Sacred Music Society. But J. B. Jeter, pastor of the First Baptist Church from 1836 to 1849, was opposed to having instrumental music in the church. His views were expressed strongly and clearly in a letter to the editor of *The Religious Herald* in which he stated: "I am not favorable to the use of instrumental music in the worship of God. . . . On this point there is but little difference of opinion among the Baptists of Virginia."[157] There was some objection among members of the congregation of the First Baptist Church to having a choir.

In July, 1837, the anti-choir members succeeded in getting a committee appointed to "consider whether or not we need a quoir [sic]." The pro-choir members were in the majority; the committee was discharged, and the matter indefinitely postponed.[158]

Agitation against the choir was again noted in 1841 when "it was proposed that the "quoir" leader be asked by the church to "raise such tunes as the congregation can

156. *Enquirer*, December 9, 1845.
157. *The Religious Herald* (Richmond), January 9, 1840.
158. White, p. 63.

sing."[159] Organized resistance to the choir dwindled afterwards, but an organ was not allowed in the church until 1861.

Marion Harland recorded her experiences as a visitor to the First African Baptist Church.

> The choir of the "Old African" was one of the shows of the city. Few members of it could read the words of the hymns and anthems. Every one of them could read the notes, and follow them aright. The parts were well-balanced and well-sustained. . . . Visitors from Northern cities who spent the Sabbath in Richmond seldom failed to hear the famed choir of the Old African. . . . George F. Root, who heard the choir more than once while he was our guest, could not say enough of the beauty of the anthem-hymn "Jerusalem, My Happy Home" as given by the colored band. He declared that one soloist had "the finest natural tenor he ever heard."[160]

Music in the Catholic Churches

St. Peter's Church was dedicated in 1834, and Father O'Brien, under whose leadership the church was built, wrote that "our Musick is very fine and attracts a pretty large congregation. . . .[161] Since few records exist, historians writing about the Catholics in Richmond have had to rely on testimonials and similar sources. Magri wrote that "Mrs. John Purcell, . . . tells us that the first organist of St. Peter's was Mrs. Gaynor, formerly Miss Picot."[162] One newspaper reference to music in the new Catholic church indicates that the church had an organ and that the Catholics offered musical leadership to the city utilizing music talent from the theatre. The organist, Mr. Daniell, from the Royal Academy of Music in London, was possibly responsible for the emphasis given to the music of Handel.

159. *Ibid.*, p. 64.
160. Harland, p. 234.
161. James Henry Bailey, *A History of the Diocese of Richmond* (Richmond: Whittet and Shepperson, 1956), p. 65.
162. F. Joseph Magri, *The Catholic Church in the City and Diocese of Richmond* (Richmond: Whittet and Shepperson, 1906), p. 55.

ORATORIO

Catholic Church—20th of February
. . . Messrs. Berg, W. Daniell, S. A. Cunnington, Blancjour
Graves, W. P. Cunnington, &c. and a considerable number
of Ladies and Gentlemen Amateurs . . . will perform. Mr.
Daniell . . . will preside at the Organ.

The whole to be under the direction of Mr. W. P. Cunnington.

PART I

Overture—Occasional Oratorio	Handel
Chorus—Hallelujah to the Father	
(From the Mount of Olives,)	Beethoven
Solo—With verdure clad,	
(From the Creation)	Haydn
Quartetto—Lord of all power and might,	Mason
Solo—Evening Prayer	C. Smith
Anthem—I will love thee O Lord,	C. S. Evans
Duette—Graceful Consort,	
(From the Creation)	Haydn
Solo—Must I leave thee Paradise,	Mr. P. King
Air—Sound An Alarm,	
(From Judas Maccabeus,)	Handel
Chorus—We hear the pleasing dreadful call,	do

PART II

Chorus—Lord in thee have I trusted,	do
Solo—Let the bright Seraphim,	do
Chorus—Lift up your Heads, O ye Gates	do
Recitative & Air—Ye sacred Priests,	
(Jeptha's Daughter.)	do
Duetto—O lovely Peace,	do
Air—Angels ever bright and fair,	do
Solo—Shall I in Mamre's fertile plain,	do
Air—Fall'n is thy throne	
Chorus—The Heaven's are telling,	Haydn[163]

Daniell had moved to Richmond from London and was

163. *Whig*, February 17, 1835.

teaching piano and voice in his new home early in 1835.[164] Three years after performing in the oratorio at the Catholic church, he performed in an oratorio at the Monumental Episcopal Church under the direction of Charles E. Horn.[165] Daniell continued to teach music in Richmond, opening a piano ware-room in which he taught, demonstrated, and sold pianos.[166] He journeyed to Europe but soon returned to Richmond to continue his career in teaching and merchandising.[167] In one of his newspaper advertisements, Daniell published a letter written by Charles E. Horn. The letter attested to the quality of pianos sold by Daniell.[168]

Singing Schools and the Richmond Sacred Music Society

A growing interest for improving congregational singing is seen in the records and literature concerning Richmond during the third decade of the nineteenth century. The beginning of the movement in Richmond is obscure, but it was undoubtedly related to the singing school movement, which began at the turn of the century and spread throughout the nation during the ensuing years, Lowell Mason becoming one of its chief proponents. The singing school played a unique role in America's history and was a precursor to and later developed contemporaneously with public school music instruction. The movement's impetus came from two sources—a genuine desire to learn and share musical experiences with a religious context and the remunerative benefits realized by teachers, publishers, and composers from the sale of singing books. It is generally agreed that much musical quality was sacrificed as the demand for quantity increased.

Amateur music societies in Richmond had been active

---

164. *Whig*, January 27, 1835.
165. *Compiler*, April 3, 1838.
166. *Whig*, October 16, 1838.
167. *Ibid.*, October 22, 1839.
168. *Ibid.*, May 17, 1841.

sporadically since the eighteenth century and had been responsible for several concerts given in churches from 1818 through 1825. One reference indicates the existence of an amateur group in Richmond in 1828, but it does not indicate whether their major interests were in sacred or secular, instrumental or vocal music.

> The honorary and active members of the Harmonic Association of Richmond are hereby notified that the regular meetings of the Association, for rehearsal, will hereafter take place every Monday evening, at Mr. Guigon's Assembly Room in the Mansion House. It is the privilege of any member to attend with his family and female acquaintants. Strangers and other persons, wishing to attend any particular evening, can procure tickets of admission from any member of the Executive Committee.
>
> CHARLES HOLT, JR.
> ELIAS REED,
> JAMES MANN,
> JAS. G. CRANE,
> GARRET V. RAYMOND,
> Executive Committee[169]

Further references to the Harmonic Association's meetings and performances were not found.

The first allusion to a sacred singing school in Richmond was an advertisement stating that Mr. A. Hudson had "again returned to the city . . . with a view of commencing another course in sacred music."[170] Hudson's instruction in sacred music apparently met with favorable patronage, and he advertised that his second quarter would begin on February 5, 1831, in the "School Room under the Presbyterian Church, on F. Street."[171] Two years later Mr. Dyer advertised that he would "re-commence his Juvenile Singing Classes . . . and commence the formation of adult

169. *Whig*, December 8, 1828.
170. *Ibid.*, September 21, 1830.
171. *Ibid.*, February 3, 1831.

classes . . . on his return from the North."[172] Another singing school teacher, Mr. Hood, is mentioned by Blanton as having begun his sacred music classes in the Presbyterian churches of Richmond in 1836.[173] Hood advertised that he would "commence an adult class in vocal music . . . in the Lecture room of the Presbyterian Church on Shockoe Hill" in 1839.[174] His fee was four dollars for twenty-four lessons—two lessons a week. Two other singing teachers using the class method of instruction in Richmond were R. Morse, who advertised that he would "resume teaching Piano Forte and singing and classes in vocal music,"[175] and S. S. Stevens, who advertised the hours that his adult and children's vocal music classes would meet in each of three Presbyterian churches in Richmond in 1845.[176]

The autobiography of Marion Harland describes her family's musical experiences in and near Richmond. She describes a singing class which, once a week, "met around our dining-table. My father led this, giving the key with his tuning-fork, and now and then accompanying with his flute a hymn in which his tenor was not needed."[177] Harland relates that a singing master, "a leader of a Richmond choir," had held a singing school the winter before, "and *The Boston Academy* was in every house in the village."[178]

> . . . There were five sopranos—we called it "the treble" then— and two women sang "the second treble." One weak-voiced neighbor helped my father out with the tenor. Until a year

172. *Ibid.*, October 3, 1833.
173. Wyndham B. Blanton, *The Making of a Downtown Church* (Richmond: John Knox Press, 1945), p. 231.
174. *Whig*, October 4, 1839.
175. *Ibid.*, October 9, 1840.
176. *Whig*, November 27, 1845.
177. Marion Harland, *Marion Harland's Autobiography* (New York: Harper and Brothers Publishers, 1910), p. 114.
178. *Ibid.* The village refers to Powhatan, Virginia.

or two before the singing-master invaded the country, women sang tenor, and the alto was known as "counter." . . . We lined both sides of the long table, lighted by tall sperm-oil lamps, and bent seriously happy faces over *The Boston Academy,* singing with the spirit and, to the best of our ability, with the understanding—"Lanesboro" and "Cambridge" and "Hebron" and "Boyleston" and "Zion," and learning, with puckered brows and steadfast eyes glued to the notes, such new tunes as "Yarmouth," "Anvern," and "Zerah."

"Sing *at* it!" my father would command in heartsome tones, from his stand at the top of the double line. "You will never learn it if you do not make the first trial."[179]

Some of the hymn tunes mentioned by Harland appear in recently published hymn books, but others have not survived. "Boyleston," "Hebron," and "Zerah," by Lowell Mason were included in the second edition (1901) of the 1866 publication: *Psalms and Hymns.*[180] These same tunes are also included in the Presbyterian *Hymn Book* published in Richmond and other cities in 1955.[181] "Anvern," a German melody arranged by Lowell Mason, was included in the *Psalms and Hymns* (1901) but is not in the *Hymn Book* (1955). "Lanesboro," written by William Dixon (1750–1825), was included in the 1901 edition of *Psalms and Hymns* but is not in the 1955 *Hymn Book.* "Zion," by Thomas Hastings, was included in the 1901 edition of *Psalms and Hymns* and the 1945 *Presbyterian Hymnal,* but is not in the *Hymn Book* (1955).[182] "Cambridge," by Ralph Harrison (*ca.* 1784), is included in the Unitarian hymn book published in 1951.[183]

179. *Ibid.,* p. 115.

180. *The New Psalms and Hymns* (Richmond: Presbyterian Committee of Publication, 1901), "Hebron," pp. 13, 56, 288, 322, 570; "Boyleston," pp. 210, 309; "Zerah," p. 66.

181. *The Hymnbook* (Philadelphia: John Ribble, 1955), "Boyleston," p. 258; "Hebron," p. 250; and "Zerah," pp. 70, 81.

182. *New Psalms and Hymns,* p. 535; and *The Presbyterian Hymnal* (Richmond: Presbyterian Committee of Publication, 1945), n.p., hymn numbers 122, 346, 394, 396.

183. *Hymns of the Spirit* (Boston: The Beacon Press, 1951), n.p., Hymn number 210.

It should be remembered that the present-day usage of the term "hymn book" differs from that of the period through 1845. Before the mid-nineteenth-century period, the title "hymn book" usually meant that the book contained words only. Several hymn books were written or compiled by Richmond ministers before 1845, but their books contained words and had no tunes nor references to tunes. Tune books were available, but until the advent of the singing school, a church congregation generally learned the tune by rote as given out by the leader of the singing. The earliest example of a book with words and tunes found in the Baptist Historical Association at the University of Richmond is *Sacred Songs for Family and Social Worship: Comprising the Most Approved Spiritual Hymns, with Chaste and Popular Tunes. . . .*[184] It is a singing school book, and the first verse of each hymn is printed with the music notation, other verses being found on the opposite page or on another page.

Singing school activities in the third decade of the nineteenth century culminated in the organizing of the Richmond Sacred Music Society. By June 1840, the society's membership was probably large enough to necessitate the publication of a notice concerning a change in the time and place of rehearsal.

Richmond Sacred Music Society
The Members of this Society are respectfully notified that as the Room they usually meet in cannot be had THIS EVENING, the meeting for the practice, will be held on FRIDAY EVENING, 12th inst.
                    by order of the President.
                    John Williams, Sec'y.[185]

By spring in 1841 the society had prepared a concert. Their advertisement indicated that the leading professional musi-

184. (New York: The American Tract Society, 1842).
185. *Whig,* June 9, 1840.

cians of Richmond had combined their talents with the amateurs of the society to present a program of music indicative of refined judgment and a desire to improve tastes.

ORATORIO

The RICHMOND SACRED MUSIC SOCIETY will give a grand ORATORIO, in St. James Church, on Friday evening, 2nd April—consisting of Solos, Duetts, Trios, Quartetts and Choruses, from the compositions of Handell, [sic], Beethoven [sic], Mozart, Haydn, Rossini, Righini, &c. On which occasion, the Society will have the valuable aid of Messrs. Berg, Damer, Dunderdale, and Signor George, of Petersburg, and Miss Sully, Messrs. P. H. Taylor, Poitiaux, Barber, Opl and others of the profession, together with the chief Amateur talent of this city.

CONDUCTOR, Mr. Evans.
LEADER, Mr. J. K. Opl.
ORGANISTS, Miss Sully and Mr. Dunderdale.
PRINCIPAL FLUTE, Mr. Taylor.
HARP, Miss Sully.

PART I

OVERTURE—Full Band	
CHORUS—Glory be to God on High	Mozart
SOLO—Thou didst not leave his soul in hell	
Signor George	Handel
CHORUS—Lo! He cometh	Haydn
RECITATIVE—Now the Philistines &c.	
SOLO—Consider the lilies-Soprano	Topliff
QUARTETTO—Almighty God	
SOLO—These as they change—Dunderdale	Calcott
CHORUS—Sing to Jehovah	Gram
SOLO—There is a stream whose gentle flow—	
Soprano	Poole
RECITATIVE—Now the work of man's redemption	
CHORUS—Hallelujah to the Father	Beethoven

PART II

OVERTURE	
CHORUS—Let us with a joyful mind	Mozart

SOLO—Deeper and deeper still, and waft her angels
Damer Handell
DUETT, TRIO, and CHORUS—Oh how beautiful
thy garments, O Zion Naumann
SOLO—Flute—P. H. Taylor Insdorff
QUARTETTO—The Prayer—Harp accompaniment by
Miss Sully Rossini
CHORUS—The Lord is great Righini
SOLO—Soprano—Song of the Hebrew Captive
Harp accompaniment by Miss Sully
CHORUS—Night's shade no longer Rossini[186]

Opl, listed as "leader," was apparently the first violinist or concert-master, and the overtures were played by an orchestra, which in the custom of that day was called a "band," the shortened form of "a band of musicians." The newspaper review of the program, an infrequent item in that period of journalism in Richmond, alludes to excellence of performance and lack of interest or lack of taste on the part of the citizens of Richmond.

THE ORATORIO

The Oratorio, Friday night, was a Musical Entertainment of the highest order. The Chorus was indeed grand, and could not, we think, be surpassed even by the Bostonians, celebrated as they are for rich Church Music. But we were really surprised to see, comparatively speaking, so few citizens in attendance. Can it be accounted for in the threatening aspect of the evening, or must it be attributed to a lack of taste in the community? We can hardly suppose the latter —yet we might be pardoned for indulging in the thought after witnessing the thin audience Friday evening and the little encouragement given to a society, or rather a band of amateurs, seeking to revive a musical taste in the city, and aspiring to excellence in the most beautiful of accomplishments.[187]

Similar programs were given by the society in March

186. *Whig*, April 2, 1841.
187. *Ibid.*, April 3, 1841.

and April 1842 at St. James' Church, in December 1842 at the Monumental Church, in January 1843 at the United Presbyterian Church, and in February 1843 at the Second Baptist Church.[188] In addition to the concerts by the Richmond Sacred Music Society in St. James' Church and the Monumental Church, there was a concert at St. John's Church in September 1842, "given by the Ladies' Benevolent Society, assisted by the Ladies and Gentlemen of the different choirs of this city."[189]

The period of musical growth in Richmond from 1826 through 1845 evinces a continual de-emphasis of the theatre-centered musical leadership that had figured prominently in the city's musical life through the first quarter of the nineteenth century. Music entertainment, music merchantry, music instruction, concerts, and church music activities all developed independently to a degree during the period, but each complemented the other in the composite musical life of Richmond's citizens. The musical practices of the several principal religious organizations are indicative of the variety of musical activities found in Richmond at that time, the Baptists, Methodists, and Presbyterians being more conservative in musical activities than the Episcopalians and Catholics—especially in regard to instrumental music in the church. At the close of the period, Richmond had developed the foundation on which soon would rest the structure for musical leadership in the South.

---

188. *Whig*, March 20, 1842; April 8, 1842; December 13, 1842; January 10, 1843; February 21, 1843. Programs for the performances of April 8, 1842, January 10, 1843, and February 21, 1843 are included in Appendix B.
189. *Whig*, September 23, 1842.

Chapter 5

Music in a Capital City of the South, 1846~1865

Over a period of 60 years, within the life span of some of its residents, Richmond had grown from a small village of limited resources to become, by 1845, a city offering economic, political, and cultural leadership to Virginia and other southern states. During the next 15 years, the city continued to develop its cultural pursuits and became a leading city of the South. By 1860,

the city was at its peak industrially and commercially. The city had built up an immense trade with South America and Australia. The ships that carried away Richmond flour returned with coffee and sugar, and Richmond was recognized as one of the leading ports. Tobacco interests were centered here largely, and iron works and mills ranked first in the South.

It was this community of culture, wealth and progressiveness that became the Confederate capital when the internecine war finally broke. In the eyes of the North, Richmond became the most desired goal for its armies, and no campaign of importance was planned that did not embrace the capture of the Southern capital.[1]

1. Francis Earle Lutz, *A Richmond Album* (Richmond: Garrett and Massie, 1937), p. xxv.

179

During the 20-year period terminating with the close of the Civil War, music activities in Richmond became more extensive and more diverse than they had been during prior years of the century. Details of all activities of the latter period are too extensive to be presented in this chapter, but the activities are described in essence and the principal personalities involved are mentioned along with citations that indicate sources for additional information.

Music on Social and Public Occasions

On a shopping or business trip to downtown Richmond during the mid-nineteenth-century period, a person might have been greeted by sounds from a variety of street musicians. A trio composed of "organ, tamborine, and bones," numerous organ grinders, and harpists are among the street musicians mentioned in the daily columns of the *Dispatch*. A writer laments that "a pair of bones had fallen from its high estate in the hands of 'Brudder B.' into the uncleansed digits of one of a triad of dirty perambulating street musicians."[2] Organ grinders are described as "the abominable pests . . . grinding out their squeaking, hissing, dolorous, discordant sounds from ill-tuned instruments."[3] The harpists are described in a more complimentary manner.

In passing some of our popular hotels, we are sometimes irresistibly drawn to see one of those wandering Bohemians —"A harper harping on his harp." . . . Most of the harps we hear are touched with skillful as with "flying fingers." The producers of the melody have mostly had their origin in the sunny land of Italy.[4]

Serenading became a popular pastime of both vocal and

2. *Dispatch*, August 20, 1852.
3. *Ibid.*, December 4, 1854.
4. *Ibid.*, July 4, 1861.

instrumental groups during the mid-century period.

> Several members of the large and talented German glee club
> of this city, made complaint to his Honor [the Mayor] yester-
> day, that about midnight on Wednesday evening, while en-
> gaged in serenading a friend, . . . the night watch had
> interfered with and put a stop to their musical performances,
> stating that they must cease their singing in the public
> streets. The Germans alleged that the Armory and other
> bands were allowed to serenade in different parts of the city,
> and were not interfered with—and desired to know whether
> they were to be made the exception, and debarred a privilege
> granted to other musical organizations.[5]

The Mayor voiced no objections to serenading at an early
and reasonable hour of the night (the Germans were
allegedly singing at one A.M.) and the regulation of serenading groups was left to the discretion of the night
police.[6]

J. B. Smith's Armory Band and E. Loebmann's Cornet
Band serenaded the *Dispatch* office on several occasions
and consequently received favorable publicity in that
newspaper's columns.[7] Smith's band was referred to as
"the head and front of musical combinations in the
South."[8] It had been formed and introduced to the public
in 1850 as the

> Richmond Independent Band! J. B. Smith has formed a
> band of 12 to 14 instruments, who [*sic*] are prepared at all
> times, to furnish music for parties, or on any public occasion,
> upon the most favorable terms, and with such a number of
> wind or string instruments as the occasion may require.
>
> .   .   .   .
>
> The Band consists of J. B. Smith, George Green, W. H.
> Harden, Jacob Miller, formerly of the Armory Brass Band;
> Thomas Hays, Jno. Boucher of Noscher's Band, attached

---

5. *Ibid.*, August 6, 1852.
6. *Ibid.*, August 7, 1852.
7. *Ibid.*, May 17 and September 19, 1853.
8. *Ibid.*, September 19, 1853.

to Robinson and Eldred's Circus, and others favorably known
as musicians.

J. B. Smith will give instructions on Wind or String instruments upon the most liberal terms, and will arrange
music for any number of instruments, as above.[9]

Smith's Independent Band was probably the first group
to give summer night band concerts in Richmond's Capitol Square, performing there first, evidently for publicity,
in June 1850.[10] That first performance, however, was
enjoyed at some distance if heard at all because of an
"over-zealous night watchman" who would not permit
citizens entrance to the grounds.[11] By the summer of 1853,
both Smith's and Loebmann's bands played evening concerts frequently in the Capitol Square.[12] Smith's band, also
known as the Armory Band, was Richmond's leading
group of musicians playing for parades, excursions, balls,
fairs, and celebrations. The Armory Band accompanied
one of Richmond's military units, the Young Guard, to
Baltimore and made a favorable impression in that city.[13]
When it accompanied the Richmond Light Infantry Blues
to Philadelphia, a newspaper account of the event included
the band's roster.

SMITH'S BAND

James B. Smith (leader), bugle.
James M. Melton, first cornet.
William Tremer, second cornet.
Frederick Fox, alto horn.
Michael Cardons, first trombone.
William Karrer, second trombone.
R. Emerson, baritone.
John Boucher, first tuba.
J. H. Knoop, second tuba.

---

9. *Whig*, May 28, 1850.
10. *Ibid.*, June 28, 1850.
11. *Ibid.*, July 2, 1850.
12. *Dispatch*, May 19, May 23, June 6, September 23, 1853 *et al.*
13. *Ibid.*, January 2, 1855.

Edward Felvy, side drum.
A. Heffron, bass drum.
W. Totty, cymbals.[14]

In describing the Armory Band's music the *Dispatch* states that "while they do not make so great a noise as bands composed of 25 men, they produce that which is much more pleasing to the ear of a musician—perfect harmony."[15] In 1858, E. Loebmann, "the well known and popular violinist" who had been one of Smith's competitors, became a member of the Armory Band, and Smith announced that he was confident that their "STRING BAND will be second to none in the city."[16] By 1860, a series of events led to the disassociation of Smith's band from the name Armory Band.[17] However, Smith continued to be a cotillion and military band leader in Richmond throughout the Civil War period.

Dancing instruction and cotillions flourished in Richmond throughout the period from 1846 to 1865, and fancy dress balls were popular.

Fancy balls are, beyond all question, doubt or demur, amusing. Their grotesqueness, odd jumble of costumes, ludicrous misconceptions of character, and exquisitely funny amalgamation of inconsistencies, make them, when most successful, most absurd. . . .[18]

Several bands other than those of Smith and Loebmann provided music at balls in Richmond during this time. Fred Dollinger published a "musical card" announcing that his "concert and cotillion band is prepared to furnish music for balls, concerts, parties, soirees, serenades, exhibits, &c."[19] Members of the band were listed as F.

14. *Ibid.*, February 21, 1855.
15. *Ibid.*, November 11, 1856.
16. *Ibid.*, January 29, 1858.
17. *Ibid.*, November 9 and 15, 1859.
18. *Ibid.*, February 22, 1854.
19. *Ibid.*, December 20, 1855.

Dollinger, R. Krausse, R. Woller, J. Beir, and S. Rosen. Their names are also associated with concert and teaching activities noted elsewhere in this chapter. Other band leaders providing music for balls and entertainments, beginning in 1860, were J. A. Rosenberger, J. Reinhardt, William Tremer, J. Kessnich, J. De Faudree, and Louis Armbrecht.[20]

The Theatre

Performances given in the Marshall Theatre during the mid-century period were much the same as those given during the previous nineteenth-century years. The principal theatrical innovation of the mid-century period was Italian opera. Operas were also given in English by touring opera troupes, the first one performing in Richmond in 1848. Resident stock companies with visiting stars also continued to give operatic adaptations, but since the star system was no longer as strong as it had been, leading roles in musicals were difficult to fill. Many persons who would have been visiting theatre stars in earlier periods were associated with traveling concert and operatic troupes in the mid-century period, and production of the more ambitious musicals was left to the touring opera troupe and seldom attempted by resident theatre companies.

The standard repertory of Shakespearean drama, melodrama, musicals, farces, and specialty entertainment was offered in the Marshall Theatre during the winter seasons from 1846 until 1862, when the theatre was destroyed by

20. Numerous advertisements of balls and other entertainments utilizing band music are given in the *Dispatch* from 1860 through March, 1865. Although there were times during the war when no cotillions or balls were advertised, in general, more activities of that nature took place during the war than during pre-war periods of comparable length. Little may be deduced from the advertisements other than a quantitative analysis of activities by various band leaders, and such statistics are deemed superfluous to the study.

fire. Opera, concert, and minstrel troupes occupied the theatre occasionally, usually staying a week or less.

English Opera Performances

The first touring opera troupe to perform in the theatre was the Sequin English troupe, who presented *The Bohemian Girl, Fra Diavolo,* and possibly other operas in March 1848, and then gave concerts of operatic selections at the Exchange Hotel.[21] Sequin's troupe returned during the next year to give the English opera adaptations—*The Bohemian Girl, Maritana, Cinderella,* and *Norma*—at the theatre, and they presented a concert at the African Church.[22] The English Opera Troupe of Pyne and Harrison performed twice in Richmond giving performances of *La Sonnambula, Crown Diamonds, Maritana, Daughter of the Regiment, The Bohemian Girl, Rob Roy,* and *Barber of Seville.*[23] Durand's English Opera Troupe made two visits to the theatre, performing *La Traviata, Il Trovatore, Der Freischutz, Barber of Seville, Don Pasquale,* and *Cinderella.*[24] "Cooper's Great American Opera Troupe" performed *The Waterman, Lucia Di Lammermoor,* and *Lucrezia Borgia* in addition to several other operas given previously by other companies.[25]

Italian Opera Performances

In 1849, an Italian opera troupe gave a concert in Richmond at the Exchange Hotel and then performed "illustrations of dramatic and Italian opera music" in the theatre.[26] The first Italian opera troupe to give complete performances of Italian opera in Richmond was Max

---

21. *Whig,* March 17, 21, 24, and 31, 1848.
22. *Ibid.,* January 23, 26, 30 and February 2 and 6, 1849.
23. *Dispatch,* April 21, 1856, and February 23, 1857.
24. *Ibid.,* June 1, 1857 and November 1, 1858.
25. *Ibid.,* October 1 and 18, 1860.
26. *Whig,* May 8, 1849.

Maretzek's company, which performed *I Puritani* and *La Favorita* in 1851.[27] Steffanoni's Opera Troupe gave the second acts of *Norma* and of *Lucrezia Borgia* in Italian "plus popular and sacred classical compositions" in 1853.[28] The "New York celebrated Italian Opera Company" of "over forty performers . . . under the direction of Signor L. Arditi" performed *Lucrezia Borgia, Lucia Di Lammermoor, Norma, La Sonnambula,* and *Belisario* in 1854. The two latter operas were given twice in probably the longest opera season held in Richmond before the Civil War.[29] Operas performed by visiting opera troupes in Richmond and their composers are listed in Table 8. They are listed in order of their first performance by the opera troupes.

Table 8

OPERAS GIVEN IN RICHMOND
1848–1860

Opera	*Composer*
Bohemian Girl	Balfe
Fra Diavolo	Auber
Maritana	Wallace
Cinderella	Rossini
Norma	Bellini
La Sonnambula	Bellini
Crown Diamonds	Auber
Rob Roy	Flotow
Barber of Seville	Rossini
La Traviata	Verdi
Il Trovatore	Verdi
Der Freischutz	Weber
Don Pasquale	Donizetti
The Waterman	(unknown)
Lucia Di Lammermoor	Donizetti
Lucrezia Borgia	Donizetti

27. *Ibid.*, October 29 and November 4, 1851.
28. *Dispatch*, May 18, 1853.
29. *Ibid.*, January 2, 4, 6, 7, 9, 11, and 13, 1854.

I Puritani .... Bellini
La Favorita .... Donizetti
Belisario .... Donizetti

Variety and Drama

In addition to presenting operatic performances of apparent quality, the theatre presented leading variety and dramatic performers of the day. T. D. Rich, "the original Jim Crow" and one of the pioneers of minstrelsy, and Edwin Forrest, America's leading tragedian, played in the theatre in 1846.[30] William Charles Macready, the English actor and rival of Forrest, performed in the theatre in 1849.[31] A newspaper article praised Macready for his acting and the correctness of his costume while indicating that the Richmond audience also complimented him highly.[32] The Forrest-Macready rivalry led to the disastrous Astor Place Opera House riot in New York four months later. As rowdy as they must have been at times, Richmond audiences can claim the somewhat negative honor of never having had a theatre riot in a day that saw many riots in the larger cities of the United States.

The Richmond theatre audience could select its entertainment from a wide variety of offerings during the mid-century period. The Nightingale Ethiopian Serenaders appeared with the Armory Band in the fall of 1849.[33] Jenny Lind, with a large supporting troupe, was in Richmond in 1850.[34] A temperance drama—*The Drunkard's Warning,* a Bohemian polka, a comedy, a comic dance, and a comic opera—*Jenny Lind in Richmond,* with Miss Sinclair as Jenny Leatherlungs, were all given during one night's performance in 1851.[35] Edwin Booth, Edwin For-

---

30. *Whig,* March 20, 1846.
31. *Ibid.,* January 5, 1849.
32. *Ibid.*
33. *Whig,* September 14, 1849.
34. See *Secular Concerts* in this chapter.
35. *Whig,* February 28, 1851.

rest, William Macready, and many other leading singers, actors, and actresses from England and the United States performed in the Richmond theatre intermittently with minstrels, ballad singers, magicians, acrobats, and trained animals. Those that did not perform music, performed to a musical accompaniment, or were associated with theatre music of some form or another.

War-Time Theatres

John Hill Hewitt, the prolific and popular American composer of sentimental and patriotic songs, was manager of the theatre from October 1861 until it burned in January 1862.[36] Within a few days after the fire, Hewitt's theatre company was performing in Franklin Hall, a building known as the "Richmond Varieties" or as the "Varieties."[37] The Varieties offered drama, singing, and dancing almost without interruption from its opening until the end of the War three years later. The emphasis of the offerings was placed on vaudeville entertainments.

Richmond Varieties—
Acting manager .... R. D'Orsey Ogden
Musical director .... C. A. Rosenberg

First Night of the Varieties Minstrels . . .
The management will spare neither trouble nor expense in getting together the best
MINSTRELS
BURLESQUE
OPERA TROUPE and
BRASS BAND
Mike Mitchell, Banjoist, Tamborinist
A. Anderson, Principal Violinist, Alto Tenor Horn, and First Solo Performer
L. Rosenberger, Second Violin and Horn Performer
J. Smith, cornet a-piston and Baritone Performer
Eugene Fenton, Accordeon Solo Performer

---

36. *Dispatch*, October 10, 1861; January 3, 1862, *et passim*.
37. *Ibid.*, January 6, 1862. See Appendix A—Franklin Hall.

C. Danvers, First Tenor
J. Baker, Violinist and Alto Singer
Morgan Kenedy, Piano Solo Performer[38]

Within a period of 13 months after the theatre had
burned, a new one built on the old foundation had opened.
The advertisement for the opening night lists 11 actors
and actresses, 12 "young ladies of the ballet," and 20
"gentlemen of the chorus and ballet."[39] Also listed in the
advertisement are two featured specialists—a vocalist and a
dancer—and the musical director. Including the orchestra
the total number of entertainers employed by the theatre
amounted to 60 or more. The opening night was to "commence with a grand overture composed by Loebman,"
and to be "followed by a grand Tableaux and chorus by
the entire company." After a dance by Miss Partington,
Shakespeare's *As You Like It* was given in five acts.[40] The
new theatre offered entertainment from its opening date
to the end of the war almost without interruption. The
prices of admission ranged from 15 dollars for private
boxes to 50 cents for the colored Gallery. The rules and
regulations published for the audience's benefit indicate
that some disorder was expected but would not be tol-
erated.

> 1st. Drunkenness, the use or sale of intoxicating liquors,
> or partaking of refreshments of any kind, to the annoyance
> of the audience—strictly forbidden.
> 2nd. Smoking, placing the feet upon the benches, or backs
> of benches, swearing, and all unnecessary noise will not be
> allowed.[41]

Musical presentations were, for the most part, overtures, songs, dance accompaniments, and melodrama ac-

---

38. *Ibid.*, February 9, 1863.
39. *Ibid.*
40. *Ibid.*
41. *Ibid.*

companiments. *Tableaux,* a popular form of entertainment of the day, were given in the theatre with musical accompaniment. Six *Tableaux* with scenery, costumes, and parlor sets were presented one evening, "the overture, incidental music and choruses composed and arranged by Mr. Robert Stopel."[42] An evening's entertainment in April 1864 included a historical drama followed by a dance by Mary Partington, and concluded with a performance by the Harmonions, consisting of

> A. Rosenberg, Leader; Harry Allen, Balladist; J. A. Clifford, Basso and Tyrolean Warbler; Sig. Malfi, Harpist; George Kemble, Banjoist; J. Wells, the inimitable Brudder Bones; E. Barker, the unequaled Tamborinist; Together with the only Orchestra in the Confederacy.[43]

Evidently all musical productions at the theatre during the war were in a light vein. The dramas, especially those of Shakespeare, provided the more serious moments of stage performances. The comic opera *Poor Soldier* was given twice as an afterpiece, but from the songs listed to be sung, the 1864 version had little in common with the ballad opera of the same name given in Richmond in 1786.[44] The opera *Guy Mannering* by Sir Walter Scott "with the original music" was given with the farce of *Jenny Lind* as the afterpiece on May 6, 1864.[45] "A Grand English dramatization of the Italian opera by G. Verdi, entitled *Il Trovatore* with the vocal and instrumental music and grand overtures selected and arranged from the opera by Richard D. Ogden, Esq.," was presented four successive times in 1865.[46] The final advertisement of the theatre during the Confederacy illustrates the frivolous nature of the musical productions.

---

42. *Ibid.,* September 25, 1863.
43. *Ibid.,* April 7, 1864.
44. *Ibid.,* January 16 and June 13, 1864.
45. *Ibid.,* May 6, 1864.
46. *Ibid.,* January 26, 27, 28, and February 10, 1865.

Richmond THEATRE,
   Corner of Seventh and Broad Streets.

Saturday Evening, April 1, 1865, FIRST NIGHT of the
   GRAND (?) OPERA OF NORMA

Singing and Dancing

Also, upon the same evening, the Operatic Play,
in three acts, of
MARATANA; or
A MATCH FOR A KING.[47]

Theatrical Entertainments in Auditoriums

Competition to the Marshall Theatre grew more keen
as several halls in the city began to offer entertainment
regularly to the public in the form of minstrels, variety,
and concerts. The three principal places of entertainment
other than the theatre were the Exchange Hotel Concert
Room, the Odd Fellows' Hall, and Metropolitan Hall.
Other places offering entertainment from 1859 through
the Civil War period were Corinthian Hall or the Mechanics' Institute Hall, Monticello Hall, and Franklin
Hall.[48] Minstrel entertainment often combined variety and
concert performances with the characteristic Negro impersonations. The intrigue of the minstrel was based not
merely on the white man's black face burlesque of Negro
mannerisms, but on the performer's sometime subtle and
sometime bland lampooning of social and political situa-
tions without involving his own personality. Variety entertainment consisted of theatre performers giving their song
and dance specialties not as added attractions between
dramatic presentations as in the theatre but in a series
of featured novelties. Concerts associated with minstrels

----

47. *Ibid.*, April 1, 1865.
48. See Appendix A for information concerning these and other public
buildings in which music was performed.

and variety entertainment were given by ballad singers and instrumentalists whose audience appeal was based on showmanship as much as, if not more than, musicianship.

The Exchange Hotel Concert Room

The Exchange Hotel Concert Room continued to provide entertainment to smaller and more exclusive audiences than the theatre. The ballad singers, family group singers, and some of the instrumentalists who performed there are classified in this study as theatrical entertainers. Tempeton, Dempster, Lover, Wilson, Hudson, and Turner were ballad singers, and most of them presented Irish characterizations along with their songs.[49] The Orpean Family, a mixed vocal quartet, performed several times during 1846, 1847, and 1848.[50] The Hughes Family, comprising six performers (three adults and three children), sang and played various instruments at the Exchange Hotel.[51] Mr. Distin and his three sons gave a vocal and instrumental concert, performing "some of the first operatic pieces on their Silver Sax-Horns and Tubas."[52] The Harmoneons and the Nightingale Ethiopians each gave several programs in the Exchange Hotel Concert Room.[53] Instrumental entertainment at the Exchange Hotel included a violinist, Desire Ikelheimer, with "his own songs, arrangements, and imitations"; the Hungarian Bell Ringers with 56 bells; and the "Baltimore Military and Orchestral Bands."[54] The bell ringers performed at the hotel on the same night that Jenny Lind was at the theatre. With

---

49. *Whig*, January 13, 1846; March 20, 1846; January 15, 1847; January 9, 1849; March 6, 1849; April 9, 1850; *Dispatch*, February 25, 1852; and July 30, 1853.
50. *Whig*, May 1, 1846; April 9, 23, 24, 1847; and June 20, 1848.
51. *Ibid.*, November 26, 1847.
52. *Ibid.*, March 6, 1849.
53. *Ibid.*, March 31, 1846; December 8, 1846; and November 1, 2, 1848.
54. *Ibid.*, March 20, 1849; December 17, 1850; and *Dispatch*, March 2, 1853.

the bell ringers was Master Theodore Thomas performing
"some of his grand Solos on the Violin."[55] Thomas, then
about 15 years of age, later became "an epic figure in
American history—one of our great heroes," laying the
foundations upon which many of our symphony orchestras
were later built.[56]

Odd Fellows' Hall

Whereas the Exchange Hotel Concert Room offered
entertainments and concerts in competition with the theatre for an audience, the entertainment offered in the
hotel would not have appealed to all patrons of the theatre.
On the other hand, the Odd Fellows' Hall began to offer
entertainment more closely associated with theatrical
presentations; and in doing so it became the first of several
halls in Richmond to offer competition to the theatre
with theatrical entertainments as the circus and Amphitheatre had done in previous years. As successor to the
circus and Amphitheatre, it may also be considered the
first vaudeville theatre in Richmond. The first of a series
of entertainments given in the Odd Fellows' Hall was
the Harmoneons' Grand Musical Soiree. The Harmoneons
gave their program at the Exchange Hotel and then moved
to the Odd Fellows' Hall, where they performed from
December 1846 through mid-February 1847.[57] The earlier
advertisements indicated only that their programs consisted of vocal and instrumental music, but by the end
of their visit, they advertised that they performed "as
citizens and Ethiopians."[58] In the middle of their visit, the
Harmoneons were replaced for three nights by the Shaking
Quakers, "the greatest Novelty of the Age," who assured

55. *Whig*, December 17, 1850.
56. Howard, p. 280.
57. *Whig*, December 8, 11, 29, 1846; January 1, 1847; February 2, 9, 1847.
58. *Ibid.*, February 9, 1847.

the public that they would give "a true specimen of the Shaker Music."[59] The Odd Fellows' Hall was used by the Washington Euterpeans and the Pee-Dee Ethiopian Opera Troupe for a few nights during that same year and at the beginning of 1848.[60] Theatrical entertainments were given during the latter part of May 1848, with drama, novelties, afterpieces, and an orchestra advertised to be "sufficiently supplied."[61] From the first of December, 1848, through February, 1849, a season of "vaudeville and light entertainment" was given, the Odd Fellows' Hall having been renovated and re-named the Odeon.[62] The Odeon presented burlesques, reviews, farces, minstrels, fire dances, magicians, and other novelty performances "with a good band of music, and an efficient Police."[63] The last entertainment given as part of the Odeon venture was a "dramatic and musical entertainment" by a group of "young gentlemen of the city . . . with some professional Ladies and Gentlemen" and the Blues' Band.[64]

After 1849 the Odd Fellows' Hall, no longer called the Odeon, periodically presented magicians, acrobats, dioramas, minstrels, and other musical entertainments. S. Samuel Sandford presented his New Orleans Opera and Ballet Troupe in 1851 and again in 1853. His presentations were advertised as

Unique and Moral Entertainments, Songs, Glees, Choruses, Refrains, Operatic Scenes, Gems, &c. from all of the principal Operas of the day, assisted by the inimitable Ballet Troupe, in their Burlesque Dances, Pas de Deuxs [sic], Flings, Cachu-

59. Ibid., January 16, 18, 19, 1847.
60. Whig, September 24, 1847; February 1, 1848; and April 4, 1848.
61. Ibid., May 23, 1848. This advertisement probably intended to apprise the reader that the orchestra would be comprised of musicians sufficient in number and possessing sufficient talent for the task at hand.
62. Ibid., December 1, 1848.
63. Ibid., January 23, and February 20, 1849.
64. Ibid., May 11, 1849.

cas, Jigs, Reels, Hornpipes, Lucy Long, &c. . . . concluding with the celebrated Burlesque ITALIAN OPERA.[65]

A burlesque Italian Opera given later by the Sandford Troupe advertised the characters as Sontag, Badiali, Pezzolini, and Biondi and the "impersonations by Collins, Rainer, Lynch, and Sandford."[66] Other troupes playing at the Odd Fellows' Hall during the 1850s were the Harmoneon Operatic Troupe composed of Richmond talent, Ned Davis's Olio Minstrels, Parrow's Minstrels, Campbell's Minstrels, The Julliens Minstrel, Burch's Minstrels, Old Joe Sweeney's Burlesque Opera Troupe, the Excelsior Minstrels, and the Empire Minstrels.[67] Concert entertainments were given by Professor Derwort with his three daughters and son; Mr., Mrs., and Master Goodall; Signor Novelli and Madame Durand; Professor and Madame Louis; and Mr. Poole assisted by his daughters and Mr. Dews. Each group presented ballads, popular songs, and instrumental novelties.[68]

The Metropolitan Hall

The Metropolitan Hall was opened in 1853, and soon became the leading place of variety, minstrel, and concert entertainment in Richmond, supplanting the Odd Fellows' Hall especially for those entertainments drawing a large audience. From the fall of 1853 to the spring of 1865 over 30 different minstrel troupes performed in the Metropolitan Hall, many of them making several return appearances and staying for several weeks. A few troupes were popular enough to draw audiences almost each night for several months. The names of minstrel leaders seen most frequently in the *Dispatch* advertisements were those of

65. *Ibid.*, June 6, 1851.
66. *Dispatch*, February 6, 1853.
67. *Dispatch*, April 26, 1852; November 20, 1859; *et passim*.
68. *Whig*, March 19, 1850; *Dispatch*, November 15, 1852; *et al.*

Kunkel, Parrow, Christy, Campbell, Sandford, and Buckley. Kunkel's troupe apparently enjoyed more popularity than other troupes from 1853 through 1856. Soon after the Metropolitan Hall had opened, a *Dispatch* article reported that "Kunkel and his Minstrels have taken our city by storm. Go where you may, turn where you will, and you hear nothing but 'Kunkel's Band!' "[69] The article also reported that 1700 people attended one of Kunkel's performances.

During the Civil War, Southern minstrel talent was popular. Buckley's Southern Nightingales apparently occupied the hall from mid-October 1862 through mid-January 1863, after which White, Wells, and Fallow leased the hall and gave minstrels to the end of February, 1863. The latter company's performers were listed as:

Bill Parrow, "Pioneer of Minstrelsy"
Jim Wood, "Brudder Bones"
Jim Wells, violinist—"Richmond's favorite"
Charley White, "South's own favorite"
T. V. Conway, "Balladist and Tenor"
Leon Roys, "Alto and Violoncello"
Mons. Faldie, Second Violinist
Harry Telto, Snare Drum
Sig. Malfi, Harpist
Rube Macon, Jig Dancer
Mdle. Amelia Wallace, Tight rope performer and dancer[70]

Buckley, White, and Allen presented the Iron-Clad Minstrels (the name probably being derived from the battle of the *Monitor* and the *Merrimac*) from December 1863 to February 1864.

Concerts were given in Metropolitan Hall by six or more ballad singers, notably Harry Macarthy, who made several extended visits. Three family groups of musicians and numerous bands, orchestras, opera troupes, magicians,

---

69. *Dispatch,* September 23, 1853.
70. *Ibid.,* January 29, 1863.

animal acts, lecturers, and dioramas were presented in the hall during the decade that terminated with the cessation of the Civil War hostilities.

Other Auditoriums

Theatrical entertainments, predominantly minstrels, were offered in several other halls in Richmond. The Mechanics' Institute Hall, also called Corinthian Hall, was used principally by concert artists at first, but from mid-June 1859 through the year 1860 several minstrel and music entertainment troupes used the building. Monticello Hall, used principally for balls and concerts, also offered minstrels and variety entertainment for about one year during the Civil War.

The last minstrel advertised in Confederate Richmond was given in the building that had been called Franklin Hall, later named the Richmond Varieties, and finally advertised as follows:

BUDD & BUCKLEY'S OPERA HOUSE
Franklin Street, next to the Exchange Hotel

———————

GRAND OPERA NIGHT

———————

Saturday Evening, April 1, 1865, First and Only Appearance of the Celebrated French Opera Singer, Mademoiselle
RACHEL

———————

A full Chorus and Orchestra have been engaged for this Occasion. . . . Remember, Mademoiselle RACHEL appears for this night only, as she will leave for Europe on Tuesday morning.

———————

The celebrated Burlesque,
RECRUITING UNBLEACHED CITIZENS OF VIRGINIA FOR THE CONFEDERATE STATES ARMY, which was received on Saturday, Monday, Tuesday and Wednesday nights with SHOUTS OF APPLAUSE.

Harry Budd and Billy Lewis every night in their Side-splitting Comicalities.
Admission, To-Night: Parquette, $4; Gallery, $3; Private Boxes, first tier, $25; second tier, $20. . . .

Highest price paid for old and new CORK at the hall.[71]

Concerts

Beginning a little more than a decade before the Civil War, Richmond's concert patrons heard numerous visitors performing music of relatively high merit. Many of the artists were Europeans touring America. They began to appear periodically during the fifth decade of the century, and a decade later the visitors were seen and heard regularly until their travel was disrupted by the war.

Visiting Artists

A chronological listing of newspaper references to concerts in Richmond by touring musicians is given in Table 9. One reference is cited for each concert or series of concerts presented, and in several instances only the principal performers are listed.

From the information given in Table 9, it is apparent that Maurice Strakosch, Amalia Patti, Adelina Patti, and Teresa Parodi were among the most frequent visitors to the city. Strakosch, a pianist and business manager of touring troupes, married Amalia Patti in 1852, a year during which they made two visits to Richmond. Adelina Patti, Amalia's younger sister, was only eight years old when she first sang in Richmond, yet her repertory included selections written for a mature voice. Parodi was possibly Richmond's favorite artist of the day. A newspaper reviewer wrote in 1852:

---

71. *Ibid.*, April 1, 1861.

Table 9

CONCERT ARTISTS IN RICHMOND
1847–1862

Newspaper Reference[a]	Artists[b]	Place of Performance
W., Dec. 10, 1847	Henri Herz, violinist Camillo Sivori, violinist	Exchange Hotel
W., Feb. 25, 1848	Instrumental concert by the *Steyermarkische*	Exchange Hotel
W., Jan. 16, 1849	Moravian Singers, vocal concert	Exchange Hotel
W., Feb. 6, 1849	Concerts of English opera[e] Mr. and Mrs. Sequin, singers Mrs. H. Phillips, singer H. W. Reeves, singer S. W. Leach, singer G. Holman, singer	African Church
W., Feb. 22, 1849	Anna Bishop, singer R. N. C. Bochsa, harpist	Exchange Hotel
W., May 1, 1849	Concerts of Italian Opera by Astor Place Opera Company Henri Hertz, violinist Franz Coenen, violinist Teresa Truñ, singer S. Benedette, singer S. Rosi, basso	Exchange Hotel

W., Oct. 30, 1849	Madame Biscaccianti, singer Maurice Strakosch, pianist Senora M. C. Casini, singer Signor Biscaccianti, cellist	Theatre
W., Feb. 12, 1850	Sconcia, singer M. De Montfort, singer	Exchange Hotel
W., Apr. 9, 1850 May 27, 1850 Nov. 19, 1850	Luigi Elena, violinist	Exchange Hotel
W., Dec. 20, 1950	Jenny Lind, singer[e] Giovanni Belletti, singer Joseph Burke, violinist	Theatre
W., Mar. 25, 1851	Teresa Parodi, singer[e] Maurice Strakosch, pianist Germania Band	Exchange Hotel
W., Apr. 4, 1851	Fortunata Tedesco, singer[e] Germania Band	Theatre
D., Jan. 21, 1852	Catherine Hayes, singer[e] Ferdinand Griebel, violinist J. A. Kyle, flutist Mengis, singer	Universalist Church and Exchange Hotel
D., Feb. 6, 1852	Teresa Parodi, singer[e] Amalia Patti, singer Miska Hauser, violinist Maurice Strakosch, pianist	Exchange Hotel

D., Jan. 17, 1853	Ole Bull, violiniste Adeline Patti, singer Maurice Strakosch, pianist	African Church
D., Apr. 11, 1853	Paul Julien, violinist	African Church
D., Apr. 25, 1853	Anna Bishop, singer R. N. C. Bochsa, harpist	Theatre
D., Nov. 3, 1853	Henrietta Sontag, singer Paul Julien, violinist Alfred Jaeli, pianist Signor Rocco, singer	African Church
D., Jan. 9, 1854	Ole Bull, violinist Adelina Patti, singer Maurice Strakosch, pianist	Metropolitan Hall
D., Apr. 7, 1854	Orchestra[c] Louis Jullien, conductor Koenig, cornet-a-piston Wuille, clarinet M. M. Lavigne, oboe S. Hughes, ophicleide Collinet, flageolet Mollenhauer brothers, violinists Anna Zerr, singer	Metropolitan Hall
D., Sept. 19, 1854	Valery Gomez, singer Sigismund Wolowski, pianist Camilla Urso, violinist	Metropolitan Hall

D., Feb. 5, 1855	Opera Troupe Rosa De Vries, singer Morino, singer Martin Lazare, singer Passarilla, singer	Metropolitan Hall
D., Dec. 7, 1855	Cecilia Young, singer Robert Heller, pianist Carlos Mahr, violinist	Corinthian Hall
D., Mar. 28, 1956	Teresa Parodi, singer Maurice Strakosch, pianist Amalie Patti Strakosch, singer Leonardi, singer	Corinthian Hall
D., May 17, 1856	Ole Bull, violinist Anna Spinnola, singer S. Anna Vail, singer	Corinthian Hall
D., May 17, 1856	Louis Schreiber Franz Roth, pianist	Corinthian Hall
D., Apr. 27, 1857	Madame D'Angri, singer Mathilde D'Angri, singer Louis Schreiber, trumpet [Theodore] Thomas, violinist Sig. Abella, pianist	Metropolitan Hall
D., Nov. 22, 1857	Maurice Strakosch, pianist Ermine Frezzolini, singer Amalia Patti Strakosch, singer Herr Kletser, violoncellist	Metropolitan Hall

D., Jan. 8, 1858	Sigismund Thalberg, pianist Henry Vieuxtemps, violinist	Metropolitan Hall
D., Apr. 26, 1858	Anna Vale, singer Mollenhauer, violinist Theodore Schreiner, pianist	Corinthian Hall
D., Nov. 1, 1858	Teresa Parodi, singer Juliana May, singer Maurice Strakosch Antonio Barili, singer Carlitto Patti, violinist E. L. Walker, pianist	Metropolitan Hall
D., Dec. 1, 1858	Durand New Orleans Opera Troupe	Corinthian Hall
D., Dec. 7, 1858	Strakosch's Grand Combined Italian Opera Company	Corinthian Hall
D., Jan. 22, 1859	Concerts by opera troupe Emanuele Muzio, conductor Maria Piccolomini, singer M'lle Ghioni, singer Sig. Maggioratti, singer Bruno Wollenhaupt, violinist Ernst Perring, singer	Mechanics' Institute Hall (Corinthian Hall)
D., Feb. 10, 1859	Ullman's Opera Company Concerts. Italian Opera performers from the New York Academy of Music	Mechanics' Institute Hall
D., Apr. 13, 1859	Maria Piccolomini, singer Sig. Maggioratti, singer M'lle Ghioni, singer Sig. Domenico, singer	Mechanics' Institute Hall

	Legendre, cornet-a-piston	
	Emanuele Muzio, conductor	
D., Feb. 14, 1860	French Opera Comique Performance of Opera	Mechanics' Institute Hall
D., Mar. 1, 1860	Opera excerpts performed	Metropolitan Hall
	Marietta Gazzaniga, singer	
	Sig. Tammaro, singer	
	Sig. Albites, singer	
	Carlos Shenal, pianist	
D., Oct. 22, 1860	Adelina Patti, singer	African Church
	Sig. Lotti, singer	
	Ettone Barili, singer	
	Nicola Barili, singer	
	Count Biscaccianti, cellist	
	Maurice Strakosch, director	
D., Oct. 24, 1860	Blind Tom, Negro pianist	African Church
D., Feb. 5, 1861	Blind Tom, Negro pianist	African Church
D., Oct. 14, 1861	Opera Excerpts in concert	African Church
	The Torriani Musical	
	Amateurs from South Carolina	
D., Jan. 30, 1862	Blind Tom, Negro pianist	African Church

a. Abbreviations for newspapers are: *W—Whig* and *D—Dispatch*.
b. Additional references concerning these artists may be found in the *Bio-Bibliographical Index of Musicians in the United States of America Since Colonial Times* (Washington, D. C.: Music Section, Pan American Union, 1956). Many are listed in *Groves Dictionary* and other standard reference works.
c. The program is given in Appendix B.

Of all the vocalists, who, in our day, have appeared before the Richmond public, Parodi has best sustained her reputation. Though she has sung here at least a dozen times, there has been, from first to last, no abatement in the desire to hear her. . . .[72]

On Parodi's return to Richmond after an absence of several years, the newspaper reported that "this is the first concert we have had in a long time in which a real prima donna sang."[73] Of Amalia Patti Strakosch it was said: "Music seems to be as natural to her as to the Virginia mocking bird."[74] After one of the earlier visits, a newspaper reported, with apparently no intentional play on words, "Mr. Strakosch paid the usual tribute to the tastes of Virginia, by executing some of the popular Negro melodies."[75]

Of the instrumental groups that appeared in Richmond, the Germania Band and Jullien's orchestra are the more notable (Table 9 and Appendix B). The Germania Band from Boston was one of the first groups in America to tour widely and offer audiences instrumental music of high quality. After an appearance in Richmond, the band was reported to be "one perfect and powerful instrument . . . commanding the whole range and compass of concord, from the highest harmonic of the violin to the deepest bass of the ophicleide. . . ."[76] Jullien also brought good music and high quality performances, but with these he mixed showmanship and novelty arrangements of music to the extent of overshadowing his better offerings. Beethoven, Haydn, and Mendelssohn were given hearings along with quadrilles, waltzes, polkas, and gallops. P. T. Barnum was Jullien's manager, and the two men appar-

---

72. *Dispatch,* May 18, 1852.
73. *Ibid.,* March 28, 1856.
74. *Ibid.,* January 19, 1853.
75. *Whig,* March 25, 1851.
76. *Ibid.*

ently shared a compulsion to amaze people with spectacular performances.

> Jullien . . . called upon his horns, and they answered him—he summoned his violins, and they came—he frowned upon his drums, and they thundered—he called spirits from the vast deep, and they were there!
>
> . . . .
>
> There was an amount of wind and catgut exhausted on the occasion, that would have served the band, for ordinary purposes, for more than six months!
>
> . . . .
>
> We have little doubt the echoes of it will be heard in Metropolitan Hall for twelve months to come.[77]

Of the solo instrumentalists listed in Table 9, Luigi Elena, Ole Bull, Paul Julien, and H. Vieuxtemps received the most favorable publicity in the press. Luigi Elena and his brother taught and performed and were welcomed into Richmond's social circles. During his stay in the city, Luigi Elena composed a concerto for the violin "dedicated to the Ladies of Richmond."[78] Ole Bull returned to Richmond three times after his first appearance in 1843. In 1853 and 1854 he performed on programs with Strakosch and Patti (Table 9). Bull was reported to be "greatly superior to, and entirely unlike any other violinist we have ever heard."[79] His concerts no longer created the furor that had accompanied his earlier concerts, however. Paul Julien was 12 years old at the time of his first performance in Richmond (Table 9). A reviewer stated that although Julien offered a "highly artistic performance on the violin," which was equaled by that of "no adult performer . . . save Sivori," his concert was thinly attended, whereas Ole Bull's concert in the same building three months

---

77. *Dispatch*, April 7, 1854.
78. *Whig*, May 27, 1850.
79. *Dispatch*, January 19, 1853.

previously had seen all seats in the house sold "some days in advance of the concert."[80] Vieuxtemps, violinist, and Thalberg, piano soloist and accompanist for Vieuxtemps (Table 9), both received excellent reviews in the newspaper.[81]

The programs in Appendix B, referred to in Table 9, give some further indication of the quality of the music performed in concerts given in Richmond. The "Grand Musical Festival" (Table 9) given by the Seguin Opera Company comprised light airs from English opera, ballads, and Scotch songs such as "Coming Through the Rye." The "Operatic Concert" by Tedesco and the Germania Band (Table 9) were of somewhat higher quality, with Tedesco singing excerpts from operas by Verdi and Donizetti and the band playing overtures, selections featuring virtuoso performers, and some lighter works.

Jenny Lind and Catharine Hayes each paid a single visit to Richmond (Table 9). Lind was well known in the city before her visit. Articles about her were published in newspapers; her music, portraits, and "medallion daguerreotypes in colours" were sold in Richmond to herald her appearance.[82] As her tour brought her nearer Richmond, the newspapers reported details of Lind's appearances in other cities. On the eve of the long-awaited event one writer called for moderation in folly and stated that gentlemen should not give more than ten dollars for music they can neither understand nor appreciate.

"The Nightingale," the "Queen of Song," the "Divine Jenney," will soon be among us, and her advent promises to be celebrated by the usual quality of Humbug, extravagance, and insane folly. As the world goes, so will Richmond go, and Dame Rumor has already announced that we have some

80. *Ibid.*, April 11, 1853.
81. *Ibid.*, January 11, 1858.
82. *Whig*, November 12, 1850.

consummate asses here, who are ambitious of playing second fiddle to the asses of New York and Boston, who gave the extravagant sums for the premium seats. . . .[83]

Tickets for Lind's concert were sold at auction by a member of P. T. Barnum's staff, the highest bid being $105, the minimum price for any ticket having been established at five. The event is recorded by many historians, one of whom relates that "no one ever visited Richmond who charmed the people more and was longer remembered than Jenny Lind."[84] When Catharine Hayes gave several concerts in Richmond (Table 9), it was reported that "we have never known a more general wish expressed by a whole community to hear a distinguished vocalist, save the case of Jenny Lind."[85] Something of the audience's mannerisms of the day are revealed in an article written on the eve of one of Hayes' concerts when the writer was "expressing the hope, that persons who have a great deal of talking to do, will do it before they go to the concert tonight."[86]

Performances by Visiting Artists Assisted by Richmond Musicians

Although many of the touring groups of concert musicians carried a full complement of performers, there were other visiting musicians who collaborated with Richmond talent to give concerts. Some of the visitors eventually made Richmond their home. Musicians who had become residents of Richmond and had performed in concerts as local professional musicians by 1845 were P. H. Taylor, E. B. Barber, John Dunderdale, Signor G. George, F. W. Rosier, J. K. Opl, and Madame Bonavita (George's daugh-

---

83. *Ibid.*, December 17, 1850.
84. W. Asbury Christian, *Richmond, Her Past and Present* (Richmond: L. H. Jenkins, 1912), p. 173.
85. *Dispatch*, January 22, 1852.
86. *Ibid.*, February 9, 1852.

ter). They continued their activities as professional musicians and, along with newly arrived resident musicians, assisted visiting artists in concerts.

A large number of musicians made Richmond their home between 1845 and 1865. Those taking part in assisting visiting musicians were T. X. Da Costa, flutist; Mr. Staddermann (apparently also spelled Stadelman, Stedman, and Stoderman), pianist and violinist; Charles William Thilow, pianist, cellist, and organist; E. Loebmann (Liebman, Loebman), violinist; and J. Kessnich (Kessnick, Kessenick, Kisnich), violinist. Table 10 lists visiting artists who were assisted by Richmond musicians during the period 1846 to 1860.

Joseph Burke, who performed in 1846 (Table 10), was considered a better performer than Ole Bull in many respects.[87] In keeping with the custom of the day, Burke's program included vocal music interspersed with violin solos. The vocal portion of the program was performed by the Richmond musician, Dunderdale, who apparently was equally talented as a pianist and organist. Dunderdale performed similar vocal duties with another violinist, Camillo Savori (Table 10). Dunderdale and George, Richmond vocalists, appeared with Rosier and Taylor, Richmond instrumentalists, in a concert given by M. A. Zani Ferranti, "first guitarist to H. M. the King of the Belgians" (Table 10). Dunderdale also played the piano in Ferranti's concert. After two other concerts in 1847 by visitors with the assistance of Richmond musicians (Table 10), no similar concerts were noted until 1852.

P. H. Taylor was the outstanding leader among the professional musicians during the second quarter of the nineteenth century. After performing in two concerts in 1847, he apparently devoted most of his time to his music store, which probably carried the most complete line of music

---

87. *Whig,* March 13, 1846.

Table 10

CONCERTS GIVEN BY VISITING ARTISTS
ASSISTED BY RICHMOND MUSICIANS
1846–1860

Newspaper Referenced	Visiting Artists	Richmond Musicians
W., Apr. 10, 1846	Joseph Burke, violinist	John Dunderdale, singer
W., Jan. 12, 1847	Camillo Sivori, violinist	John Dunderdale, singer
W., Jan. 19, 1847	M. A. Zani De Ferranti, guitarist	John Dunderdale, singer pianist Signor G. George, singer F. W. Rosier, cellist P. H. Taylor, flutist
W., Nov. 23, 1847	F. Rieman, singer	J. K. Opl Signor George John Dunderdale Charles Rosen The Armory Band The Gray's Band
W., Dec. 31, 1847	George Knoop, celliste Miss De Jeune, pianist Mr. Buck, pianist	P. H. Taylor, flutist J. K. Opl, violinist
D., May 13, 1852	Jenny Busk, singer Mrs. Muller, singer F. Kley, pianist	T. X. Da Costa, flutist

D., Sept. 27, 1852	Anna Widemann,[e] singer Mons. Genibrel, singer	Mr. Staddermann, pianist T. X. Da Costa, flutist E. Loebmann, violinist F. W. Rosier, cellist
D., Apr. 22, 1853	Mrs. Bostwick, singer Julius Seide, flutist Mr. Appy, violinist and singer Little Annie Oliver, concertina	C. W. Thilow, pianist
D., May 3, 1853	Anna Bishop, singer R. N. C. Bochsa, harpist	T. X. Da Costa, flutist
D., Jan. 27, 1854	Amalia Siminski, flutist and singer Joseph Borra, violinist C. Bottesini, pianist Prof. Millar, singer	C. W. Thilow, pianist
D., May 29, 1854	Cecilia Young, singer[e]	T. X. Da Costa, flutist C. W. Thilow, pianist
D., Jan. 31, 1855	Mara De Estvan, singer L. De Lacy, singer	F. W. Rosier, cellist C. W. Thilow, pianist
D., May 22, 1856	Adeleni Lohse, singer	Charles Rosen, flutist J. Kessnich, violinist
D., Oct. 18, 1859	Charles Elliott, singer	G. George, singer Madame Bonavita, singer
D., June 15, 1860	Pauline Colson, singer Signor Stigelli, singer	C. W. Thilow, pianist

---

d. Newspaper abbreviations: *W—Whig* and *D—Dispatch.*
e. Program is given in Appendix B.

merchandise in the city, and he relinquished his role as the city's principal concert flutist to T. X. Da Costa, who moved to Richmond to teach music in 1852.[88] Da Costa was referred to as "a distinguished flutist of this city" when he assisted Jenny Busk in a concert in 1852 (Table 10). Staddermann and Loebmann were active as professional musicians in Richmond, but their only appearance with a visiting artist was made with Da Costa and Busk (Table 10).

C. W. Thilow made his first Richmond appearance as accompanist for Mrs. Bostwick's concert in 1853 (Table 10). Thereafter, he was one of the leading pianists, organists, and teachers in the city. Thilow's second performance with a visiting artist was in a concert by Amelia Siminski, "said to be the greatest flutist in the known world" (Table 10). Among other visiting artists accompanied by Thilow were Mara De Estvan and her sister L. De Lacy (Table 10), both of whom resided, taught music, and performed in Richmond from 1855 through the Civil War. Kessnich, violinist and teacher in Richmond for many years, made only one concert appearance with a visitor, that one being with Adeleni Lohse (Table 10).

Sacred Music Concerts by Richmond Musicians

Concerts by the Richmond Sacred Music Society during 1840, 1841, and 1843 are described in Chapter 4. The society apparently became inactive after their concert given in February 1843, but music instruction continued to be offered to classes meeting in churches. S. S. Stevens, who in 1845 advertised singing classes for both children and

---

88. *Dispatch,* April 10, 1852. For additional information on music merchantry in Richmond from 1846 through the Civil War the reader is referred to several Richmond Directories listed in the Bibliography, to the *Dispatch,* which includes advertisements of music merchandise in each issue, and to Richard B. Harwell, *Confederate Music* (Chapel Hill: The University of North Carolina Press, 1950), a book containing excellent material on Richmond publishers.

adults to be held in Richmond's Presbyterian churches, later became the director of the Richmond Sacred Music Society and served as conductor during its most productive years from 1852 to 1856. The society was apparently inactive from its last concert in 1843 until 1851. In the interim, Stevens continued his classes and "gave his first Juvenile Concert for the Season" in March 1847.[89] Another singing school was conducted in the "vestry of the Presbyterian Church on Church Hill" by Harriet M. Jones in 1852.[90] In February of that year the *Dispatch* announced that an "Oratorio" was in preparation by a "number of Amateur Musicians" under the direction of "Mr. Stadelman."[91] In May the performance was erroneously advertised as a "first" performance of its kind.

> ABSALOM, (the first Oratorio ever performed in this city,) composed by Haydn, Handel, Mozart, Beethoven, &c. &c., Arranged by Woodbury, conducted by Mr. S. S. Stevens, to be performed by Professors and Amateurs, at the 1st Presbyterian (Rev. Mr. Moore's) Church, for the benefit of Mr. Michelbacher's Synagogue, on Tuesday, May 11, at 8 o'clock.
>
> Price of Admittance $1. . . .[92]

A newspaper writer reviewing the concert was most liberal in his praise of the performance, and his article clarified the role played by Mr. Stoderman or Stadelman, who was a violinist rather than the director, as previously announced.

> Many of the young ladies had voices which would do no discredit to the Italian Opera, and wanted nothing but a little more confidence to make them perfect in their *role*.
> The instrumental music was very fine. The leader and

---

89. *Whig,* March 2, 1847.
90. *Dispatch,* February 19, 1852.
91. *Ibid.,* February 14, 1852.
92. *Ibid.,* May 11, 1852.

first violin was Mr. Dollinger, who, also, we understand, drilled the corps of singers and brought them to sing together. He was assisted by Messrs. Loebman, and Stoderman, also violinists of great taste and execution. Mr. Joseph Ritterhouse performed on the Bassoon with great effect.[93]

The same music was again performed by the ensemble in June 1852, as a benefit for its conductor, S. S. Stevens.[94]

The Richmond Sacred Music Society applied to the Richmond City Council for permission to use the municipal lecture hall, the Athenaeum, for rehearsals, but the request was not granted for several reasons: among them, because the library was upstairs, rehearsals would disturb the library users and, too, scientific equipment was sometimes stored in the room between lectures.[95] The society received more favorable publicity as a result of having presented the request to the City Council, and it was described as "a new and commendable organization, which has in view the acquisition of a thorough knowledge of sacred music, its promotion in the community, and the instruction of the young, without regard to the denominational distinctions. . . ."[96]

On the last program given by the society in 1852, "upwards of 100 vocal and instrumental performers" were to take part.[97] Having experienced a successful year with the Sacred Music Society, Stevens continued his singing school activities, organizing a school for adults in the Second Presbyterian Church and a school for children in the Third Baptist Church early in 1853.[98] In the spring, the Society was again liberally supported by the press.[99] The

93. *Ibid.,* May 13, 1852.
94. *Ibid.,* June 3, 1852.
95. *Ibid.,* July 3, 1852 *et al.*
96. *Ibid.,* September 27, 1852.
97. *Ibid.,* December 17, 1852.
98. *Ibid.,* January 28, 1853.
99. Two additional articles describing their activities and giving more praise to the society were printed in the *Dispatch,* April 29 and May 3, 1853.

program of their concert given in May at the First Presbyterian Church was published,[100] and a review stated that "80 members of the society, half ladies, were present."[101] There was a "full and most efficient orchestra" under the leadership of Dollinger and Loebmann. Dunderdale was the pianist, and Stevens directed the performance, in which the solos, quartettes, and choruses were reported to have been "uniformly excellent."[102] On December 24, 1853, the society gave another concert of sacred music,[103] but "owing to the extreme inclemency of the weather, . . . the concert was attended by a thin audience."[104]

The society was again praised and encouraged by the press in the spring of 1854, but for the first time there was an ominous undertone in the writings.[105]

Richmond Sacred Music Society.—This Society has been struggling on for some years under great difficulties, and it deserves to be encouraged. It has contributed largely to the public enjoyment in this city, and done a great deal to encourage and improve the taste for music.[106]

The group evidently disbanded during the summer, to reorganize in the fall of the same year. An article in the *Dispatch* in September states that the Society was to resume its weekly practice at the Second Presbyterian Church, and the purposes of the organization were: (1) self-improvement and enjoyment of music, especially church choir music, (2) cultivation and improvement of public taste, and (3) "to cheapen the price of music study."[107] A note of bitterness implied that some persons, including ministers, had not yet realized the value of the society and its

100. *Ibid.,* May 3, 1853.
101. *Ibid.,* May 5, 1853.
102. *Ibid.*
103. *Ibid.,* December 24, 1853.
104. *Ibid.,* December 26, 1853.
105. *Ibid.,* March 6, 1854.
106. *Ibid.,* May 27, 1854.
107. *Ibid.,* September 27, 1854.

objectives: "It is, we learn, the experience of nearly all the churches in Richmond, that the attendance at their weekly choir practice is very small. . . ."[108]

Apparently the members of the society felt that, although they themselves had experienced success in their concert ventures, music in the churches had seen little improvement, and therefore one of their objectives remained unfulfilled. In desperation, perhaps, they turned elsewhere for help, for during the next year two conventions were held, and support from the North was called in.

The Music Conventions

The members of the Richmond Sacred Music Society met with various church choirs early in 1855 to plan a convention. The purposes of the convention were probably (1) to revive the waning interest in sacred music, (2) to receive some expert instruction and advice, and (3) to attract the attention of the public with hope of gaining their support. They engaged George F. Root, of the Normal Musical Institute, New York, and W. C. Van Meter, lecturer, for the convention. It was reported that "everyone seems determined that this, the first Musical Convention ever held in Virginia, shall be worthy of the cause."[109] The convention ran from Saturday evening, March 17, 1855, through the following Tuesday. At the first meeting, which was held at the Second Baptist Church, officers were elected, and there were "Choruses, solos and musical criticism by Root."[110] Principal officers elected were Moses D. Hogue, president; R. B. C. Howell and Charles H. Read, vice-presidents. The three men were ministers in Richmond churches. Root and Van Meter were elected as musical directors; T. M. Gallaher and James Gordon, secretaries; and L. M. Harrold, treasurer.

---

108. *Ibid.*
109. *Ibid.*, March 13, 1855.
110. *Ibid.*, March 24, 1855.

A committee headed by Stevens recommended that a second convention be held in December of the same year and that it should be the beginning of "a Southern Musical Institute for imparting more thorough music education and especially for teacher training."[111] The second convention was held in the First Baptist Church and headed by Lowell Mason and George Root. It ran from Friday, December 14 through December 20, 1855, and culminated in a public performance given under the direction of Root. Dunderdale was the piano accompanist. "Sittings of the convention" were held every morning beginning at 10 o'clock, and at the first meeting Lowell Mason spoke on "Congregational Singing."[112] Marian Harland (nee Mary Virginia Hawes) gives a personal account of the Hawes family's role in the convention. This account, which exemplifies the meaning of mid-century southern hospitality, follows:

> My father, my sister, my brother Herbert, and myself were members of a flourishing Sacred Music Society, composed principally of amateurs, and we had engaged the distinguished leaders in the profession to preside over the conference, by which it was hoped public taste in the matter of choir and congregational singing might be improved. Classes were formed for the study of methods and for drill in vocalization. The course would be closed by a grand concert, in which no professional would take part.
>
> The thought that the imported leaders in the programme should be allowed to put up at a hotel was opposed to the genius of Southern hospitality. Doctor and Mrs. Lowell Mason were the honored guests of Mr. Williams, the President of the Society. My father invited Mr. Root "to make our house his home while he was in our city."
>
> That was the old-fashioned form of asking strangers to take bit and sup and bed with us. We made good the words, too. The "home" was theirs as truly as it was ours. The Convention was advertised to last ten days. When the time

111. *Ibid.*
112. *Ibid.*, December 17, 1855.

was nearly expired, the extraordinary success of the experiment induced the projectors to extend the time to a month. Mr. Root was for removing to a hotel, but we arose up in arms and forbade it. His bonhomie, intelligence, and general attractiveness of manner and disposition had endeared him to us all.[113]

After the second convention, the Sacred Music Society did not appear again before the public, but the organization and its officers were listed in the Richmond City Directory in 1856. With the listing was the information that the Society "meets every Monday night at Second Presbyterian Church."[114] The officers were: John Williams, president; P. R. Keach, treasurer; S. S. Stevens, conductor; James Evans, assistant conductor; E. M. Harralle, librarian: J. M. Tyler, J. P. Hanlon, William Mingle, S. P. Hawes, James Gordon, and R. A. Rhodes, managers.

Another music convention was held in Richmond at the beginning of 1857 in the Sycamore Disciples of Christ Church, but the names of the participants differed from those in the previous convention. Ministers elected to office came from Richmond's First Baptist, First Presbyterian, Monumental Episcopal, and United Presbyterian churches. The proceedings were apparently instigated by two men, A. N. Johnson and E. H. Frost, who had written a book or a series of books on singing. The two men with Miss S. E. Whitehouse and Miss E. E. Rawson had given vocal quartette concerts and lectures in Richmond prior to the convention.[115] The quartet also participated in a concert presented at the conclusion of the convention when "hymn tunes sung by a select choir of nearly 100 singers" were heard.[116] The musical convention of 1857 marked the end of interdenominational sacred music gatherings in Richmond until after the Civil War.

---

113. Harland, pp. 297–98.
114. *Richmond Directory 1856*, n.p.
115. *Dispatch*, December 23, 1856.
116. *Ibid.*, January 19 and January 23, 1857.

Secular Concerts by Richmond Musicians

The city's own professional musicians, who had given concerts in 1845 and before, did little afterwards in the way of producing concerts other than to perform with visitors until 1856, at which time the professional musicians combined with Richmond amateur groups to give concert performances. Various factors contributed to the activities of Richmond musicians, which culminated in the series of secular instrumental and vocal concerts given during 1856. The increasing quantity of minstrel entertainment and band music, plus the concerts by visiting artists, stimulated interest in music, and the instruction given to citizens by the excellent musicians residing in and visiting the city had probably inspired and developed native talent. A decade or more of work by people interested in improving sacred music performances played an important part in preparation for those concerts given in 1856.[117] The final factor supplying the musicians with inspiration and leadership was the arrival of German and Scandinavian immigrants who brought their love and talent for making music with them. These immigrants had apparently organized small amateur vocal and perhaps instrumental groups during the early part of the mid-century decade.

Volkmar Busch, "late titular orchestra-conductor to H. M. the King of Denmark," made the first public move to organize Richmond's musicians for secular concerts when he announced his plan to form a small amateur orchestra.[118] Soon after Busch's announcement was published, a "Grand Vocal and Instrumental Concert" was given by "many of the leading professors, assisted by the Armory Band . . . for the benefit of the suffering poor of

---

117. A concert given by Dunderdale, Rosier, and their pupils on December 25, 1849, is included in Appendix B. The music on the first part of the program is sacred, and that on the last part is secular.

118. *Dispatch*, February 5, 1856.

our city."[119] The professors and other musicians are not named, but a composition by Busch and several selections by the Virginia Verein, composed of 20 members, are listed on the program.[120] An arrangement by C. W. Thilow is also listed.

The next concert by Richmond musicians was given a week later by De Estvan and De Lacy, both of whom were residing and teaching in Richmond. Assisting on that second concert during 1856 were G. George, T. K. Da Costa, and C. W. Thilow. The program lists music comparable to the better music performed by visiting artists of the period.[121]

The third concert by Richmond musicians in 1856 was directed by Busch. His program, published in the *Dispatch,* is unusual in several ways.[122] Described on the program is an orchestra of "more than twenty performers" composed of the theatre orchestra, Busch's newly organized Musical Amateur Club of Richmond, and "some of the musicians of the Armory Band." Members of the Musical Amateur Club of Richmond are listed as featured instrumentalists, one member being Mr. Ericsson of Stockholm, who is scheduled to play a trombone sole with orchestra accompaniment arranged by Busch for that concert. A composition by John J. Fry, "of Richmond," is listed as arranged by Busch and to be performed by members of the amateur club. Several other compositions are listed as having been arranged by Busch, and a description of each is given.[123] The *Dispatch* printed the following review of the concert:

> Mr. Busch's concert . . . [was a] fine musical treat, reflecting high credit on the musical talent and the accomplishments

---

119. *Ibid.,* February 15, 1856. Program—Appendix B.
120. *Ibid.*
121. *Ibid.,* February 21, 1856. Program—Appendix B.
122. *Ibid.,* March 27, 1856. Program—Appendix B.
123. *Ibid.*

of this city as well as upon the accomplished conductor. . . .
The pieces were admirably played, and the spirit and concord of the instrumentation showed that the performers were
practiced and well educated musicians; for they had but
one rehearsal previous to the performance. The house was
a fair one; but not such as should have been present to encourage those musicians whose residence among us adds so
much to the interest of public ceremonials and festivities,
and helps so much to inspire and improve the taste for
music.[124]

The last concert by Richmond musicians in 1856, given
in May, was called the "first grand festival of the three
united singing societies of Richmond."[125] The vocalists,
40 in number, were assisted by the theatre orchestra and
the Armory Band, but neither the individual musicians
nor the conductors are listed on the program. The *City
Directory, 1856* lists three German Societies and their
officers.

Singing Society of Virginia. . . . Dr. Wm. Grebe, President;
A. Cipperich, Secretary; B. Brauer, Treasurer.
Quartette Club. . . . H. C. G. Timmerman, President; A.
Rich, Secretary; A. Schad, Treasurer.
Concordia Singing Society. . . . E. Loebmann, Leader; C.
Emminger, Secretary; A. Schad, Treasurer.[126]

In 1857 there were two concerts by groups of Richmond
musicians, one given in February and the other in December. Busch was the conductor and "arranger of the
music" for the February concert, which was given by the
Richmond Amateur Instrumental Club.[127] Selections from
operas, songs by Schubert, and compositions by members

---

124. *Ibid.,* March 31, 1856.
125. *Ibid.,* May 26, 1856. Program—Appendix B.
126. One of the three groups, probably the "Concordia Singing Society," became known as the *Gesangeverein* after the Civil War. They
contributed much to the development of Richmond's musical culture
during that later period.
127. *Dispatch,* February 10, 1858. Program—Appendix B.

of the club were included on the program. Busch probably left Richmond during 1857, and the program given in December was directed by J. A. Rosenberger, leader of the theatre orchestra. Whereas other concerts in 1856 and 1857 by Richmond musicians had been given in Metropolitan Hall, Rosenberger's concert was given in Steinlien's Hall.[128] Called a "grand sacred concert," the program included only one composition with a sacred text, a selection from Haydn's *Creation* sung by the Cecilia Society, possibly an amateur vocal group making their only public appearance in Richmond. The remainder of the music listed on the program consists of selections from operas, Schubert's "Serenade," solos for trumpet, clarinet, and flute, and one composition by Rosenberger. The soloists listed are Baier, trumpet; Baumann, clarinet; Krausse, vocal; and Rosenberger, flute—all apparently from the theatre orchestra.

Evidence of activities by Richmond amateur vocal groups is found in two concerts in 1859, one by groups of German musicians and one by another group of Richmond musicians. The first, a "Grand May Festival," was given at the Volk's Garden by the Gesang-Verein Quartette Club, the Virginia Verein Club, and the German Turner Society.[129] The second was a "Grand Gift Concert" by Joseph P. Hanlon at the Mechanics' Institute Hall.[130] The concert was sponsored by a committee and announced by publication of a proposal addressed to Hanlon.

> Desiring to show some small token by which you may in some degree be remunerated for the many efforts on your part at charitable concerts and many other occasions, . . . we propose to you to give a complementary concert at which time and place as may suit your convenience. . . .

128. *Ibid.*, December 19, 1857. See Appendix A—Metropolitan Hall and Steinlien's Hall. Program—Appendix B.

129. *Ibid.*, May 9, 1859.

130. *Ibid.*, June 28, 1859. Program—Appendix B.

N. J. Willis,
Miles Turpin,
T. J. Starke,
and others.[131]

The offer was accepted by Hanlon, and the concert was reportedly "one of the most delightful entertainments of the season," the additional attraction of distributing prizes to the "holders of luckey numbers" having been provided by Hanlon.[132] The performers, all amateurs, are identified by initials only. The music consisted of popular songs of the day.

Professional and amateur musicians gave concerts in 1860 both separately and in combination. A concert by the German Independent Turners Association was given in January for the benefit of the widow of a German newspaper editor in Cincinnati.[133] Soon thereafter, a new organization, the Richmond Philharmonic Association, began a series of public activities. They first "dedicated the new and beautiful hall in Belvin's Block on twelfth street."[134] Two other projects of the association were concerts, one in February, the other in March, both at the Mechanics' Institute Hall.[135] A. Gebhardt was named as conductor of both concerts, but the performers were identified only as members of the association, "some of the principal professors of the city," and, for the second concert, "several lady artistes of our city."[136] The first program published in the *Dispatch* stated that "the music will be entirely of a Classical Character, the object of the Association being the cultivation of an improved taste in that elevating science."[137] Selections from operas by the or-

131. *Ibid.*, June 16, 1859.
132. *Ibid.*, June 29, 1859.
133. *Ibid.*, January 11, 1859. The program, given in Monticello Hall, was not published.
134. *Ibid.*, January 21, 1860.
135. *Ibid.*, February 2 and March 9, 1860. Program—Appendix B.
136. *Ibid.*
137. *Ibid.*, February 2, 1860.

chestra, vocal compositions of Beethoven and Schubert, and a string quartet by Haydn were included on the first program. The second concert included instrumental and vocal ensembles performing opera selections and called for solos on the clarinet, violin, and bassoon. Teachers and other professional musicians organized under the name of The Richmond Academy of Music presented their first and only concert before the Civil War in June 1860. The program published in the *Dispatch* contains the essential facts known about the academy. Apparently an outgrowth of the Philharmonic Association, the Richmond Academy of Music was probably established in conjunction with the Mechanics' Institute, in which some of the music teachers had studios. Members of the orchestra, predominantly German, were the principal musician-teachers of Richmond, and the compositions played were selections from the repertory of instrumental literature popular in Germany at that time.

RICHMOND ACADEMY OF MUSIC
————
First Concert
For the Benefit of the orphans of the city,
at the
HALL OF THE MECHANICS' INSTITUTE
Thursday, 7th June, 1860.
————

President—Dr. James Beale,
Vice President—Dr. Charles L. Mills

Violins—A. Gebhart, E. Loebmann, Jno. Metz, Jno. Werth,
        R. Mayr, W. Fran——[illegible].
Viole—F. W. Rosier, C. C. Mera.
Violoncello—C. W. Thilow.
Bassi—B. Krausse, J. A. Knop, R. Wooler.
Flutes—Tillander, Jo. H. Hewett.
Clarionets—Schneider, J. Baumann.
Bassoons—J. C. Rittershause, O. A. Ericsson.
Horns—E. Stein, H. Shaltz.

The Katy-Did Polka *by Jullien is a typical instrumental music composition of the mid-nineteenth century. Jullien's orchestra played this music in his Richmond concert, and the sheet music was available for all those who wished to purchase it and try it on their piano. (Photo: from a New York City Public Library microfilm)*

Jenny Lind's appearance in Richmond (1850) was well heralded by P. T. Barnum's staff. Tickets were auctioned, the highest bid being one hundred and five dollars. The minimum price for any ticket had been established at five dollars. (Photo: Virginia State Library)

When Catharine Hayes gave several concerts in Richmond (1851), a newspaper reported that "we have never known a more general wish expressed by a whole community to hear a distinguished vocalist, save the case of Jenny Lind." (Photo: Virginia State Library)

Ole Bull, violinist, performed in Richmond in 1843 and again several times during the 1850s. Of the earlier visit, a newspaper reported: "Such extraordinary tones, so sweet, so rich and so soft, we could have not believed it possible, to proceed from a merely mortal instrument, touched by a merely human hand." (Photo: Virginia State Library)

Amalia Patti was among the most frequent artist-visitors to Richmond during the 1850s. She married Maurice Strakosch, pianist and business manager of touring troupes. Of Amalia Patti Strakosch it was written: "Music seems to be as natural to her as to the Virginia Mocking bird." (Photo: Virginia State Library)

Adelina Patti, Amalia Patti's younger sister, was only eight years old when she first sang in Richmond during the 1850s, yet her repertory included selections written for a mature voice. (Photo: Virginia State Library)

Richmond Theatre notices and advertisements in newspapers from 1819 to 1865 referred to activities in this building. Edwin Booth, Edwin Forrest, William Macready, and other leading actors, actresses and musicians from England and the United States performed here intermittently with minstrels, ballad singers, magicians, acrobats, and trained animals. (Photo: Virginia State Library)

This Richmond Theatre photograph was probably taken late in the century. The building was torn down in 1896. Built in 1819, remodeled in 1838, burned in 1862, rebuilt on the same foundations in 1863, it had offered culture and entertainment to several generations of Richmond citizens. (Photo: Virginia State Library)

The White House of the Confederacy is viewed, in this mid-twentieth-century photograph, looking from the southwest toward the northeast. It is located in what is now the Medical College of Virginia complex. (Photo: Courtesy the Confederate Museum, Richmond, and the Virginia State Library)

Lewis Miller sketched this scene from life in 1853. Violin (fiddle), banjo, and bones are played for dancers. (Photo: Virginia State Library)

A Civil War camp scene shows Joe Sweeney (with banjo) entertaining Confederate soldiers. Sweeney became a legendary figure because of his virtuosity as a banjoist. (Photo: Virginia State Library)

Pray, Maiden, Pray *was one of a large quantity of patriotic songs inspired by the Civil War. It was lithographed and published in Richmond, Virginia, of the Confederate States of America. (Photo: from a Library of Congress microfilm)*

St. John's Church, Richmond, built in 1741, is perhaps best known as the meeting place of the Colonial Virginia General Assembly in 1775 where ideologies of independence were debated. After the American Revolutionary War, the building fell into relative disuse, but it has been used for services continually since 1814. The church had an organ that was sold in 1790, and the next organ to be installed, during 1816–17, preceded other church organ installations in Richmond. (Photo: Virginia State Library)

St. John's Church now stands in splendor, remodeled and refurnished, with a proud history of service dating back more than two and a half centuries. (Photo: The Virginia State Chamber of Commerce)

St. Paul's Episcopal Church   *Richard L. Mays Jr 32.*

St. Paul's Church was consecrated in 1845 with music by the choir and organ. The organ was described as being "among the largest built on this continent." President of the Confederacy, Jefferson Davis, was attending church services here when he was called out to be notified of the impending capture of Richmond by the Union Army. (Photo: Virginia State Library)

Trumpets—J. Beier, G. Bonsack.
Trombone—G. Voelker.
Kettle Drum—F. Grabau.
Triangle—Chas. Seibert.
Bass Drum—Fr. Seibert.
Pianists—E. Barber, C. W. Thilow, Chas. Seibert, F. Seibert,
    F. Grabau, Rob. Woller, Schneider.

PROGRAMME
Part First

1. Grand Overture—"Stradella."   Flotow.
2. Quartetto—Piano Forte, Violin, Viole and Violoncello.
    Messrs. Grabau, Stein, Rittershause and Rosier. Mozart.
3. Solo—Violoncello, from "I Puritani,"
    Mr. Thillow.   Piatti.
4. Trio, (Andante,) —Piano Forte, Violin and Violoncello.
    Messrs. F. Seibert, Loebmann and Thillow.   Reissiger.
5. Grand Athalia March.   Mendelssohn.

Part Second

1. Grand Overture—"Felsenmuhle."   Reissiger.
2. Solo—Clarionet, Mr. Baumann.   Beer.
3. Grand Duett, for two Piano Fortes.
    Messrs. C. and F. Seibert.   Herz.
4. Trio—Allegro—Piano Forte.
    Messrs. Fred Seibert, Loebmann and Thillow. Reissiger.
5. Coronation March, from the Prophete.   Meyerbeer.

Conductor—Mr. F. Seibert.[138]

Possibly all of the members of the orchestra were music
teachers, and many of them were associated with the
numerous female academies in Richmond.[139]

The students of the Richmond Female Institute, which
later became the Woman's College of Richmond and is
now a part of the University of Richmond, gave a "Soiree
Musical" in conjunction with the Institute's sixth annual

---

138. *Dispatch*, June 7, 1860.
139. The *Dispatch* (1846–1865) advertises a large number of private
schools located in and around Richmond. The advertisements by female
academies generally state that music is taught by the professional musicians and music teachers of Richmond, and in some instances the
teachers are named.

commencement in June 1860. The music, directed by Nathan B. Clapp and performed by student pianists and vocalists, included a wide variety of selections from popular operas and other songs composed or arranged for pedagogical use.[140]

Late in the fall of the same year, a series of "Soirees Musicale" by Richmond musicians was given, similar programs by professional musicians not having been offered for over a decade.

> These Classical Concerts take place every Thursday Evening, at the School Room of Mrs. Pellett, commencing at 8 o'clock, under the direction of Messers. F. W. Rosier, F. N. Crouch, and John Metz.[141]

A fee of five dollars admitted a lady and a gentleman to five performances of this, probably the first series of subscription concerts given in Richmond. Rosier had been teaching and performing in Richmond for 15 years or more, but Crouch and Metz were recent arrivals. Crouch had migrated from England, where he had already won some recognition as a singer and composer.

The last concert by Richmond musicians before the Civil War was given in February 1861, by the United Musicians of Richmond, directed by Rosenberger of the theatre and Loebmann of the Armory Band. The concert, which was followed by a ball, was held in Monticello Hall and offered opera medleys, solos for clarinet, bassoon, and trumpet, and popular dance tunes.[142] The *Dispatch* reported that "we have not heard such charming instrumental music since the days of Jullien."[143]

---

140. The Program—Appendix B. Source of the material: the files of the Virginia Historical Society.
141. *Dispatch,* November 22, 1860.
142. *Ibid.,* February 11, 1861.
143. *Ibid.,* February 13, 1861.

War-Time Concerts

Nine or more concerts were given by professional and amateur musicians of Richmond between the end of September 1861 and mid-February 1862, after which concert activities in Richmond ceased for a year and a half. Most of the war-time concerts given in 1861 and 1862 were designated as benefits for soldiers or their wives and children. Rosier and one of his pupils, identified only as Miss H., played prominent parts in the first two concerts.[144] Rosier conducted the first concert, and F. N. Crouch was featured in both concerts. Soon thereafter, Crouch gave a farewell performance as he prepared to leave the city to join Shield's Battery of the Confederate Army.[145] Others appearing in the first two concerts who had performed on previous occasions were B. Krause, John Hewitt, Madame D'Estvan, and Miss De Lacy. Giving their first performances in Richmond were Mons. D'Alfonce and Mr. Eggeling, singers, and Mr. Herman Bishop " (of the Jeff. Davis Flying Artillery,) ," who performed solos on the violin, piano, and clarinet. Amateur singers also performed. The program included selections from operas; English, Irish, and German songs; and patriotic Confederate songs, one by a young lady of Virginia and another by John Hewitt. A newspaper report of the second concert praised several amateurs' performances and Hewitt's singing and complimented Rosier and Crouch "for the manner in which they presided over the affair."[146] A committee of patrons headed by "Mrs. President Davis" was named for the second concert.[147]

Signor George and his daughter, Madame Bonavita, gave a concert in Richmond as part of their tour of the

---

144. *Ibid.,* September 25 and October 24, 1861. Program—Appendix B.
145. *Ibid.,* November 4, 1861.
146. *Ibid.,* October 26, 1861.
147. *Ibid.,* October 24, 1861. The entire committee is listed on the program in Appendix B.

Confederacy "for the benefit of the Southern soldiers."[148] George was referred to as a former resident of the city. Piano accompaniment for the concert was provided by J. R. Borrage, of Richmond.[149]

The *Dispatch* announced that the Richmond Philharmonic Association, "whose pleasing rehearsals and concerts a year since are fresh in the memory of many of our readers, contemplate giving an entertainment shortly for the benefit of the Maryland volunteers."[150] The association advertised later that a concert for the benefit of the wives and children of the Richmond Volunteers was to be given in Franklin Hall, and that O. A. Ericsson was to conduct.[151] Madame Estvan, Miss Lacy, Mr. Wildt, an orchestra, and a male chorus were the performers. Most of the program consisted of opera selections somewhat higher in quality than other local efforts at that time. The concluding selection was listed as a "Southern Anthem" by Ericsson.

C. T. De Coeniel, teacher and aspiring composer making his home in Richmond, advertised that he would give a concert "assisted by M'dlle Alboni De Vries, of New Orleans, combined with the best talent of this city."[152] De Coeniel's name is first seen in an advertisement in the *Dispatch* in 1861, which states that he has "resumed his professional services in the city."[153] He advertised a "full course of musical instruction," which included the art of teaching music, and was the only teacher in the city whose advertisements placed emphasis on teacher training before 1865.

Two weeks after De Coeniel's scheduled concert there began a series of concerts held by "ladies and gentlemen

---

148. *Ibid.,* November 7, 1861.
149. *Ibid.,* November 12, 1861.
150. *Ibid.,* October 18, 1861.
151. *Ibid.,* November 12, 1861. Program—Appendix B.
152. *Ibid.,* November 28, 1861.
153. *Ibid.,* September 27, 1861.

amateurs, assisted by able professors and a full orchestra."[154] The first two concerts, held in the United Presbyterian Church, reportedly raised $1500 for the wives and children of the Richmond Volunteers and for Maryland soldiers.[155] Two more concerts, given by the same performers, were held at the Second Baptist Church, one a benefit for a Kentucky regiment, the other a benefit for volunteers from western Virginia.[156] Although theatrical entertainments were offered nightly except possibly on Sunday, no concerts can be noted in the newspapers for the next year and a half (from March 1862 to September 1863).

In the fall of 1863, Madame Bertha Ruhl, "the Southern Cantatrice, from New Orleans, a refugee and exile," gave a series of concerts assisted by performers from New Orleans and residents of Richmond.[157] From that time to the end of the war, Ruhl was the leading figure in the numerous concerts of the city. Her first appearance was in Metropolitan Hall where she was featured as a singer with the other entertainments regularly offered there. Ruhl's performances in Metropolitan Hall were described as "one of the very few opportunities the public have had since the war to hear the performance of an artiste who has strong claim to excellence."[158] On her first formal concert, which was given at the Exchange Hotel, Ruhl was assisted by Miss Rosa Fay, singer; Herr H. Braun, violinist, cellist, and pianist; and C. W. Thilow, piano accompanist.[159] Ruhl, Braun, and Thilow shared honors in the concert, giving a variety of meritorious instrumental and vocal selections, many of which had probably been performed with the French opera company of New Orleans.

154. *Ibid.*, December 17, 1861.
155. *Ibid.*, December 24, 1861.
156. *Ibid.*, January 16 and February 4, 1862.
157. *Ibid.*, September 25, 1863.
158. *Ibid.*
159. *Ibid.*

Following the first formal concert was a "last concert" by Ruhl, which was in turn followed by a "farewell concert."[160] Ruhl's assistants were the same in each instance with the addition of J. Reinhardt, Richmond pianist, for the farewell concert. Three days after Ruhl's farewell concert Herr Herman Braun presented a "grand concert" at the Exchange Hotel, assisted by Ruhl, Fay, Thilow, F. Seibert, C. Seibert, and "several of the best amateur singers of this city."[161] That concert was Braun's last performance in Richmond.

The next "grand vocal and instrumental concert" was given "for the benefit of the poor and soldiers' families, under the direction of the Army Committee of the Young Men's Christian Association, at the African Church."[162] The list of participants, all of whom had "volunteered their services," was headed by Ruhl and included Richmond's leading musicians—Thilow, Loebmann, Reinhardt, Gebhardt, and Rosier—in addition to three persons who had not appeared on previous concerts in Richmond —Miss Rosetta Dale, Major M., and Mr. A. R. Vocal solos, duets, and a quartet were performed intermittently with two piano, violin, and cello trios, a piano duet, and a string quartet. Compositions performed showed good taste in their selection. Popular operatic airs, sentimental songs, and technically uncomplicated instrumental music by popular but noteworthy composers were performed. Composers represented on the program were Reissiger, Paisiello, Rossini, Haydn, Arne, Foster, Schubert, Thalberg, Verdi, and Balfe.

Mr. and the Misses Sloman—pianists, harpists, and vocalists—were the next group to give a series of concerts in the Exchange Hotel. For their first appearance it was announced that

160. *Ibid.,* September 30 and October 2, 1863.
161. *Ibid.,* October 5, 1863. Program—Appendix B.
162. *Ibid.,* October 22, 1863. Program—Appendix B.

between the first and second parts of the Concert a Solo and
Chorus,
  "Our National Confederate Anthem,
      God Save the South,"
will be introduced for the first time, accompanied by the
composer, Prof. De Coeniel.[163]

After five performances by Mr. and the Misses Sloman, a
sixth and final concert of that series was given with Ruhl.[164]
The final concert of 1863 was "Madame Ruhl's Grand
Concert, assisted by some of the most accomplished artistes
of the city."[165]

Madame Ruhl retained her position of leadership to the
end of the war. Assuming concert leadership along with
her but playing supporting roles were Thilow and Reinhardt. Also assuming prominent positions in Richmond's
concert life during 1864 and to the end of the war in 1865
were J. Kessnich, violinist and cotillion bandleader, and
Heinrich Schneider, clarinetist and harp teacher. These
four performers appeared in most of the concerts given
from April 1864 through March 1865; yet judging from
the musical selections listed on concert programs, they
seldom equaled and possibly never surpassed the quality
of those given in October 1863 by Ruhl, Thilow, Loebmann, Reinhardt, Gebhardt, Rosier, and others.

Concert performers continued their activities through
1864, but during the year there was a trend to modify the
programs by including entertainment other than music.
A concert for the benefit of Ruhl and Thilow was given
in January with the assistance of Kisnich (Kessnich), Fay,
and Reinhardt.[166] The instrumental portions of the program were possibly superior to the vocal portions. Two

163. *Ibid.*, November 6, 1863. Both the Valentine Museum and the
Virginia Historical Society have copies of De Coeniel's composition
"God Save the South."
  164. *Ibid.*, November 9, 11, 13, and 14, 1863.
  165. *Ibid.*, December 25, 1863. The concert was given at the Exchange
Hotel.
  166. *Ibid.*, January 5, 1864. Program—Appendix B.

concerts were given in March. The first, apparently given by amateurs since the performers were not named, was presented at the Second Baptist Church for the benefit of refugees.[167] Vocal solos, duets, and one selection by a chorus were given intermittently with instrumental selections by a pianist and a clarinetist. Opera excerpts dominated the program, but a ballad and the popular "Serenade" by Schubert were also listed. The second concert in March was given by Ruhl, "assisted by the best professional and amateur talent of this city" and by some of Ruhl's pupils.[168] April 1864 was a busy month for Ruhl, Miss M. (Ruhl's pupil), Kessnich, Reinhardt, amateurs, and Kessnich's orchestra, all of whom combined with Professor J. St. Maur Bingham and members of his dancing academy to give a series of "grand combination amusements," each consisting of music selections interspersed with "moving comic and sentimental *tableaux*" and followed by a "grand ball."[169] Along with the opera excerpts, ballads, and sentimental songs by the singers and instrumentalists was a guitar solo by Bingham. The entertainment, which was held in the Exchange Hotel concert room (Bingham's dancing academy room), was repeated several times during the week following the first performance. Ruhl and the amateurs next gave two concerts in the African Church for the benefit of soldiers' families.[170] The following week, Bingham gave a program similar to the "combination amusements," and he was assisted by Ruhl, Kessnich, Thilow, and amateurs.[171] The last program published in April 1864, a "grand classical concert" given by Thilow with the assistance of Ruhl, F. Seibert, Schneider, Kessnich and Reinhardt, is indicative of the more refined musical taste of Thilow.[172]

167. *Ibid.*, March 8, 1864. Program—Appendix B.
168. *Ibid.*, March 21, 1864.
169. *Ibid.*, April 1, 1864.
170. *Ibid.*, April 12 and 15, 1864.
171. *Ibid.*, April 21, 1864.
172. *Ibid.*, April 29, 1864. Program—Appendix B.

After April no more concerts are noted in 1864 until December when four are announced in the *Dispatch*. Each advertisement includes the names of Ruhl, Schneider, and Kessnich. Several members of Armbrecht's Post Band are listed on the first concert, and the entire Post Band "assisted by a full orchestra" is scheduled to perform in the second.[173] Also listed as performers for the second concert in December are Blanch Middleton, Reinhardt, Smith, Rosenberger, and Rittershaus. In the third December concert, Miss Blanch Middleton, currently appearing as a theatre entertainer, and F. N. Crouch, performing "before his Richmond friends after a three year absence in camp," are listed to perform with the assistance of Reinhardt and amateurs.[174] The last program of December 1864 was a concert given by the "Nineteenth Georgia Band" assisted by Ruhl, Schneider, Kessnich, and O. L. Siegel.[175]

A series of concerts, the last of the secular ones in the capital of the Confederacy, took place during the first three months of 1865. Ruhl, Kessnich, Reinhardt, Thilow, amateurs, and members of the Armory and Post bands were the performers. After Thilow, Kessnich, and Schneider had each given a benefit concert assisted by the others, the amateurs gave two concerts with the assistance of the professional musicians and "other talented performers" for the benefit of "the soldiers' families."[176]

Music of the Church

From the end of the eighteenth century to the beginning of the Civil War, Richmond had grown from a city with a few church congregations worshiping in temporary

---

173. *Ibid.*, December 12 and 16, 1864. Second program—Appendix B.
174. *Ibid.*, December 20, 1864. Program—Appendix B.
175. *Ibid.*, December 22, 1864. Program—Appendix B.
176. *Ibid.*, January 17, 26, February 7, March 14 and 16, 1865. Programs of January 26 and February 7, 1865—Appendix B.

quarters to a city with over 40 churches of various faiths and denominations. In 1861, the *Dispatch* published an article about Richmond's churches listing ten Baptist, nine Methodist, six Episcopal, five Presbyterian, three Catholic, two Lutheran, and five other churches, each of a different Christian denomination.[177] Three of the Baptist churches and one Methodist church were known as African churches, their congregations being composed entirely of Negroes.

Music customs and practices in the churches varied. Prior to the mid-nineteenth-century period the Episcopal, Presbyterian, and Catholic churches had sponsored concerts and had used musical instruments in their services, and the Presbyterians had been especially active in the singing school movement. On the other hand, the Baptists and Methodists were probably no less exuberant in the musical practices that were their media of religious expression, but they were reluctant to accept departures from their established traditions. For example, many Baptists and Methodists retained the custom of lining out hymns and singing without instruments or choirs up to the Civil War period. However, beginning in the mid-century period, Baptists and Methodists church leaders began to give in to the pressures of those persons demanding changes, and choirs, organs, and singing schools found their way into the churches.

Church Music Instruction for Children

Sacred music instruction had been given to children and adults in Richmond's churches during the third and fourth decades of the nineteenth century, and during the fifth decade, the emphasis had shifted to adult societies. However, the teachers of children were still active, and in the year that the first musical convention was held in

---

177. *Dispatch,* December 7, 1861.

Richmond (1855), Mr. Kemmer's singing classes gave two programs. Of the first it was reported that "some of the children sang most artistically, while the greater portion of them sang well."[178] The same group gave a second concert at the Odd Fellows' Hall, where there were between one and two hundred children "beautifully arranged by elevated seats. . . . The pupils, thoroughly trained in separate classes, sang together in perfect time."[179] The audience was "pleased and astonished at the progress the children made in vocal music."[180] Mr. Kemmer's class of 148 pupils gave a "musical entertainment at Leigh Street Baptist Church" in 1859.[181] He advertised his singing school for children, which met at various times during the week in the First Baptist, Trinity Methodist, and Third Baptist Churches in 1860.[182] Tuition was "twenty-five cents for twelve lessons to close with a concert."[183] During the next two months his class gave "musical entertainments" in five churches.[184]

Mr. T. L. Gallaher organized his "second Juvenile Class, for instruction in vocal music, in the Lecture Room of the First Presbyterian Church" in 1855.[185] The editor of the *Dispatch* pointed out that Gallaher was a native Virginian, "now permanently located in our city, where he designs establishing a 'Musical Institute' of the highest order."[186]

Vocalism—It is gratifying to notice the interest now manifested in this city on the subject of "musical education," and to witness the liberal support tendered to Mr. Gallaher, in

178. *Ibid.*, April 6, 1855.
179. *Ibid.*, April 12, 1855.
180. *Ibid.*
181. *Ibid.*, August 11, 1859.
182. *Ibid.*, January 26, 1860.
183. *Ibid.*
184. *Ibid.*, February 20, February 25, February 27, March 5, March 7, and March 8, 1860.
185. *Ibid.*, March 7, 1855.
186. *Ibid.*

his musical academy, for many of the church congregations are quite deficient in the art of vocalism, and are therefore deprived of cultivated church music during their periods of divine worship. Mr. G. is said to be a teacher of great proficiency, and as he is an enthusiast in his profession, the public have every reason to believe that he will advance his pupils to perfection as rapidly as possible. . . .[187]

The young ladies who met in Gallaher's Richmond Musical Academy performed George Root's Cantata "The Flower Queen" in the Metropolitan Hall in 1858 and C. C. Converse's Cantata "Spring Holiday" in 1859.[188] Gallaher also taught adults in the Second Presbyterian Church.[189]

Another teacher of singing, William Mingle, taught in the Leigh Street Baptist Church. The young ladies "connected with the Sabbath School" of that church gave a "Grand Floral Concert" under Mingle's direction, and they were accompanied by Professor F. A. Newhiser, who presided at "the splendid instrument used on the occasion."[190]

Hymn Books and Singing School Books

Hymn books containing music notation in four-part harmony with words printed between two staves are in common usage today, but they did not come into general use in churches until the latter part of the nineteenth century. During the mid-nineteenth-century period, the format of hymn books was undergoing a gradual transition from the practice of printing hymns and tunes in separate books, through a second stage wherein hymns and tunes were in the same book but were printed separately in various arrangements, to the final stage, in which words and music notation were printed together as a unit.

Basil M. Manly, who was the minister in Richmond's

187. *Ibid.*, March 12, 1856.
188. *Ibid.*, June 17, 1858, and June 14, 1859.
189. *Ibid.*, March 12, 1856.
190. *Ibid.*, January 7, 1857. The instrument was presumably a piano.

First Baptist Church from 1850 to 1854, published a hymn book entitled *Baptist Psalmody* in 1850. The book contained words only and made no reference to tunes. In 1859 Manly published *Baptist Chorales: a Tune and Hymn Book Designed to Promote General Congregational Singing, Containing One Hundred and Sixty-four Tunes adapted to about Four Hundred Choice Hymns.*[191] One verse of each hymn was printed with the music notation. The other verses of each hymn were printed at the bottom of the page. The hymns were selected by Manly and were adapted to music by Asa Brooks Everett. Manly wrote in the introduction of the book:

> It seems to be common to imagine that the singing of God's praise in public worship is a matter of indifference; that it is valuable principally as a sort of agreeable relaxation from the tediousness of other services, and that no particular obligation rests on any to join in it. It is, therefore, not unusual for the whole business of worshipping God in song to be committed to a few, sometimes to a hired company, whose voices are trained in the theatre all week, to perform, with about as much devotion, in the church on Sunday.

> . . . The object of this volume is not to come in competition with hymn books now in circulation, but to render them more useful by supplying tunes adapted expressly to some of the choicest hymns; while for convenience's sake, the words are printed on the same page, so that embarrassment may be removed likely to hinder those who are slightly skilled in musical science.

> . . . The simple design of this work is to provide, as far as possible, congregational singing in the use of the ordinary hymn books. Hence hymns have been selected, almost exclusively, which are to be found in both the *Baptist Psalmody* and *The Psalmist*, the two books most extensively used in the Baptist churches in the United States.[192]

191. B. Manly, Jr., *Baptist Chorales* (Richmond: T. J. Starke, 1859). Copies of the *Baptist Psalmody* and the *Baptist Chorales* are in the Virginia State Library, Richmond, Virginia.
192. *Ibid.*, p. ii.

L. C. Everett and Asa Brooks Everett, who adapted the music used in Manly's *Baptist Chorales,* organized a system of singing instruction at Richmond. "In 1861 they had fifty teachers of singing-schools representing them and using their publications."[193] The Virginia State Library has two of Everett's books: *The New Thesaurus Musicus, or United States Collection of Church Music . . .* , and *Everett's Sabbath Chime.*[194] They are illustrative of the changing format found in hymn books of the period. The *New Thesaurus . . .* has four-part harmony with a staff for each part, but only one verse of a hymn is printed with the music. Other verses were to be found in a separate book. In *Everett's Sabbath Chime,* four vocal parts are written on three staves in most of the musical arrangements, but several four-part arrangements are written on two staves with the words of all verses printed between the treble and bass notation, as in the present-day format used in hymn book publication.

Two books by Bradbury in the Virginia Baptist Historical Association's collection, University of Richmond are: *The Singing Book for Boys' and Girls' Meeting* and *Oriola: a new and complete Hymn and Tune Book for Sabbath Schools.*[195] These books, which contain music notation for children's voices in two- and three-part harmony as well as having the words printed with the notation, were apparently used in Richmond's Baptist Sabbath Schools.

During the War years a book written in the older style was printed, *The Army and Navy Prayer Book.*[196] The

193. *Groves Dictionary, American Supplement,* p. 23.

194. L. C. and A. B. Everett, *The New Thesaurus Musicus* (Richmond: published by the authors, n.d.) ; and L. C. Everett, *Everett's Sabbath Chime* (Richmond: George L. Bidgood, 1860) .

195. William B. Bradbury, *The Singing Book for Boys' and Girls' Meetings* (New York: Ivison and Phinney, 1854) ; and Bradbury, *Oriola* (Cincinnati: Moore, Wilstach, Keys and Company, 1860) .

196. Diocesan Missionary Society of the Protestant Episcopal Church of Virginia (Richmond: Charles H. Wynne, Printer, 1864) .

first half of the book contains prayers; the second half, hymns and Psalms. No tunes are specified, but the meters of the hymns are indicated.

Music in the Baptist Churches

The progress in congregational singing made by the Baptists under the leadership of Basil M. Manly during the mid-century period was hampered by many obstacles. While Manly was pastor of the First Baptist Church, a motion was made in the church business meeting that a committee consider the subject of singing in the church.[197] Later, the committee on singing reported that they "had revived the weekly practicing of the choir, and were looking for some suitable person to take charge of the choir. . . ."[198] In February 1854, J. F. C. Potts of Portsmouth, Virginia, was engaged "to lead the singing in the choir and Sunday school at the rate of $250 per annum."[199] After two years, Potts handed in his resignation, but the minutes of the church meeting indicate that the resignation was not accepted until October 1858. New rules governing the choir stated that disputes would be settled in the future by three church members who were not members of the choir.[200] At the November 1859 meeting it was reported that the choir had elected H. Eldridge as leader and they asked the approval of the church. "Brother Ryland moved the adoption of the report," but another member of the board of directors "moved the abolishment of the choir with the view of trying congregational singing."[201] After much discussion the initial resolution passed and the choir remained intact.

Requests for allowing an organ to be brought into the

197. "Minutes of the First Baptist Church, Richmond City Book 4," 1851–1860, July 25, 1853.
198. *Ibid.*, September 26, 1853.
199. *Ibid.*, February 27, 1854.
200. *Ibid.*, September 27, 1858.
201. *Ibid.*, January 24, 1859.

First Baptist Church were denied or tabled periodically throughout the 1840s and 1850s, but a small organ was used in the church beginning in 1861.[202]

> In 1863, it was reported to the church that "J. P. Ballard had caused the organ to be moved to the choir." So far as we know, the question of the orthodoxy concerning the use of an organ or the leadership of the congregational singing by a choir was never again seriously challenged. Sometime prior to 1864, two melodeons were acquired by the church, for in that year the minutes record the statement that they had been insured "for one thousand dollars each."[203]

Other Richmond Baptist churches experienced similar difficulties in getting choirs started. Mrs. John B. Harvie, historian for the Pine Street Baptist Church, reports that in 1859 a committee of five were appointed to start a choir. "The choir was authorized to sing from note books, but not hymn books," but contrary to the committee's expectations, "the soothing effect of music on the minds and hearts of men was not experienced. The choir was discharged."[204] When the Leigh Street Baptist Church congregation moved into its new sanctuary in 1854, "dissension was created by an element in the church which insisted upon forming itself into a choir occupying seats in the gallery and from that elevation leading the congregation in its singing."[205] Ensuing developments saw the self-appointed choir move to the main floor and later to the balcony, taking the melodeon with them, and still later "the church voted that these leaders of the singing should return to the main floor and the janitor was instructed

---

202. White, p. 115.
203. *Ibid.*, p. 65.
204. Mrs. John B. Harvie, ed., *Beacon on a Hill* (Richmond: The Williams Printing Company, 1955), p. 17.
205. W. C. James, compiler, *Leigh Street Baptist Church, 1854–1954* (Richmond: Whittet and Shepperson, 1954), p. 80.

to return the melodeon likewise."[206] The pastor was eventually to settle the dispute in 1860. Part of his written report is interesting because it reveals the problems faced by congregations using hymn books which did not give music notation or tune indications.

As we have no choir, nor any leaders of the congregational singing and are therefore liable to the confusion which would be produced by having several tunes raised at the same time by different persons in the congregation, and are subjected also to that unpleasant feeling produced by hesitancy in raising the tunes; in order to prevent these unpleasant circumstances and to ensure the selection of suitable tunes, and have them properly raised, it is indispensably necessary that someone should be designated for that purpose. Therefore, *Resolved* that Brother Miles Turpin be requested and he is hereby appointed to raise or to secure the assistance of someone to raise the tunes sung as part of the devotional exercises of this church and if any of the brethern and sisters choose to sit with him and sing, they have the right to do so.[207]

Music in the Methodist Church

The lack of references to Methodists having taken part in public performances, singing schools, and hymn book writing in Richmond during the mid-nineteenth-century period, coupled with a knowledge of their traditional love of hearty singing, suggests that their musical activities continued to be carried out in the older tradition of lining out the hymns by the preacher or song leader. Henry E. Johnson, recalling his experiences in the Clay Street Methodist Chapel, wrote:

The singing at the Chapel was a power in the work. It was not artistic, but very hearty and earnest. The emphasis was put on praising God and winning sinners to repentance.

---

206. *Ibid.*, p. 81.
207. *Ibid.*

There was no choir and no instrument. Francis T. Isbell, or some other with strong voice, led and all the people sang.[208]

Isbell is mentioned as a trustee of the Chapel in 1856.

At the ceremonies for the laying of the cornerstone of the Broad Street Methodist Episcopal Church, South, June 30, 1859, the "choir and audience sang" Masonic odes and the doxology."[209] Centenary Methodist Church had a choir in 1853 that gave a concert of sacred music for the benefit of the Parsonage Society. They were "assisted by a number of amateurs."[210] Centenary Church had no organ until the 1870s when they used a reed organ before the installation of a larger one.[211]

Music in the Presbyterian Churches

The Presbyterians were active in the Richmond Sacred Music Society and in Richmond singing schools. Singing schools were held in the Presbyterian churches from the third decade of the century. There was apparently no general disdain of instrumental music, as was found in the Methodist and especially the Baptist churches, but there is little reason to believe that the Presbyterian churches in Richmond had or wanted organs in their churches before the 1860s.

It has been noted that concerts were given in the First Presbyterian Church, the first one having been given with instruments in 1824. The new Third Presbyterian Church, built in 1850, had a choir that gave a concert in the church "assisted by distinguished Musicians and Amateurs of the city" in 1852.[212] The Second Presbyterian Church had no

---

208. Asa Johnson, *A History of Clay Street M. E. Church (South) Richmond, Virginia 1844–1918* (Richmond: Whittet and Shepperson, 1919) , p. 1.

209. *Dispatch,* July 1, 1859.

210. *Ibid.,* June 14, 1853.

211. Georgia C. West, *Gifts to Centenary* (Richmond: Centenary Methodist Episcopal Church, South, 1937) , p. 14.

212. *Dispatch,* February 4, 1852.

organ until 1861, "then an organ of the old type, hand blown, and none too powerful."[213] In his diary, Michael Gretter, a member of the Second Presbyterian Church, wrote that he "raised the first tune and requested Dr. Moore to raise the second" at a funeral service in 1855.[214] There had probably been a choir in the church for some time by 1855, but at the Sunday services "it served the simple purpose of leading the congregation in the singing of hymns and only that. There were no solos, no amens, no recessionals."[215] Moses Drury Hoge, their pastor, was of the Old School and a conservative Presbyterian. "He did not believe in church music to attract crowds or to entertain the people or as a filler-in of the service."[216] On one occasion early in his career, he allowed the Orphean Family to sing in his church, and afterward he warned his uncle in Raleigh, North Carolina, a city of the Orphean's itinerary:

> One of the young men is an imposter, he pretends to be a vocalist, but he carries a private trombone in his belly, and makes believe he is singing. Mrs. Ham I fear conceals a little octave flute in the roof of her mouth, as you will discern when she sings the Tyrolese March.[217]

Music in the Episcopal Church

It appears that other than in the Catholic and Hebrew religious services, of which few records exist, the Episcopalians were the only religious organization utilizing a formal music ritual in their services. Their organs, organists, and choirs described in previous chapters continued to play an active role in the services throughout the mid-century period.

James Evans, who had been organist at St. John's Church

---

213. Blanton, p. 229.
214. *Ibid.,* p. 228.
215. *Ibid.,* p. 229.
216. *Ibid.*
217. *Ibid.,* p. 230.

and was active in the Richmond Sacred Music Society, was chosen as organist at the Monumental Church in 1853.[218] His salary was $100 per year in 1857.[219] Evans resigned in 1860 and was replaced by W. T. Grabau, a music teacher who had recently taken up residence in Richmond.[220] His yearly salary was $200.[221] Grabau resigned in 1863 to move to Gloucester County, Virginia. His successor is not named but the organist's salary was stated as being $1,000 in 1864, and Mrs. Lockerman, chief singer, was paid $1,200 the same year.[222] The salary was paid in the then inflated Confederate currency.

One of the few sacred concerts given during the Civil War was advertised as a public rehearsal.

> The choir of the Monumental Church, assisted by several amateur friends, respectfully announce that they will give a PUBLIC REHEARSAL OF SACRED MUSIC, at the CHURCH, on TUESDAY EVENING, November 1st, commencing at 8 o'clock, for the benefit of the FEMALE ORPHAN ASYLUM.
> Tickets of admission, Five Dollars, to be obtained at the Music and Bookstores and at the door.
> Programs will be furnished at the church.[223]

The last concert given in the Confederacy was held at St. James' Church. The Capitol was evacuated two days later after President Davis was called from worship in that church.

CONCERT

> The Concert of St. James CHURCH, for the benefit of the Orphans, will take place THIS EVENING, March 31.

---

218. George D. Fisher, *History . . . Monumental Church . . .* , p. 251.
219. *Ibid.*, p. 255.
220. *Ibid.*, p. 266.
221. *Ibid.*
222. *Ibid.*, p. 305.
223. *Dispatch*, November 1, 1864.

Programme:
1. Organ—Voluntary.
2. Chorus—12th Mass: "Glory be to God."
3. Duet and Chorus: "The Lord is My Shepherd."
4. Solo: "Consider the Lillies."
5. Quartette for Male Voices: "The Sabbath Call."
6. Solo and Quartette.

1. Strike the Cymbal.
2. Duet: "Arrayed in Clouds."
3. Duet and Chorus—Evening Hymn: "Fading, still Fading."
4. Solo: "Flee, as a Bird, to your Mountain."
5. Quartette for Male Voices: "O Sanctissima."
6. Doxology: "Praise God."[224]

224. *Dispatch*, March 31, 1865. The Valentine Museum has an original printing of the program.

Chapter 6

In Retrospect

The preceding chapters reveal the development of the Old South's musical culture in two of its principal urban areas. Since Colonial Williamsburg and Richmond are the sites of the capitals of Virginia, and Richmond is also the ultimate site of the capital of the Confederacy, those places are viewed as exemplary cultural centers of the Old South.

Carefully researched information on people, places, and events and pertinent evidence of musical activities and interest in music provide the key to bring out a story that until now has been hidden in countless archives, rare publications, and artifacts. Descriptions of available musical instruments and music scores, and enumerations of the availability of instruction in music and related arts such as dancing help provide insights into the Old South's cultural development through the years. Above all, the people who sang and played the instruments, read and wrote the musical scores, and danced to the music roam through the pages of the preceding chapters.

We discover a prevalent dissimilarity of attitudes toward music performances in northern and southern English colonies during the eighteenth century. No effective resistance was offered to music activities and theatre en-

246

tertainments in the south, whereas much animosity toward similar events, particularly the theatre, was predominant in the north. Although communication and cultural exchange between the two sections of the country were effectual, the development of the southern music culture in the colonies and the new republic was rather independent of northern developments through the eighteenth century and well into the nineteenth century. Nevertheless, both the north and the south developed music cultures based on their common European and especially their English heritage.

We find that as the nineteenth century began, northern cities such as New York, Boston, and Philadelphia no longer strenuously resisted musical and theatrical progress, and before the mid-century period, the South was looking toward these cities as well as to Europe for leadership in music. But the Civil War, stemming from the political division of the country into the North and the South, found Richmond, the South's capital city, utilizing essentially indigenous southern talent in its musical endeavors.

European Influences on the South's Cultural Development Noted

English culture and customs dominated Virginia during the colonial period, and the colonists' musical interests and activities were influenced from the outside chiefly by the musical events of London. The English composers and arrangers utilized music idioms and materials from continental Europe, and therefore, while the music of colonial America was predominantly English in character, it was representative of a fusion of European national styles. The colonial centers of culture were principally Williamsburg and the larger plantations.

Richmond began to develop as a cultural center after the American Revolution. The dominant musical influence affecting Richmond's cultural growth during the two final decades of the eighteenth century emanated from the theatre, which offered drama, music, and other entertainment derived almost exclusively from English sources. Concerts were similar to theatrical offerings, and the performers were usually also associated with theatrical activities.

Social and public events of late eighteenth-century Richmond likewise followed the traditions of English heritage. Music merchandise and materials for instruction were imported from London, although some music and dancing teachers were apparently of French and German extraction. The two principal church organizations in late eighteenth-century Richmond were Episcopal and Presbyterian congregations, and since they worshiped together in the Capitol, the music of the two denominations was similar if not identical. Other religious groups were organizing, but nearly all had only temporary meeting places during the eighteenth century. It is evident that, as Richmond began to develop as a center of culture, the dominant influences on musical entertainment, concerts, merchantry, instruction, and the church were of English origin.

By the beginning of the nineteenth century, Richmond was serving as a business, entertainment, and cultural center for the surrounding area of Virginia. From the nature of music activities in the city it is apparent that the theatre played the dominant role in influencing musical tastes during the first quarter of the nineteenth century, and the dramatic and musical repertory of the theatre continued to be predominantly English. The performers, both English and American, emulated the theatrical, concert, and entertainment offerings of London. Concerts, music instruction, and music merchantry were also allied with theatre activity.

The first quarter of the century was a period of rapid

growth for Richmond's church organizations, with the
Episcopal church providing musical leadership by install-
ing organs and presenting sacred music concerts in their
churches. Instrumental music was provided with Episcopal
Church services and concerts, and in at least one instance
near the end of the first-quarter-century period, instrumental music was heard in a Presbyterian church concert,
although the Presbyterian churches apparently had no
organs at that time. Methodists and Baptists opposed the
use of instrumental music in their services but were active
as writers and singers of hymns.

Throughout the second quarter of the nineteenth century there was a gradual transition from the English domination of music activities toward a more cosmopolitan
European influence. Consequential to the city's growth
in population, there was a diversification of music activities, and the theatre became less prominent as an influen-
tial center of music. During the two decades prior to 1850,
the theatrical performers exerted progressively less influence on Richmond's musical tastes, while concert performers and music teachers who were not primarily
associated with the theatre began to offer more musical
leadership. English influence in the theatre also lessened
as the American form of entertainment, the minstrel,
became popular.

The European influences on cultural activities began
to reach Richmond by way of New York after the latter
city had become established in a position of economic and
social leadership in America. From the fourth decade of
the century to the Civil War period, entertainments, fads,
and merchandise from the north, especially from New
York, were the epitome of fashion. Therefore, musical
entertainment, instruction, concerts, and merchantry developed somewhat according to the dictates of the prevailing tastes in New York. New York, in turn, looked to

London and Paris for social and cultural leadership. The music of the church also began to feel an influence from the north through the singing schools that were organized in Richmond's churches by men from northern cities bringing music publications from the north.

The 15-year period before the Civil War was an era of rapid growth for Richmond. There was more of a diversity of music activities than during previous years, and the city experienced an infusion of musically talented Europeans into its social structure. Richmond's newly arrived German immigrants organized amateur and professional music groups and provided inspiration and assistance to other musicians of the city. An amateur interdenominational sacred music choral society flourished under local leadership during the mid-century period until 1856, when the emphasis of local music activity shifted to combined instrumental and vocal secular music. There were two component types of theatrical music performances during the period: one was concerned with artistic endeavors in serious drama and opera; the other offered entertainment consisting of minstrel and variety performances. Possibly the principal influences on musical tastes of the period were (1) the minstrels in which sentimental, jubilant, and comic songs were performed, and (2) the European concert artists' performances on which were offered selections from popular operas and other art music, some of which was notable for its adaptability to spectacular performance.

Local concert ventures increased in scope during 1860 and were continued into the Civil War period after travel restrictions had curtailed performances by visiting artists. All concert activity ceased early in 1862, but local performances were revived in the fall of 1863 under the leadership of newly arrived immigrants from New Orleans. Music was heard with theatre entertainments and at social functions throughout the war period.

Musical Leadership in Richmond Disclosed

Although the best known musicians of the day visited and performed in the city, the resident musicians who performed and taught in Richmond for an extended period of time claimed no universally recognized fame. However, many were apparently superior musicians and a large number of them contributed their talents in providing musical leadership for the city. Among the early musical leaders was Mrs. Sully, who gave what was perhaps the first formal concert to be held in Richmond while she was traveling with a theatre troupe in 1793. She later became a resident of the city and provided musical leadership as a singer, pianist, and church organist during the first quarter of the nineteenth century. Another outstanding musician of that period of Richmond's cultural development was Charles Southgate, possibly a native of Richmond, who served the city as a teacher, cellist, singer, music editor of the city's first magazine, and who was the first resident composer whose published music is preserved today.

A few of the other numerous resident musicians whose activities are cited in the preceding chapters are: William H. Fitzwhylsonn, amateur musician, music merchant, and mayor of the city; P. H. Taylor, theatre flutist who became the leading music merchant in the city; E. B. Barber and John Dunderdale, pianists who performed as soloists and accompanied many distinguished visiting artists; T. X. Da Costa, Charles F. Rosen, F. W. Rosier, Charles W. Thilow, Nathan B. Clapp, and C. T. De Coeniel, some of the leading music teachers of the city; E. Loebmann, J. A. Rosenberger, and J. B. Smith, bandleaders and music entertainers; William Daniell, and F. William Grabau, two of the city's many excellent church organists; J. P. Hanlon, James Evans, and S. S. Stevens, prominent leaders of the

Richmond Sacred Music Society; Volkmar Busch and A. J. Gebhardt, two of the numerous active musical European immigrants of the mid-century period; and John Hill Hewitt, Frederick Nicholas Crouch, and Bertha Ruhl, Civil War period residents and music leaders in Richmond.

Social Predilection Toward Musical Events Revealed

Richmond newspaper journalism, the principal source of information concerning music activity and public reaction to music events, provides an insight into audience behavior and attitudes toward theatre performances before *ca.* 1840, but is rarely concerned with other musical events before that date. The theatre audience sought entertainment, and reviews of performances were reported in terms of entertainment values rather than in terms of artistic merit. After the fourth decade of the nineteenth century, when the theatre was no longer the principal center of Richmond's music life, concert performances were reviewed by the newspapers partially in terms of their artistic merit but also in terms of their success as social events. News items concerning operas and concerts by visiting European artists report attendance by large and fashionable audiences. Many persons appeared apparently not so much for the hearing of music as for the preservation and elevation of their social status, and when the newspapers periodically reported excellent performances by local musicians, a commentary on the thin attendance was not unusual. An indication of the existence of public apathy toward genuine appreciation of music performances of merit other than those of social significance is seen in announcements by local performing groups that their aims include the improvement of musical tastes in the city. Richmond newspapers of the mid-nineteenth-century period indicate that musical entertainments such as minstrels, theatre novelties, concert novelties, parades, and celebrations utilizing music attracted large audiences and created wide-spread interest in music of that caliber.

In Conclusion

Music does not live apart from people. It may exist or be preserved on the printed page or be otherwise recorded, but it is not alive unless it thrives in a cultural setting. Much of the music discussed here can come to life again only in juxtaposition with the lives of the people in this book. Some of the music discussed and listed in Appendix B still lives or has been brought back to life by people of our era. However, most of the music is historically rather than artistically relevant today.

As in other civilized cultures, the Old South had a multitude of social milieu, each enjoying its own type of music, but all sharing each other's music to some extent. The slaves sang and played various instruments. A young lady's education was incomplete if she could not sing or play a socially acceptable instrument for parlor guests. Itinerant actors and musicians brought the latest tunes and compositions to town from far away places. The opera, the recital, the church service, the minstrel, the circus, the serenade, the parade, the music of the street, and numerous other modes of performance provided music to suit the wide variety of musical tastes of the community.

We observed that the Old South assimilated the music of other cultures, particularly those of Europe and especially England. It produced some music of its own but not without drawing heavily from the fundamental idioms of European music. Although there must have been elements of uniqueness in the indigenous music, they are most elusive since most evidence left behind is silent. The traditional Negro spiritual that we do hear today and that came out of the Old South evinces a unique flavor. However, "Dixie" and "Suwannee River," tunes from the minstrel era that are associated with the Old South, are compositions by men who lived in the North.

Both North and South were culturally dependent upon Europe for artistic leadership and remained so well into the twentieth century. It is doubtful that a leading composer or musician was nourished by the southern culture for two reasons. First, a professional musician, while being admired and praised by the upper echelons of society, was seldom admitted to its ranks. Therefore, talented young men with parents who could afford to provide a musical education in Europe would not make such an investment on a career with a social stigma attached to it. The announcements of performances made careful distinctions between "gentlemen amateurs" and "musicians." Second, if a native of the South became famous as a musician, he no doubt had found it necessary to change his name, claim to be from Europe, and thus deny his southern legacy.[1]

The activities of a substantial number of musicians from the eighteenth-century period throughout the Civil War era are described in this book. They performed well, taught, and composed music. That none became a Beethoven or a Paganini does not indicate the lack of an existing or thriving musical culture. It does, however, lend substance along with other evidence available here that the musical culture, while thriving, had not reached its apex at the termination of the Civil War, which closed the era of the Old South. That era is an integral part of our cultural heritage, and it was a noble era.

---

1. An exception may be Louis Gottschalk, who was born in New Orleans in 1828 and who studied and performed in Europe with extraordinary success before coming back to America to be enthusiastically received by audiences. New Orleans, of course, was under French rule until 1803 and, while it is definitely "South," there may be some dispute as to whether it is "Old South." Gottschalk's mother was French and his father was English of Germant descent. Nevertheless, Louis Gottschalk was born in a city that became part of the Confederacy, and that fact may qualify him as a citizen of the "Old South."

Appendixes

A. *Public Buildings Used For Music Performances*[1]

Academy of Sciences and Fine Arts
Location: South side of 12th Street between Broad Street and
   Marshall Street.
Structure: Frame building. Built in 1786. Burned in 1789.
Use: The Academy was founded by a Frenchman, Quesnay de
   Beaurepaire and was intended to be an institution of
   higher learning (academy) in science and the arts. To
   meet financial needs, the building was rented from the
   beginning as a theatre, concert hall, and dancing assembly.

Amphitheatre
Location: Opposite Tanbark Hall.
Structure: Frame. Built in 1829. No longer used *ca.* 1840.
Use: Constructed specifically for circus and theatrical perfor-
   mances in competition to the Theatre.

Athenaeum
Location: Corner of Marshall and 10th Streets.
Structure: Frame. Opened in 1854. Torn down in 1858.
Use: Municipally owned and operated, it housed the library
   and was used for lectures.

---

1. The information was compiled from material in the files of the
Valentine Museum in Richmond and from sources cited in the text
of this study.

Broad Street Theatre
See *Monticello Hall.*

Circus, The
Location: Near the site of the Richmond Theatre.
Structure: Temporary—frame. Torn down when the Richmond
     Theatre opened in 1819.
Use: It was a temporary theatre or circus building used by the
     acting company until the theatre was completed.

Corinthian Hall
Location: On Main Street, south side, between 9th and 10th
     Streets.
Structure: Built in 1854. Burned in the Evacuation fire in 1865.
     Probably a frame building.
Use: Also known as the Mechanics' Institute Hall, concerts,
     amateur dramatic performances and dancing schools were
     held there.

Eagle Tavern
Location: On Main Street near the Capitol.
Structure: Frame. Built during the eighteenth century. Torn
     down *ca.* 1840.
Use: Balls, concerts, and theatrical entertainments were given
     there in the late eighteenth century and into the nineteenth
     century. It was renamed the Richmond City Hotel and
     the Eagle Hotel after 1817. It was probably the principal
     hotel in Richmond from the time it opened until about
     the end of the third decade of the nineteenth century.

Exchange Hotel
Location: Franklin and Pearl Streets.
Structure: Masonry. Built *ca.* 1840.
Use: It was one of the finest hotels in the city prior to the Civil
     War. The Concert Room was used for concerts, balls, and
     dancing academies.

Franklin Hall
Location: On Franklin Street—"The first door beyond the Exchange Hotel."
Structure: Masonry. Built as Trinity Church in 1828. Converted for use as a theatre in 1861—renamed Franklin Hall.
Use: Minstrel and variety entertainment were given there after it was converted to a theatre. It was called the Richmond Varieties when the acting company took it over after the Theatre burned in 1862. Beginning in February 1864 the building was called the Opera House by the managers, and Ethiopian operas (minstrels) were performed there.

Hay-Market Gardens
Location: Between 7th and 8th Streets and Byrd and Arch Streets, south of the basin.
Structure: Livery stables, inn, and formal garden were built *ca.* 1785, and to this was added a large frame building for balls and concerts. The gardens were sold at auction in 1814.
Use: Pleasure resort. The central building was advertised as the largest ballroom in the State "with a music gallery, in the center above, containing an elegant organ, in an Orchestra sufficient to hold a Grand Piano and twelve performers."

Marshall Theatre
See *Richmond Theatre.*

Masons Hall
Location: On Church Hill at 25th Street.
Structure: Built during the eighteenth century.
Use: Entertainments were given there occasionally. It was used as a hospital during the Civil War.

Mechanics' Institute Hall
See *Corinthian Hall.*

Metropolitan Hall
Location: On the north side of Franklin Street between 13th

and 14th Streets, "within a half a square of the Exchange Hotel."

Structure: Built in 1828 as the First Presbyterian Church. In 1853 the building was converted into a concert hall. It had a stage 20 x 30 feet and seats for 1500. Torn down during 1882–1883.

Use: Concerts and operas were given there. After 1855, minstrels and variety entertainments were offered regularly.

Monticello Hall

Location: On Broad Street near the Richmond Theatre.

Use: Balls, concerts, variety entertainments, and minstrels were given there from 1857 through 1865. The building was also called Steinlien's Hall, Broad Street Theatre, and the Richmond Lyceum by its various proprietors.

Odd Fellows' Hall

Location: At Mayo and Franklin Streets. (Mayo Street was between 14th and 15th Streets.)

Structure: Frame. Probably built during the first quarter of the nineteenth century, the building was torn down recently.

Use: Entertainments and concerts were given there occasionally from the third decade of the nineteenth century through the Civil War. Variety and theatrical entertainments were given regularly in the building from December 1848 to May 1849, during which time the building was called the Odeon.

Odeon, The
See *Odd Fellows' Hall.*

Opera House, The
See *Franklin Hall.*

Philharmonic Hall

Location: On 12th Street between Main and Franklin Streets.

Structure: Probably frame. Built in 1858, burned in April 1865.

Use: Dedicated in 1860 as the hall of the Philharmonic Society which had been organized in 1859.

Richmond Lyceum
See *Monticello Hall.*

Richmond Theatre
Location: On the southeast corner of 7th and Broad Streets.
Structure: Brick. Built in 1819. Remodeled and renamed the
    Marshall Theatre in 1838. Burned in 1862. Rebuilt on
    the same foundations in 1863. Torn down in 1896.
Use: All Richmond newspaper references to the theatre be-
    tween 1819 and 1865 referred to activities in this building.
    References to the building were given as: the theatre, the
    Theatre, the Marshall Theatre, and the Richmond The-
    atre. Although there were other buildings used periodically
    as theatres before 1865, this building was apparently the
    only one associated with the word "theatre" after 1819.

Richmond Varieties
See *Franklin Hall.*

Steinliens Hall
See *Monticello Hall.*

Tanbark Hall
Location: On Main Street, south side, near 8th Street.
Structure: Frame. Built *ca.* 1800 either as an enlargement of
    or adjoining a dwelling erected there as early as 1796. A
    tannery had been on the site, and from that association
    the building derived its name. It was torn down *ca.* 1835
    and replaced by a row of dwellings built by James Bosher
    and called Bosher's Row or Tanbark Row. The row was
    replaced by the Spotswood Hotel in 1859.
Use: The Musical Society described by Mordecai met at Tan-
    bark Hall for its regular concerts, and other concerts and
    entertainments were held there in the early part of the
    nineteenth century. One variety entertainment was given
    in Bosher's Hall in 1850.

Terpsichore Hall
Location: On the northeast corner of 7th and Grace Streets.

Structure: Frame. Built by a French dancing master, John Bossieux, in 1830. Its dimensions were 80 x 50 feet, and it contained a large ballroom and separate rooms for refreshments, ladies, and gentlemen. It burned in 1843.

Use: The owner established dancing classes and cotillions, and sponsored public balls in the building. It was used as the principal concert hall in Richmond by theatre performers who gave concerts outside of their appearances in the theatre.

Theatre, The

Location: On Academy Square, Broad Street below 12th.

Structure: Brick. Completed in 1806, burned in 1811.

Use: It was the second theatre in Richmond to house resident acting companies over a period of years, the first having been the Academy of Sciences and Fine Arts. Its burning resulted in a great loss of life and was one of the major tragedies in Richmond's history. Monumental Church, which still stands today, was built on the site in memory of those who perished in the fire.

Virginia Museum

Location: On 12th Street facing F. Street, near the Governor's Mansion.

Use: It opened in 1817 and was used for various exhibitions including objects of curiosity, handicraft, and art. Music was often provided as an added incentive to visitors, and concerts were held perhaps with reciprocal benefits for the curators. Apparently the museum declined in popularity and was abandoned after 1840.

B. Selected Programs Representative of Concerts in Richmond, 1797–1865

A concert given at the Eagle Tavern, Richmond, Virginia—1797.[2]

---

2. Sonneck, *Early Concert Life* . . . , p. 59.

Part 1.

A Grand Sonata of Pleyel's on the Piano Forte, accompanied
  on the violin—By Mrs. Sully and Mr. Pick.
A Favourite Song "Whither my love"—By Mrs. Pick.
A Favourite Scotch Reel, with variations—By Mrs. Sully.
The Favourite Duett of "the Way worn traveller"—
  By Mr. and Mrs. Pick.
A Grand Sonata of Steibelt's, to conclude with the favourite
  Air of "The Rose Tree" with variations—By Mrs. Sully.
The Marseilles Hymn, in English—By Mrs. Pick.

Part 2.

A Grand Sonata of Clementi's on the Piano Forte, accompanied
  on the Violin—By Mrs. Sully and Mr. Pick.
A French Song—By Mr. Pick.
The Favourite Air of Lira Lira, with variations, from
  the Surrender of Calais—By Mrs. Sully.
An Italian Duet, sung by Mrs. Sully and Mr. Pick.
The Favourite Air of Moggy Lauder, with variations on the
  Piano Forte—By Mrs. Sully.
The Hunting Song of Tally Ho!—By Mr. Pick.
Sonata on the Italian Harmonica, with several known airs.

*A concert given by R. Shaw at the Eagle Tavern, Richmond—
1797.*[3]

Part 1.

Overture	
Song, "Primroses deck the bank's green side,"	Linley
by Mr. Bartlett	
Sonata on the Grand Piano Forte, by Mr. Frobel	Pleyel
Song, "Amidst the illusions," by Mrs. Shaw	Shield

---

3. *Ibid.,* p. 61.

Concerto, German flute, by Mr. Shaw   Devienne
Song, "Twins of Latona," by Mr. Robins   Shield

Part 2.

Song, "Love sounds an alarm," by Mr. Bartlett   Randel
Quartetto, oboe, violin, viola & bass   Bach
Song, "Loose were her tresses," by Mrs. Shaw   Giordani
Glee, "Sigh no more ladies," by Messrs. Bartlett,
    Robins, Shaw, and Mrs. Shaw
Symphony—Finale
Between the first and second parts, the facetious history
    of John Gilpin will be recited by Mr. Green.

A concert given at the Eagle Tavern, May 30, 1812.[4]

Part First

Overture of Lodoiska on the Harp—Signor Pucci.
English Song, "The Bird Duet," accompanied on the
    Piano and Harp.
Rondo, on the Forte-Piano—L. Boucherie.
Italian Song, . . . accompanied on the Harp.
English Song, "Henry," accompanied on the Piano—Boucherie.

Part Second

Fantasia, on the Forte-Piano—Boucherie.
English Duet, "All's Well," accompanied on the Harp
    & Piano—Boucherie & Pucci.
Song, accompanied on the Harp—Signor Pucci.
    To conclude with Variations, Harp & Piano by S. P.
    and L. B.

---

4. *Argus,* May 30, 1812. Throughout Appendix B, spellings, italics, and
quotation marks, except for obvious misprints, are cited as found in
the source.

Mr. Gallaher's grand concert given at the Eagle Tavern, 1814.[5]
Act I.

Overture,	Haydn.
A Comic Song by Mr. West.	
Quartetto—Violin principal, Mr. Stephan,	Pleyel.
Andante,	Haydn.
Quartetto on the Flute, by Mr. Weidemeyer,	Pleyel.
Minuetto,	Haydn.
Finale,	do.

Act II.

Grand Concerto on the Clarionet by Mr. Gallaher,	Michel.
Andante	Pleyel.
Song, "The Girl of my heart," by Mr. Maher,	Shield.
Minuetto,	Pleyel.
Duet, "Could a man be secure," by Charles Southgate and Mr. Gallaher,	Corfe.
Quartetto, Violin principal, Mr. Stephan,	Pleyel.
Song, "Hull's victory," by Mr. Gallaher,	Bray.
Finale,	Pleyel.

Mr. Twibill's concert at the Eagle Hotel, 1819.[6]

Part I.

Song, The Star Spangled Banner, written by Francis S. Key, Esq.
Song, The Young Son of Chivalry, composed by M. P. King.
Song, He was Famed for Deeds of Arms, written by Mr. Cherry, composed by Corri.
Song, The Girl of my Heart, the music by W. Shield.

Part II.

Song, Bright Phoebus, written by Hook . . . .
Song, The Wood Pecker, music by Kelly, words by T. Moore, Esq.

5. *Ibid.*, April 9, 1814.
6. *Compiler,* April 2, 1819.

. . . Robin Adair—Jessie O'Dumblaine—The Minute Gun at Sea—and The Light House.
To conclude with the much admired Melos-cosmiotis
(as arranged by Mr. Twibill) called
The Four and Twenty Fiddlers.

Grand vocal and instrumental concert for the benefit of Mrs. Green at the Eagle Hotel, 1819.[7]

Part the 1st.

Simphony—By Mozart,	Full Band.
Song—I never will prove unkind to thee, (J. Parry,)	Mr. Nichols.
Song—Softly waft ye Southern breezes, (by Hood)	Mrs. Green.
Solo—On the Piano, accompanied on the violin,	Mrs. Sully and Mr. De Bihl.
Song—Will you say farewell my love, (Moore,)	Mrs. Green.
Concerto, for the Violin (Viotti)	Mr. De Bihl.
Song—Whilst with Village Maids I stray, from the favorite Opera of Rosina, (by desire,)	Mrs. Green.
Bird Duette,	Mr. Nichols and Mrs. Green.

Part the 2nd.

Overture, Mozart,	Full Band.
Song—Why did she give this flow'ry Wreath, (Phillips)	Mr. Nichols.
Song—Tuneful Lark, (Shield,)	Mrs. Green.
Duetto,	Mr. Nichols and Mrs. Green.
Song—The celebrated Song like Love is yonder Rose (by Braham,)	Mrs. Green.
Variations for the Violin, to the favorite	

---

7. *Ibid.,* August 9, 1819.

Ballad of Robin Adair, composed and played by
Mr. De Bihl.
A new Patriotic Song, called the Genius of
 Columbia, or Strike the Heart,   Mrs. Green.
Finale   Full Band.

Concert given by Mrs. French assisted by Mrs. Sully, 1822.[8]

Part I.

Song,—My Henry is gone.   Stevenson.
Song,—My Jockey is the blythest Lad. Scotch Air.
Song,—My native land good night. Miss Fowler.
Song,—The celebrated Echo Song,
  (the echo performed by herself.) Bishop.

Part II.

Song,—As down the Bannas banks I stray'd. Irish Ballad.
Song,—Dulce Domum (by particular desire,) Braham.
Song,—Scots wha hae we' Wallace bled. Scotch Air.
Song,—Robin Adair (by request,) Irish Air.
Song,—Love sounds the trumpet of joy. Shield.

*Vocal concert by Thomas Philipps given at the Great Room in
the Eagle Hotel, 1822. His pupil, Miss Davis from Dublin, was
introduced to the audience.*[9]

Part First

Song—Mr. Philipps—"Said a Smile to a Tear." Braham.
Air—Miss Davis—"The Shamrock." Irish Melodies, T. Moore.
Duett—Mr. Philipps and Miss Davis—"Oh Maiden
  Fair"—from the Opera of the Barber of Seville. Paisiello.
Song—Miss Davis—"Di Placer mi Bal zarl Cor." [*sic*] Rossini.

8. *Ibid.,* February 19, 1822.
9. *Ibid.,* June 20, 1822.

New Ballad, MS.—Mr. Philipps—
    "Where Hudson's murm'ring billows."
    Words by Mr. Woodworth   Philipps.
Sonata, piano forte—Miss Davis—Variations on
    "Scots wha hae wi' Wallace bled."   Panormo.
Irish Melody—Mr. Philipps—"Love's young Dream." T. Moore.
Duett—"La ci darem la Mano"—from the
    Opera of Don Juan.   Mozart.

Part Second

Song—Mr. Philipps—"Pomposo, or a Receipt for an
    Italian song," (mock Bravura, introduced by
    him in the Barber of Seville.)   Altered from Dibdin.
Song—Miss Davis—"Oh say not Woman's Heart
    is Bought."   Whitaker.
Duett—"Love in thine Eyes."   Jackson.
Air—Miss Davis—"The Castilian maid."
    accompanied by herself on the Spanish guitar. Spanish Air.
Storm Concerto—Miss Davis,   Steibelt.
Song—Mr. Philipps—"Is there a heart"—from
    the opera of the Devil's Bridge.   Braham.
Song—Miss Davis—"The Mocking Bird."   Bishop.
Song—Mr. Philipps—"Love has Eyes."   Bishop.

Vocal concert by Mr. Keene, theatre performer, given at the Museum, 1823.[10]

Part I.

Sinfonia,   Orchestra.
Song—Love's Young Dream,   Moore.
Ballad—Robin Adair,   Irish Melody.
Waltz—Arranged by Mr. Berg,   Orchestra.
Song—A Temple to Friendship (by request,)   Moore.

---

10. *Ibid.,* January 31, 1823.

Part II.

Sinfonia,   Orchestra.
Song—Eveleen's Bower,   Moore.
Polacca—The Bed of Roses, composed expressly for
    Mr. Keene by   C. Gilfert, Esq.
Waltz—Arranged by Mr. Berg,   Orchestra.
Song—Cushlamachree, or Dear Erin.
Song—Sam Jones the Fisherman, a parody on the
    Knight Errant, (by particular request,)

Part III.

Sinfonia,   Orchestra.
Song—The Parting Kiss,   Tyrolese.
Song—Fanny Dearest,   Moore.
Waltz—Arranged by Mr. Berg,   Orchestra.
Finale—THE HUNTERS OF KENTUCKY

*Mrs. Sully's vocal and instrumental concert at the Eagle Hotel,
1823.*[11]

Part 1st.

Symphony   *Haydn.*
Song, Flow, flow, Cubanna,   Mr. Milon.
Favorite Scotch Airs on the piano forte   Mrs. Sully.
Romance, La Rose a lagonic,
    accompanied on the guitar   Mr. Milon.
Favorite Air, "Huntsman Rest,"
    Piano, Harp and Flute   Mrs., Miss and Mr. Sully.
Variations on the Violin
    Friend of my soul   Mr. Milon.
Concertante, Piano Forte with accompaniments   *Kalkbrenner.*

---

11. *Ibid.,* May 21, 1823.

Part 2nd.

Symphony   *Haydn.*
Sonata, Harp with Violin accompaniment,   *Naderman.*
                                        Miss Sully and Mr. Berg.
Italian Cavatina, composed by the celebrated   *Rossini.*
                                                   Mr. Milon.

Favorite Tyrolese, Song of Liberty
          arranged as a duet for Piano Forte,   Mr. and Miss Sully.
Fantasia and Variation for the Guitar,   Mr. Milon.
Favorite Airs of Mrs. McDonald and
          Ye banks and Braes,   Mrs. Sully.
The Whole to conclude with a grand Concerto for
          two Piano Fortes, with accompaniments,
          composed by *Mozart.*   Mr. and Miss Sully.

The Oratorio performed at the Monumental Church, 1823.[12]

Part First

An introductory piece on the Organ.
Chorus—Awake the harp, awake the lyre,
          in shout and joy, your voices raise,
          &c. from the Oratorio of the "Creation,"
          by *Haydn.*
Duet—Sweet as the Shepherd's tuneful reed, &c.
          Anonymous.
Solo—O Zion, O Jerusalem, when I forget thy glory,
          &c. by *Carr,* of Baltimore.
Anthem—Holy Lord God of Hosts, &c. by *Mozart.*
Solo—Angels ever bright and fair, &c. by *Handel.*
Chorus—The Heavens are telling the Glory of God,
          &c. from the "Creation," by *Haydn.*

Part the Second

An introductory piece on the Organ.

12. *Ibid.,* December 20, 1823.

Chorus with an introductory Solo—Break forth into
   joy, glad tidings of salvation, &c. from the
   Oratorio of the "Messiah," by *Handel*.
Solo—Rolling in foaming billows, &c. from
   the "Creation," by *Haydn*.
To conclude with the Hallelujah Chorus, from
   the "Messiah," by *Handel*.

*The oratorio performed at the First Presbyterian Church,
1824.*[13]

Part I.

Adams.—Come let us sing unto the Lord, &c.
Magdalin Ode; By *Madin*.—Grateful notes and numbers bring,
Drummond; *Dr. Miller*.—See how beauteous on the mountains,
Anthem: *J. Arnold*—I beheld, and lo a great multitude,
Duet; *Beaumont*.—Although the fig tree,
Strike the Cymbal; Pucitta.—Strike the Cymbal, roll the
   timbrel,
Solo. Father thy word is past,
Hymn for Christmas; *Leach*.—Shepherds rejoice, &c.

Part II.

Anthem; *Handel*.—O praise the Lord,
Vesper Hymn; *Russian Air*.—Hark the vesper Hymn is stealing,
Anthem; *S. Chapple*.—I waited patiently, &c.
Solo, Sun is Rising; *Handel*.—Hail to thy brightness
   glorious Sun.
The Last Day; Whitaker.—That day of wrath, that dreadful
   day,
Chorus Anthem; *Rev. C. Gregore*.—Hosanna, blessed is
   he that comes, &c.
Anthem; *Chapple*.—O come let us sing unto the Lord,
Anthem; *Rev. Mr. Mason*.—Lord of all power and might, &c.

---

13. *Whig,* May 11, 1824.

N. B. The above pieces will be accompanied with a variety of Musical Instruments that have been judiciously selected for the occasion.

A Grand Vocal Concert given by the Miss Gillinghams and Mr. Paddon at the Eagle Hotel, 1827.[14]

Part First

Grand Overture. Zauberflote, for two performers on the Piano Forte—	Mozart
Song. Quel Pallor. Miss Gillingham—	Portogallo
Duett. When thy Bosom. Miss E. Gillingham—Mr. Paddon—	Braham
Trio. La Mia Dorabella. Miss Gillinghams—Mr. Paddon—	Mozart
Song. Fly, soft ideas. Miss Gillingham—	Arne
Song. Eccesso di Contendo. Miss E. Gillingham—	Portogallo
Ballad. Old Robin Gray. Miss Gillingham—	Lindsay
Trio. Cruda Sorte. Miss Gillinghams—Mr. Paddon.	Rossini

Part Second

Duett. Care Zittelle. [sic] Miss Gillingham—Mr. Paddon	Curcio
Ballad. Down the Burn. . . .	Scottish
Song. Di Tanti Palpiti. . . .	Rossini
Song. The Soldier Tir'd. . . .	Arne
Duett. Ah Se Di Mali Miei—	Rossini
Ballad. Kate Kearney. . . .	Irish
Trio. Fra Quai	Rossini

---

14. *Ibid.,* February 20, 1827.

Miss George's concert of vocal and instrumental music given in the Eagle Hotel, 1829.[15]

Act 1st.

Overture arranged for five instruments, by
  Mr. Parnell.   Composed by Parnell.
Song, Miss George, Araby, dear Araby.   Carl Von Weber.
Ballad, Mrs. Gill, Light Guitar, accompanied
  on the Spanish Guitar by Mr. Andre.   Barnett.
Cavatina, Miss George, Una Voce poco, fa.   Rossini.
Quartett, Violin Obligato.   Rode.
Duett, Mrs. Gill and Miss George, I know a Bank.   Horn.
Song, Miss George, My Bonny Lad.   Lee.

Act 2nd.

Quartett, clarionett obligato, Mr. Harman,   Kuffner.
Grand Scena Reutva and Air a Compir Gia Vo
  L'Imprisa, Violin Obligato, Mr. Parnell,
  from the Italian Opera of *La Vendetta de Nino,* Guglielmi.
Ballad, Mrs. Gill, Maid of Lucern,   Barnett.
Duett, Oh no, we never mention her,
  Miss George and Mrs. Gill, arranged by Miss George.
                                                   Bishop.
Fantasia, Violin and Guitar,
  Messers. Andre and Parnell.   Kuffner.
Song, Miss George, by particular request,
  The Soldier Tir'd,   Dr. Arne.

The Farewell Ballad Concert given by Mrs. Knight in Terpsichore Hall, 1832.[16]

Part I.

Overture to the Slave   Bishop
English Song, Cease your Funning
  Mrs. Knight

15. *Ibid.,* March 6, 1829.
16. *Ibid.,* February 13, 1832.

Solo, Piano Forte; La Ricordauza—   Czerny
    Mrs. Knight
Scotch Ballad, Nid Noddin
Recitation. . . .
Trio, Piano, Violin, and Violoncello
    Mr. Knight, Mr. Berg, and Mr. W. Cunnington   Mozart
Irish Ballad, the last Rose of Summer
    Mrs. Knight

Part II.

English Song, Crazy Jane—
    Mrs. Knight
Overture to Il Barbiere de Siviglia   Rossini
Ballad, Home Sweet Home—
    Mrs. Knight   Bishop
Trio, Piano Forte, Violoncello, and Horn—
    Mr. Knight, Messers. W. and S. Cunnington   Knight
Recitation. . . .
Scotch Ballad, All the Blue Bonnets are over the Border
    Mrs. Knight   Lee

Mr. Schmidt's concert given at Mr. Blondel's ball room, 1835.[17]

Part I.

1. Overture to the Caliph of Bagdad; for the Piano
    Forte and Violin; by a   Young Lady and Mr. Schmidt
2. Grand Variation a la Paganini, for the Violin; by
                              Mr. Schmidt
3. Oft in the Stilly Night; by   Mr. Schmidt
4. Imitation of the Church Organ on the Violin; by
                              Mr. Schmidt
5. Strike the Cymbal, with variations for the
    Piano Forte; by a   Young Lady
6. Song. The Swiss Boy in Tyrolesse; by   Mr. Schmidt
7. Grand Variation, of Away with Melancholy, for
    the Violin and Piano Forte,
    accompanied by a   Young Lady and Mr. Schmidt

17. *Ibid.*, January 2, 1835.

Part II.

1. Overture to Lodowiski, for the Piano Forte,
   by a   Young Lady and Mr. Schmidt
2. Favorite American, Scotch and Irish Airs,
   by   Mr. Schmidt
3. Scotch Song—My Love is like a red, red rose;
   sung by   Mr. Schmidt
4. Grand Sonata for the Piano Forte, by a Young
   Lady, accompanied on the Violin by   Mr. Schmidt
5. Song. The Spanish Serenade by   Mr. Schmidt
6. Grand Variations a la Paganini on one String
   only; by   Mr. Schmidt
7. Song. The Watchman; sung by   Mr. Schmidt

To conclude with Mr. Schmidt's celebrated

STORM

In which he will imitate the Storm, Lightning, Sun rising, village people dancing, Engine Running, Pipe and Bugle sounding, Pigs squealing, cry of old woman, speaking of a Landlord, etc., on the Violin.

Soiree Musicale given by Mr. and Mrs. Morley at Terpsichore Hall.[18]

PROGRAMME
Part First

Overture—Mr. Barber, Piano Forte   Rossini
Duetto—Mr. and Mrs. Morley, "Crudel Perche Finora." Mozart
Ballad—Mrs. Morley, "The Banks of the Blue Moselle."
                                         Rodwell
Song—Mr. Morley, "Come brothers arouse."   Russell
Fantasia—Flute, Mr. P. H. Taylor, accompanied
    by Mr. E. B. Barber   Nickolson
Song—Mrs. Morley, "Meet me in the willow Glen."
    (Composed for her.)   Lee
Old Song—Mr. Morley, "The fine old English Gentleman,"

18. *Ibid.,* November 14, 1837.

taken from the Gregorian Chants of A.D. 1200,
arranged by   Dewar
Comic Duet—Mr. and Mrs. Morley, "Master and Scholar."
                                                           Barnett

Part Second

1. Extemporaneous effusion on the Piano Forte   Mr. Barber
2. Duett—Mrs. Morley and Mr. Taylor,
   "When thy bosom."   Braham
3. Aria Buffo—Mr. Morley, "Miei rem polu Femminini,"
   (From Cinderella)   Rossini
4. Southern Refrain. Mrs. Morley, "O'er the lake where
   droop'd the willow." Arrang'd from the old song
   "Long time ago," by   C. Horn
5. Scena—Mr. C. W. Taylor, "Isabel."
   (From the opera Il pirati)   Bellini
6. Piano Forte. Mr. Barber, La Violette,
   (with variations)   Hertz
7. Irish Ballad. Mrs. Morley, "Young Rory O'Moore,"
   (Or good omens) From the Irish superstitions.   Loder
8. Song—Mr. Morley, "The Brave Old Oak,"
   (composed for him.)   Loder
9. Laughing Ferzetto—Mr. and Mrs. Morley and
   Mr. Taylor, "Vadasi via diqua."   Martini

Henry Russell's concert at Terpsichore Hall, 1838.[19]

PROGRAMME
First Part

Introduction—Piano Forte   Russell.
Some Love to Roam—composed by   Russell.
The Brave Old Oak—Arranged by   Russell.
Wind of the Winter Night   Russell.
The Ivy Green   Russell.
Arm Brothers Arm   Cooke.

---

19. *Ibid.*, February 2, 1838.

Second Part

The Wreck of the Mexico	Russell.
Come, Brothers Arouse	Russell.
Woodman, Spare that Tree	Russell.
The Fine Old English Gentleman	Martin Luther.
Comic Song—Largo al Factotum della cita	Rossini.

Soiree Musical given by C. E. Horn and Miss Horton
at Terpsichore Hall, 1838.[20]

. . . assisted by Mr. E. B. Barber and Mr. P. H. Taylor. . . .
Mr. Horn will preside at the Piano Forte.

Overture. Piano Forte. Messrs. Horn and Barber	Bellini.
New Song. Miss Horton. The Land of the West. . . .	C. E. Horn.
Ballad. Mr. Horn. Sing away, Sing away.	A. Lee.
Duetto. Miss Horton and Mr. Horn.	
Sweet on the Thorn.	C. E. Horn.
Divertisement. Piano Forte and Flute.	
Messrs. Barber and Taylor.	Tulou.
Cavatina. Miss Horton. Se M'Abban S'doni.	Mercadante.
Song. Mr. Horn. "Still so gently o'er me	
stealing." From the Sonnambula.	Bellini.
Trio. "O dolce cara istante."	Cimarosa.

Part II.

Duetto, with Variations, Messrs. Horn and Barber.	
From the French in Guilliam Tell, by Rossini	Hertz.
Ballad. Miss Horton. O'er the Lake where	
droops the willow.	C. E. Horn.
Song. Mr. Horn. Death of the Smuggler.	C.E. Horn.
Duetto. Forbear, let nothing fear thee—	
From the opera of Armida.	Rossini.
Solo. Piano Forte. Mr. Barber.	Czerny.

---

20. *Ibid.*, March 6, 1838.

Song. Miss Horton. Why don't the men propose?
   By desire.   Blewitt.
Cantata. Mr. Horn. Rosalie.   Beethoven.
Finale. The celebrated Laughing Trio.   Martini.

    It is Mr. Horn's intention to devote his time to giving Lessons in Singing during his short stay in Richmond.

A Grand Vocal and Instrumental Concert given by Madame Brengeri at Terpsichore Hall, 1839.[21]

Madame Brengeri will be assisted by Signor Fabj, First Tenor of the Italian Opera in New York and Philadelphia, and by Mr. Barber, Professor of the Piano Forte.

PROGRAMME
Part I.

1. Introduction; Piano Forte, Mr. Barber.
2. Recitative Air, How gently was my slumber,
   Opera Der Freischutz, Madame Brengeri.   Weber.
3. Di Piacer, Opera La gazza Ladra,
   Madame Brengeri.   Rossini.
4. Aria, "Perche non posso odiarti," [*sic*]
   Opera Sonnambula, Signor Fabj.   Bellini.
5. Duo, "Mira la bianca luna," from the
   Soiries Musicales of Rossini,
   Madame Brengeri and Signor Fabj.   Rossini.

Part II.

1. Fantasia, Piano Forte, Mr. Barber.
2. Should he upbraid, Madame Brengeri.   Bishop.
3. Bollero, Vieni o Ruggiero, Signor Fabj.   Rossini.
4. 'Tis the last rose of Summer, Madame Brengeri.   Moore.
5. Comic Neapolitan Tarantella, Signor Fabj.   Rossini.
6. Duo, "ultimo addio, Opera la Straniera,   Bellini.
   Madame Brengeri and Signor Fabj.

---

21. *Ibid.*, March 12, 1839.

Mr. Barber will preside at the Piano Forte.

Madame Dussek O'Connor's concert at Terpsichore Hall, 1839.[22]

Signor Fabj and Mr. E. B. Barber have . . . volunteered their services.

PROGRAMME
Part I.

Introduction, Piano Forte, Mr. Barber.	
Aria, "I o l'undia," Madame D. O'Connor.	Donizetti.
Aria, Signor Fabj.	Donizetti.
Irish Ballad, "Kathleen Mavourneen," Madame O'Connor.	Crouch.
Serenade, "Buona Notte," Signor Fabj.	
Ballad, "Grace Darling," Madame O'Connor.	Linley.
Duo, "Opera Norma," Madame O'C. & Signor F.	Bellini.

Part II.

Duet, Harp and Piano Forte, by Madame O'Connor and Mr. Barber.	Steibelt.
. . . "Still so gently," . . . Signor Fabj.	Bellini.
Bolero, "Ouvres Donc," Madame O'Connor.	Dessaurer.
Song, Signor Fabj.	Bellini.
Irish Ballad, "Savourneen ma Dellish," Madame O'Connor, accompanied by herself on the harp.	Knight.
Duo, "Amor che nasce," Madame O'C. & Signor F.	Blangini.

Mrs. Martyn's benefit performance given in the Theatre, 1841.[23]

The performance will commence with . . .
A GRAND
VOCAL AND INSTRUMENTAL CONCERT
in two parts.

---

22. *Ibid.,* April 2, 1839.
23. *Ibid.,* April 8, 1841.

PART I.

OVERTURE, from the Opera of Fra Diavolo—Auber.

GLEE, "Here in cool grot," Mr. and Mrs. Martyn, Miss Inverarity, and Mr. Pearson—Lord Mornington.

CAVATINA, "Joy inspires my bounding heart," (De Placer,) Mrs. Martyn—Rossini.

SONG, "Erin is my home," Mr. Pearson—Moschelles.

DUETT, "Take them, I implore thee," from Bellini's celebrated Opera of Norma. . . . Mrs. Martyn and Miss Inverarity.

SONG, "The Shepherd's Evening Bell," Miss Inverarity—Barnett.

DUETT, "When thy bosom heaves the sigh," Mrs. Martyn and Mr. Pearson—Braham.

GLEE, "And we're a'noddin," Mr. and Mrs. Martyn and Miss Invererarity—Scottish.

PART II.

OVERTURE, from the Opera of Tancredi—Rossini.

GLEE, "Come o'er the brook," Mr. and Mrs. Martyn and Miss Inverarity, and Mr. Pearson—Ford, 1660.

RONDO, "Come, friends, and listen to the story," (from the Opera of the Postillion of Longjumeau,) Mr. Pearson—A. Adam.

DUETT, "The happy Savoyards," Mrs. Martyn and Miss Inverarity—Bishop.

BALLAD, "My boy Tammie," Miss Inverarity—McNeil.

GLEE, " 'Twas on a Simmer's afternoon," Mr. and Mrs. Martyn and Miss Inverarity—Scottish.

BALLAD, "Whistle and I'll come to ye, my lad," Mrs. Martyn—Burns.

LAUGHING FINALE—"Come, and with us be gay," Mr. and Mrs. Martyn, Miss Inverarity, and Mr. Pearson—Martini.

————

After which the Comedietta of the
BARRACK ROOM
The whole to conclude with the popular Farce of
THE SWISS COTTAGE

Vocal and instrumental concert given by Madame Pardi Marras at Terspichore Hall, 1841.[24]

... assisted by Messrs. P. H. Taylor, E. B. Barber, and C. Bassini.

1. SOLO, on the Harp—The Garland of Shamrocks   Bochsa.
2. DUETT, from Norma—on the Violin. Mr. Bassini

                    Bellini.
3. ROMANZA, from the Opera Otello. Madame Marras

                    Rossini.
4. DUETT, from the Opera Moise. P. H. Taylor,
  flute, and E. B. Barber, piano   Tulou and Herz.
5. INTRODUCTION AND AIR, with variations on the
  Harp

                    Bochsa.

Part II.

6. GRAND FANTASIA—on the Harp   Alvars.
7. TRIO—Le Souvenir de Naples. P. H. Taylor, flute;
  E. B. Barber, piano; and C. Bassini, violin Bassini.
8. SONG—We have lived and loved together   Herz.
9. POT POURRI—on the violin   Bassini.
10. GRAND MARCH—on the Harp   Alvars.

John Braham's concert at Terpsichore Hall, 1841.[25]

... Assisted by Mr. and Mrs. Watson.
The following are the principal Songs which will be sung in the course of the Evening.

Mr. Braham's Songs
Mad Tom—Composed by Purcell in 1695.
Kelvin Grove; Scot's wha ha'e; Blue Bonnets; Bay of Biscay, &c.

Mrs. Watson's Songs
Kathleen O'Moore; She wore a wreath of Roses.

---

24. *Ibid.,* May 10, 1841.
25. *Ibid.,* May 29, 1841.

My Beautiful Rhine.
On the lake where droops the willows
And on the Mountain high, my love and I.

Duett—Mr. Braham and Mr. Watson—Come brave with me
    the sea, my love.
Duett—Mr. and Mrs. Watson—The celebrated Singing Lesson,
    composed by Ficravante.
The celebrated Laughing Trio— . . . Vada si via diqua.

Mr. Watson will preside at the Piano Forte.

Oratorio given in St. James Church, 1842.[26]

| Organ and Harp | Miss Sully |
| Conductor | Mr. Evans |

Part I.

Chorus—Old Hundred	Luther
Duett—Go thy way—thy son liveth	Evans
Solo—Fallen is thy throne, oh Israel	Martini
Quartette—Bow down thine ear O Lord	Rossini
Solo—Oh Zion! Oh Jerusalem (Harp)	Carr
Duett—Hear my Prayer	Kent
Chorus—Hallelujah to the Father	Beethoven

Part II.

Chorus—The Heavens are telling	Haydn
Solo—Evening Hymn	Smith
Duett—Oh Praise the Lord	Bassini
Solo—Angels ever bright and fair	Handel
Trio and chorus—Night, shades no longer	Rossini
Solo—He was despised	Handel
Finale—Grand Hallelujah	Handel

---

26. *Ibid.,* April 8, 1842.

Concert of sacred music given at St. John's Church, 1842.[27]

To be given by the Ladies' Benevolent Society, assisted by the Ladies and Gentlemen of the different Choirs of this city.

Part I.

100th Psalm.
Prayer.
Anthem—Sing O Heavens.
Duett—Thy Son Liveth.
Anthem—When the Lord shall build up Zion.
Solo—The Sabbath Bells.
Duett and Chorus—I will wash my hands in Innocency.
Anthem—Hark the Herald Angels Sing.
Trio—The Sky Lark.
Anthem—I waited patiently.

Part II.

Anthem—O praise ye the Lord.
Trio—Guide me o thou Great Jehovah.
Anthem—Daughter of Zion.
Quartette—Lord of all power and might.
Anthem—How beauteous upon the mountains.
Solo—Consider the Lilies.
Anthem—Sons of Zion come before Him.
Duett—O Lovely Peace.
Quartette—Where withall shall a young man cleanse his way.
Anthem—The Lord's Prayer
Benediction

Soiree Musicale given at the Exchange Hotel, 1842.[28]

C. BASSINI informs the amateurs of Music, that he intends giving a Soiree Musicale . . . assisted by Messrs. E. B. Barber

27. *Ibid.,* September 23, 1842.
28. *Ibid.,* November 18, 1842.

and P. H. Taylor, who have kindly volunteered their valuable services.

PROGRAMME
Part I.

1. Trio—From the Overture of "La Norma,"	Bellini.
2. Grand Concerto—Mr. Bassini,	Paganini.
3. Duetto—from "Moses in Egypt,"	Herz & Tulou.
Messrs. Barber and Taylor	
4. Brilliant Variations—on a theme by Bellini,	Dohler.

Part II.

1. Trio—from "La Norma,"	Bellini.
2. Pot-Pourri—from "La Sonnambula,"	Bassini.
3. Fantasia—on a beautiful Italian Air,	Nicholson.
Mr. Taylor	
4. Una Bagatella Italo Galia	Bassini.
Mr. Bassini.	Bassini.

Program given by the Richmond Sacred Music Society in the United Presbyterian Church, 1843.[29]

Part 1st.

Old Hundred.	
Prayer	
Chorus—Glory be to God on high.	Haydn.
Duett and Chorus—How beautiful upon the Mountain.	
Trio—Earth with her ten thousand flowers.	Winter.
Duett and Chorus—I waited patiently.	Chapple.
Chorus—Blessings and honour.	Mozart.
Duett—All things bright and fair are thine.	Shaw.
Chorus—Grand Hallelujah Chorus.	Handel.

Part 2d.

Chorus—Sing to Jehovah.

---

29. *Ibid.*, January 10, 1843.

Duett and Chorus—I will wash my hands in innocency. Chapple.
Quartette—"Where withall shall a young man cleanse
    his way."
Solo—The Prayer.   Bellini.
Anthem—Hark the song of jubilee.
Duett—Heavenly home.   Swiss Air.
Duett and Chorus—Soon shall the Trumpet sound   Dixon.

Benediction

*P. H. Taylor's first Soiree Musicale: given at the Exchange
Hotel.*[30]

. . . assisted by . . . Mr. Bassini, Violin; Mr. Barber, Piano;
Mr. Berg, Alto; Mr. Ulmo, Violoncello; and an Amateur on
the Clarionet.

PROGRAMME—Part I.

1. Overture—Piano Forte, Violin, Alto, Flute, Clarionet
    and Violoncello (Torvaldo e Dorliska)   Rossini.
2. Melange—Flute, Mr. Taylor introducing Coming Thro'
    the Rye, L'pipe du tabac, Durandarte and Balerma,
    and my Nannie O.   Taylor.
3. Bagatelle—Violin, Mr. Bassini introducing a Neopolitan
    air, La Cachucha, 'Twere vain to tell, and with
    rapture dwelling.   Bassini.
4. Variations—Clarionet, Mr. _____ on a favorite
    air.   Muller.
5. Fantasia—Piano Forte, Mr. Barber, introducing
    Kate Kearney and Chopin's favorite Mazurka.   Barber.

Part II.

6. Sestetto—Violin Imo, violin 2do, Alto, Flute,
    Clarionet and Violoncello, introducing John
    Anderson, Kitty Tyrell, Believe me if all those

---

30. *Ibid.,* January 12, 1843.

endearing young charms and the Union Waltzes. Bassini.
7. Cavatina—Flute, Mr. Taylor, Una voce poco fa.   Furstenau.
8. Solo—Violin, Mr. Bassini   De Beriot.
9. Aria—Flute, Mr. Taylor, Robin Adair, with variations,
    as performed by the celebrated Drouet.   Drouet.

Program by the Richmond Sacred Music Society given at the Second Baptist Church, 1843.[31]

ORATORIO OF SACRED MUSIC
Part I.

Old Hundred.
Prayer.
Chorus—Now elevate the sign of Judah.   Haydn.
Trio—Earth with her ten thousand flowers.   Winter.
Anthem—When the Lord shall build up Zion.   Cole.
Anthem—Sing unto God.
Solo—Evening Prayer.
Anthem—O Sing unto the Lord, a new song.   Clarke.
Duett—We'll rest in thy Love.   P. A. Andreau.
Chorus—Holy Lord God of Hosts.   Mozart.

Part II.

Chorus—Let us with a joyful Mind,   Mozart.
Solo—Let not your hearts be troubled.   J. K. Opl.
Anthem—Praise the Lord O my soul.   Chapple.
Collect—Lord of all power and might.   Wm. Mason.
Solo—With verdure clad.   Haydn.
Anthem—Daughter of Zion.
Duet and Chorus—Night shades no longer   Rossini.
Anthem—Sweet is the scene when Christians die.
Solo and Chorus—Luther's Judgment Hymn.   Luther.
Benediction.

---

31. *Ibid.*, February 21, 1843.

Soiree Musicale given in the Exchange Hotel, 1843.[32]

E. B. Barber, C. Bassini, and P. H. Taylor . . . assisted by Mr.
Ulmo . . . and AN AMATEUR, on the clarionet, the gentleman
whose performance was so much admired at P. H. Taylor's
Concert.

PROGRAMME
Part I.

Overture . . . Lodiska.   Kreutzer.
Concertante Duett—Clarionet and Piano Forte
    from Rossini's Matilde de Sabran,   Behr and Fessy.
Duett—Violin and Piano Forte . . . from
    Donizetti's Philtre   Burgmuller and Lafonte.
Fantasia—Flute, . . . on the favorite Irish
    air Durandarte and Belerma   Tulou.
Quartett—Violin, Violoncello, Flute and Piano, . . .
    from the opera Norma   Bassini.
Pot Pourri—Violin . . . introducing La Cachucha,
    with Rapture Dwelling, and a Swiss air   Bassini.
Solo—Piano Forte, . . . on a favorite Scotch air   Dohler.
Divertisement—Clarionet, Amateur, with Quartet
    Accompaniment   Kuffner.

Ole Bull and company at the Theatre, 1843.[33]

Programme—Part I.

Overture—by the Orchestra.
Song—"Ah! Come Rapida"—Air, Dans L'opera Il
    Crociato in Egitto—Mrs. Bailey.   Meyerbeer.

GRAND CONCERTO IN THREE PARTS

Allegro Maestoso; Adagio Sentimentale; and Rondo Pastorale!

32. *Ibid.,* February 27, 1843.
33. *Ibid.,* December 27, 1843.

Composed and executed by Ole Bull, and accompanied by the whole orchestra.

Song—"Come to me at Morning"—Mrs. Bailey.   Wade.
Overture—by the Orchestra.

Part II.

Adagio Religioso (a mother's prayer) composed and performed
  by Ole Bull.
Song—"Auld Robin Gray"—Mrs. Bailey.
Overtures—by the Orchestra.

Part III.

Grand Polacca Guerriera! Composed and executed by Ole Bull.
Music by the Orchestra.
The evening entertainments to conclude with "Il Carnivall di
  Venezia"—composed by Paganini and performed by Ole
  Bull.

*P. H. Taylor's Soiree Musicale given at the Exchange Hotel,
1845.*[34]

Part I.

1. Overture—Piano Forte, Violoncello, Clarionet and Flute—
     Messrs. Knecht, Dunderdale, Rosier, Amateur and Taylor.
2. Song—The War Song from "Norma,"—"On the Field,"
     Mr. Dunderdale.   Bellini.
3. Fantasia—Flute and Piano Forte, from the Opera
     "Il Tasso,"—Messrs. Taylor and Dunderdale. Donizetti.
4. Cantata—"The May Queen," . . .   Dempster.
5. Divertisment and Theme with variations—
     Clarionet, and Piano Forte—Amateur and
     Mr. Knecht.   Barmann.

---

34. *Ibid.*, March 17, 1845.

6. Song—"John Anderson my Joe,"—
   Mr. Dempster.   Scottish Ballad.
7. Romance—Violoncello and Piano Forte—
   Messrs. Rosier and Dunderdale.   Ganz.

Part II.

1. Theme with Variations—"Hope told a flattering Tale,"—
   Flute, Violoncello, Clarionet, and Piano Forte—
   Messrs. Taylor, Rosier, Amateur, and Dunderdale.
2. Song— (first time in public) "The Grave of the Departed,"—
   Mr. Rosier   Schubert.
3. Song—The "Star Spangled Banner,"— (by particular
   desire) Mr. Dunderdale.
4. Song—The "Lament of an Irish Emigrant,"—composed
   and sung by Mr. Dempster.
5. Concertante—Piano Forte and Clarionet—Mr. Knecht
   and Amateur.   Behr and Fessy.
6. Song—The Savoyard—"Ah! I Wander,"
   with guitar accompaniment,   Rosier.
7. Adagio and Polonaise—Flute and Piano Forte—
   Messrs. Taylor and Dunderdale.   Boehm.

F. W. Rosier's Soiree Musicale at the Exchange Hotel, 1845.[35]

   Mr. P. H. Taylor,
      Mr. Dunderdale,
         and several Gentlemen Amateurs. . . .

PROGRAMME
Part I.

OVERTURE—Piano Forte, Flute, and Violoncello—
   Messrs. Dunderdale, Taylor and Rosier.
GLEE—"Hail Smiling Morn,"—by the Gentlemen
   Amateurs,   Spofforth.

---

35. *Ibid.,* April 14, 1845.

"SONG WITHOUT WORDS,"—for the Violoncello,
   Mr. Rosier.
SONG—"The New Year's Come,"—Mr. Dunderdale,   Knight.
FANTASIA—Flute and Piano Forte—Messrs. Taylor
   and Dunderdale.
GLEE—"Crows in a Cornfield," by the Gentlemen
   Amateurs,   Phillips.

Part II.

HUNTING CHORUS—"The Sun's Gay Beams,"
   from Euryanthe.   Weber.
FANTASIA—Flute and Piano Forte, introducing a
   Favorite Air—Messrs. Taylor and Dunderdale, Nicholson.
SONG—"The Serenade," Mr. Rosier, accompanied by
   two Flutes, obligato—Messrs. Taylor and
   Dunderdale, arranged by,   Rosier.
AIR, with variations—Violoncello—"Hope told a
   Flattering Tale," (by request)   Muntzberger.
IRISH BALLAD—"Molly Bawn,"—Mr. Dunderdale,   Lover.
FINALE—Laughing Trio—by the Gentlemen
   Amateurs,   Martini.

*Mr. W. L. Bloomfield's concert with the Band of the Fourth
Regiment of Artillery, 1845.*[36]

. . . given at the Exchange Concert Room.

Programme,
Part I.

1.—The Portuguese Reveille   Caprara.
2.—The celebrated Challenge Duett (David
   and Goliath) in the Oratorio of David   Newkomm.
3.—The White Squall (Barry Cornwall)   Barker.
4.—"vivi tu," from Anna Bolena   Donizetti.

---

36. *Ibid.,* October 20, 1845.

5.—"Hear me, Norma," (Duetto)   Bellini.
6.—Capt. Ro. O. Scott's Jr. Quick Step   Bloomfield.

Part II.

1.—Hark! The curfew's solemn sound (glee)   Atwood.
2.—Cavatina, "Through the wood,"   Horn.
3.—Miss Richie's Gallopade,   Bloomfield.
4.—Thou art gone!   Rooke.
5.—Cruda sorte, from L'Italiana in Algeri   Rossini.
6.—Tu Vedrai [sic], from Il Pirata   Bellini.
7.—Quick Step from the overture
      Robert le Diable   Bloomfield.

*Concert at the Exchange Hotel, 1847, given by George Knoop
with assistance from Miss De Jeune, Mr. Taylor, Mr. Buck, and
Mr. Opl.*[37]

PROGRAMME.
Part I.

1. Grand Potpourri for the Violoncello, composed and executed
   by Mr. Knoop.
2. Grand Fantasia, for the Piano, . . . Mr. Buck.
3. Grand Duett Concertante, for Piano and Violoncello, . . .
   Miss De Jeune and Mr. Knoop.
4. Fantasia for Violoncello, (by request) in which he will introduce a Virginia Reel, with different comic imitations,
   composed and executed by Mr. Knoop.

Part II.

1. Grand Duette, for Violin and Violoncello, (by particular
   request,) . . . Mr. Opl and Mr. Knoop.
2. Grand Terzetto, for Piano, Flute, and Violoncello, . . .
   Messrs. Buck, Taylor, and Knoop.

---

37. *Ibid.*, December 31, 1847.

3. Grand Waltz, for Piano, . . . Mr. Buck.
4. Grand Fantasia on a Russian air, for Violoncello, (by request,) introducing "The Last Rose of Summer," composed and executed by Mr. Knoop.

A program given at the African Church in 1849.[38]

Grand Musical Festival!
by the
OPERA TROUPE
Consisting of Mrs. Seguin, Mrs. H. Phillips, Mr. W. H. Reeves, Mr. S. W. Leach, Mr. G. Holman, Mr. Seguin. . . .

Part I.

1. GLEE—The Chough and Crow . . .   Bishop.
2. NEW BALLAD—Woman's Love . . .   Kiltz.
3. SONG—Coming thro' the Rye . . .   Scotch Air.
4. BALLAD—My soul in one unbroken sigh . . .   Balfe.
5. ROMANCE—It is in Vain . . .   Auber.
6. SONG—My Boyhood's Home . . .   Rooke.
7. NEW GLEE—The lass of Gowrie   Scotch Melody.

Part II.

1. QUINTETTO—With wonder, I'm astounded . . .   Auber.
2. BALLAD—My Pretty Jane . . .   Bishop.
3. MY FAVORITE DUET—Take them, I implore
   thee . . . From NORMA   Bellini.
4. BALLAD—Farewell to the Mountain . . .
   from THE MOUNTAIN SYLPH   Barnett.
5. BALLAD—On the mountain high . . .   Swiss Air.
6. SONG—Let the toast be dear woman . . .   Rodwell.
7. MADRIGAL—Oh, by Rivers, by whose falls,
   Melodious birds sing Madrigals.

---

38. *Ibid.*, February 6, 1849.

accompanied on the piano forte by Mr. Leach.   Savile.
A vocal and instrumental concert given by John Dunderdale,
F. W. Rosier, and their pupils at the "New Church on Church
Hill," 1849.[39]

Part I.—Sacred.

Quartette—"Bow down thine ear, Oh Lord" . . .	Rossini
Recit. and Air—Mr. Rosier, . . . "Comfort ye my people" . . .	Handel
Song—"The Infant's Prayer" . . .	Novello
Song—Mr. Dunderdale—"Angel of Life" . . .	Callcott
Duett—"Forsake me not"— . . .	Spohr
Recit. and Air—"Then shall the eyes of the blind" . . .	Handel
Song—"The Funeral Bell"— (words by F. W. R.) . . .	Schubert
Quartette—"Deep within thy narrow chamber," (words by F. W. R.) . . .	Fuss

Part II.—Secular.

Grand Fantasia, from the Opera Maritana— Piano Forte . . .	W. V. Wallace
Ballad—"The Reconciliation" . . .	Peters
Duett—"When thy bosom heaves the sigh" . . .	Braham
Song—Mr. Dunderdale—"What is the spell,"—from Amilie . . . 	Rooke
Song—"The Soldier Tired" . . .	Arne
Solo—Violoncello—Mr. F. W. Rosier, (by request,) — Recollections of Savori and Knoop . . .	F. W. R.
Duett—"Hear me Norma" . . .	Bellini
Ballad—"On the banks of Guadalquiver"	Bochsa
Quartette—"The Roses," (words by F. W. R.) . . .	Werner
Reminiscences of the Opera "Lucrezia Borgia"— Piano Forte . . .	M. Strakosch
Trio—"The Curfew" . . .	Bishop

---

39. *Ibid.,* December 25, 1849.

Jenny Lind's concert at the Richmond Theatre, 1850.[40]
Programme.
Part I.

Overture, (La Dame Blanche,)	Boieldieu.
Aria, "Sorgete," (Maometto Secondo,)	
Signor Belletti,	Rossini.
Aria, "Perche non ho," (Lucia di Lammermoor)	
Mad'lle Jenny Lind	Donizetti.
Fantasia on the Violin, (Il Tremolo) —	
Mr. Joseph Burke	De Beriot.
Trio for the Voice and two Flutes, written expressly	
for Mad'lle Jenny Lind, (Camp of Silesia) —	
Mad'lle Jenny Lind	Meyerbeer.

Part II.

Overture, (Fra Diavolo,)	Auber.
Cavatina, "Largo al Factotum" (Il Barbiere) —	
Signor Belletti	Rossini.
The Bird Song—M'lle Jenny Lind	Taubert.
La Tarantella—Signor Belletti	Rossini.
Home, Sweet Home, (Clari,) —the words by	
J. Howard Payne—M'lle J. Lind	Bishop.
The Herdsman's Song, commonly called the Echo	
Song—M'lle Jenny Lind.	

Conductor—Mr. Benedict.

An orchestra composed of the most eminent solo performers, from . . . New York, led by Mr. Joseph Burke, is engaged.

A concert given in the Theatre, 1851.[41]

Theatre—Grand Musical Festival—

OPERATIC CONCERT!—By particular request TEDESCO appears again . . . assisted by the Germania Musical Society, and Signor Guilio Macchi.

---

40. *Ibid.*, December 20, 1850.
41. *Ibid.*, April 4, 1851.

Amongst the pieces of the Programme are three in full costume: Favorita, Linda, and Colasa.

PROGRAMME.
Part I.

1. Grand Overture, Alessandro Stradella, Flotow;
   . . . Germania Musical Society.
2. Rondo Finale, from Donizetti's Opera Elixir d'Amore, . . .
   Signora Tedesco.
3. Brilliant Variations, with full orchestra accompaniment,
   Cavallini, for the clarionet, Signor Macchi.
4. Cavatina, from Ernani, (Verdi) . . . Signora Tedesco.
5. Introduzione and Variations for the trumpet, Mr. Haase,
   Grantz.
6. Recitative and Aria, from I Masnadieri, Signora Tedesco,
   Verdi.

Part II.

7. Grand Overture, Oberon, Germania Musical Society,
   Weber.
8. Cavatina, from Linda di Chamounix, . . .
   Signora Tedesco, Donizetti.
9. Ideal Waltz, . . . Germania Musical Society, Lanner.
10. Cavatina, from Opera LaFavorite, . . .
    Signora Tedesco, Donizetti.
11. A Summer Night in Denmark, . . .
    German Musical Society, Lumbye.
12. The much applauded Spanish Song, La Colasa,
    Signora Tedesco.

Catherine Hayes' concert given at the Universalist Church, 1852.[42]

PROGRAMME
Part I.

---

42. *Dispatch,* January 21, 1852.

Scena and Aria, "Vienila ma vendetta,"
(Lucrezia Borgia,) Donizetti—Herr Mengis.
Cavatina, "Ah, mon fils" (Le Prophete) Meyerbeer—
Miss Catherine Hayes.
Solo on the Violin—Herr Griebel.
Aria Buffa, "Il Bivacci," Battista—Herr Mengis.
Song, "Happy Birdling," (Wallace) with flute obligato
accompaniment, by Mr. Kyle—Miss Catherine Hayes.

Part II.

Duette, "Quanto Amore" (L'Elisir d'Amore,) Donizetti.
Miss Catherine Hayes and Herr Mengis.
Solo on the Flute, (G. Loder) —Mr. Kyle.
Aria Buffa, "Miel Rampoli," (Cenerentola,) —Herr Mengis.
"Auld Robin Gray"—a Scotch Ballad—Miss Catherine Hayes.
Swiss Song, "The Happy Switzer," (Mengis,) —Herr Mengis.
"The Last Rose of Summer"—an Irish ballad—
Miss Catherine Hayes.
Conductor—Mr. Lavenu.

Concert by Teresa Parodi at the Exchange Hotel, 1852.[43]

. . . ASSISTED BY Signorina Amalia Patti, Miska Hauser, and Maurice Strakosch.

Programme—Part I.

1. Fantasia on favorite airs from "La fille du Regiment," composed and executed by
Maurice Strakosch.
2. Neapolitan, I am Dreaming of Thee, an English Song, by Alexander Lee, sung by
Signorina Amalia Patti.
3. Fantasia on airs from "Lucrezia Borgia," by Donizetti, composed and executed on the Violin by
Miska Hauser.

43. *Ibid.*, February 6, 1852.

4. The celebrated Cavatina from Rossini's grand opera
Tancredi, sung by

Mad'lle Teresa Parodi.

Part II.

1. "By the sad Sea Waves," composed by Benedict, sung by
Signorina Amalia Patti.
2. "Adagio religioso," Ole Bull's masterwork, executed by
Miska Hauser.
3. The favorite Cavatina from "La Sonnambula," sung by
Mad'lle Teresa Parodi.
4. "The Magic Bell," a reverie sentimentale;
composed and executed by   M. Strakosch.
5. The grand duetto from Rossini's "Sabat Mater," sung by
M'lles Teresa Parodi and Amalia Patti.

Part III.

1. "The Bird on the Tree," a Capriccio written for
little children, composed and executed by

Miska Hauser.
2. "Comin' through the Rye," a Scotch song, sung by
Signorina Amalia Patti.
3. The famous Ricci Valse, sung by

M'lle Teresa Parodi.
4. "Kossuth's Gallop," composed and executed by
M. Strakosch.
5. Grand Duetto from Bellini's Grand Opera "Norma," sung by
M'lles Teresa Parodi and Amalia Patti.

*Concert given by Madame Anna Widemann and others at the
Universalist Church, 1852.*[44]

PROGRAMME—Part I.

1—Trio, for Piano, Violin and Violoncello,   Hummel.

44. *Ibid.,* September 27, 1852.

Messrs. Staddermann, Lobmann, and Rosier.

2—Grand Air, from Jerusalem   Verdi.
Mr. Genibrel

3—Aria, from the Capuletti   Bellini.
Mad. Widemann

4—Beatrice Di Tenda   Donizetti.
Mr. Genibrel

5—Fantasio, for Flute and Piano, upon
Themes from Lucia di Lammermoor,
Messrs. De Costa and Staddermann.

6—Il Canto d'Italia   Gordigiani.
Mad. Widemann

7—Grand Duo, from Semiramide
Mad. Widemann and Mr. Genibrel   Rossini.

Part II.

1—Trio, Second Part

2—Ma Paquita   Hanau.
Mr. Genibrel

3—Grand Aria Della Semiramide   Rossini.
Mad. Widemann

4—Stances a L'Eternite   Delsarte.
Mr. Genibrel

5—Florita   Vimeux.
Mad. Widemann

6—Grand Duetto, from Puritani   Bellini.
Mad. Widemann and Mr. Genibrel

Ole Bull's concert at the African Church, 1853.[45]

. . . assisted by Signora Adelina Patti and Mr. Strakosch.

PROGRAMME
Part I.

1. Fantastic Dramatique on airs from Lucia di Lammermoor,
composed and performed by H. Strakosch.

---

45. *Ibid.,* January 17, 1853.

2. The Grand Aria from "Ernani," by Verdi,
   sung by Signorina Adelina Patti.
3. Bravura Variations on "L'Amo, ah! L'Amo," from Bellini's
   Romeo e Guiletta, composed and performed by Ole Bull.
4. "Home, Sweet Home," composed by Sir Henry Bishop,
   sung by Signorina Adelina Patti.
5. Introductione de Capriccio e Variosiane on "helcepin,"
   from Paisiello, composed for the violin alone by
   N. Paganini, performed by Ole Bull.

Part II.

1. The Nightingale, a woodland scene,
   composed and performed by M. Strakosch.
2. Trip! Trip! Trip! an English Ballad, composed by Kacher,
   sung by Signorina Adelina Patti.
3. Notturno Amoreso e Rondo, Giocoso,
   composed and performed by Ole Bull.
4. Jenny Lind "Echo Song," sung by Signorina Adelina Patti.
5. "The Carnival of Venice" by Ole Bull.

A concert by Louis Jullien and orchestra at the Metropolitan Hall, 1854.[46]

Part First.

The whole of the incidental descriptive music to
   MIDSUMMER NIGHTS DREAM . . . Mendelssohn.
   1. Overture. . . .
   2. Scherzo. . . .
   3. Interlude in A Minor. . . .
   4. Comic March. . . .
   5. Notturno. . . .
   6. The Grand Wedding March.

Grand Scena—From "Robert le Diable,"   Meyerbeer.
   M'lle Anna Zerr.

---

46. *Ibid.,* April 7, 1854.

Valse—"Farewell Valse," or "Adieu to America"
   ... solos by Herr Koenig   Jullien.
Solo oboe—"La Sonnambula,"   Lavigne.
Quadrille Nationale   Jullien.
   "The American"

Part Second.

Grand Operatic Selection and Fantasia   Bellini.
   From the Opera of "Les Huguenots," arranged by
   Jullien ...   Horn.
Ballad—"I've been Roaming," ...
   Mad'lle Anna Zerr.
Duo—Two Violins   Mollenhauer.
   The Brothers Mollenhauer.
Polka—"The Katy Did," or Souvenirs of Castle
   Garden in Autumn   Jullien.
Solo—Clarionet   Wuille.
Polka—"The Sleigh Polka"   Jullien.

Mrs. Cecilia Young's concert at the Metropolitan Hall, 1854.[47]

   ... assisted by Signor Da Costa and Herr Thilow.

Programme:
Part I.

1. Piano Solo   Mr. Thilow.
2. Qui La Voce, Cavatina per Puritani   Bellini.
   Mrs. Cecilia Young.
3. I'll Pray for thee—for Flute & Piano   Donizetti.
   Messrs. Da Costa and Thilow.
4. Kate Kearny, Irish Ballad,
   Mrs. Cecilia Young.

Part II.

5. Piano Solo   Mr. Thilow.

47. *Ibid.*, May 29, 1854.

6. The Harp that once Through Tara's Hall   Moore.
   Mrs. Cecilia Young.
7. Variations for the Flute
   Composed by   D. X. Da Costa.
8. Gratias Agimus Tibi—with Flute obligato
   Mrs. Young and Mr. Da Costa   Guglielmi.

Charity concert at the Metropolitan Hall, 1856.[48]

Many of the leading Musical Professors, assisted by the Armory Band . . . will give a Grand Vocal and Instrumental concert for the benefit of the suffering poor of our city. . . .

PROGRAMME.
Part I.

1. Grande Marche Triomphall—By the Armory Band,
                                           V. Busch.
2. Chorus—By the Virginia Verein, (twenty in number,)
                                           Beethoven.
3. Solo—Song, Woman,   Withers.
4. Duo—Song,   De Weber.
5. Solo—Violoncello,   Servais.
6. Trio—Violoncello, Piano, Violin,   Reissiger.
7. Chorus, by the Virginia Verein,   Kreutzer.

Part II.

1. Cavatina—Armory Band,   Donizetti.
2. Duo—Song,   Kucken.
3. Solo—Flute,   De Beriot.
4. Solo—Song, Up to the Forest High,   Bennett.
5. Trio—Song, Freischutz,   De Weber.
6. Overture of Stradella—Piano, Violin,
     Viola, Violoncello, and Flute; arranged by   C. W. Thilow.
7. Chorus—By the Virginia Verein,
8. Edinburg Waltz—Armory Band,   Labitzky.

---

48. *Ibid.,* February 15, 1856.

Madame De Estvan's concert given at the Metropolitan Hall, 1856.[49]

  . . . Assisted by Mademoiselle De Lacy, Soprano
        Signor George, Tenor
        Signor Da Costa, Solo Flute
          Mr. C. W. Thilow, Violoncello and Piano

PROGRAMME
Part I.

1. Overture from the Opera "Martha," by   Flotow.
   For four hands on the Piano, executed by
   Mad. L. Lacy and Mr. Thilow.
2. Song—"Kathleen Mavourneen," Ballad, by   Crouch.
   Sung by Mad. De Estvan and Mad. Lacy.
3. Duo—"Of the Knights," from the Opera "Martha" by
                                     Flotow.
   Sung by Mad. De Estvan.
4. Solo Violoncello, "Le Desire," by   Servais.
   Executed by C. Thilow.
5. Grand Air from the Opera "Robert Le Diable," by
                             Meyerbeer.
   Sung by Mad. L. Lacy.

Part II.

1. Song—"As I view these Scenes so Charming,"
   from the Opera "La Sonnambula," by   Bellini.
   Sung by Signor George.
2. Air and Prayer, from the Grand Opera, "Holofernes," [*sic*]
   by   Concone.
   Sung by Madame De Estvan.
3. Solo Flute—Variations Brilliantes, by   Tulou.
   Executed by Signor Da Costa.
4. Terzett—"Oh! Di quall sei tu vitima," from
   the Opera "Norma,"   Bellini.
   Sung by Mad. Estvan, Mad'lle Lacy and Signor George.

---

49. *Ibid.*, February 21, 1856.

5. Duet—"Master and Scholar," by   Horn.
   Sung by Mad'lle Lacy and Signor George.

A concert by Volkmar Busch, 1856.[49a]

Volkmar Busch, (of Copenhagen) Titular Orchestra Conductor
and Composer to H. M. the King of Denmark, for the present
Professor of the Piano Forte, Harmony and Instrumentation
in the city of Richmond . . . will give a
                          GRAND CONCERT!
                                 in the
                          Metropolitan Hall. . . .
                             Assisted by
                  An Efficient Instrumental Orchestra,
        Numbering more than twenty performers, composed of all
the members of the EXCELLENT ORCHESTRA OF THE
RICHMOND THEATRE, of some of the members of the
MUSICAL AMATEUR CLUB OF RICHMOND, lately
established and conducted by him, and of some of the musicians
from the ARMORY BAND.

                            PROGRAMME:
                     Part First— (Semi-Sacred.)

Principally consecrated to connoisseurs and lovers of the
    Musical Art.

1. FUNERAL MARCH   V. Busch.
    Composed to the memory of a distinguished warrior and
        awarded the first Musical Prize of the three Scandinavian
        Kingdoms, Denmark, Sweden, and Norway.
        Performed by the Orchestra.
2. DUO CONCERTANTE, for Flute and Clarionet.
    Composed for a Soprano and Contralto voice to Piano
        accompaniment, by John J. Fry, of Richmond. Arranged
        for the above two instruments by V. Busch, and per-

49a. *Ibid.,* March 27, 1856.

formed by two gentlemen, members of the Musical Amateur Club of Richmond.

3. THE SERENADE, by   Schubert.
   The unrivalled and most charming of all this celebrated composer's songs for a single voice. By general request arranged for this occasion, by V. Busch, and performed by the Orchestra.

4. SOLO, for the original Trombone Basso,   V. Busch.
   Composed for this concert.
       Introducing themes from Meyerbeer's Robert le Diable; Rossini's Otello; and as a conclusion, the grand American National Anthem, Hail Columbia. All solo for the above majestic instrument, to accompaniment of the Orchestra. Performed by Mr. Ericsson, of Stockholm, member of the Musical Amateur Club of Richmond.

5. L'ADIEU. (The Last Greeting)   Schubert.
   One of the most beautiful compositions of that immortal composer. Arranged by V. Busch. Performed by the Orchestra.

6. THE XXIII. PSALM OF DAVID, "The Lord
   is my Shepherd"   Schubert.
       Composed for two Soprano and two Contralto voices to accompaniment of the Piano, the four parts for the voices, arranged for two Cornets and two Alto-Horns, will be performed (to accompaniment of the Orchestra, arranged by V. Busch) by four gentlemen, members of the Orchestra.

Part Second— (Secular.)
For the Million.

1. OVERTURE   Boieldieu.
   From the comic Opera, Jean de Paris. Performed by the Orchestra.

2. COPENHAGEN CASINO WALTZES.   Lumbye.
   Performed by the Orchestra.

3. SOMMER'S SALON POLKA   Gungl.
   Performed by the Orchestra.

4. EL JALEO DE PARIS   V. Busch.

Dance, composed in the Spanish popular style, and
  dedicated to H. M. Eugenie, Empress of the French.
  Performed by the Orchestra.
5. FLORA QUADRILLE   Strauss.
  Performed by the Orchestra.
6. EPILOGICAL PIECE: SIC SEMPER TYRANNIS,
  Or the Invincibility of the Union! Grand March of
  Homage. Composed for this occasion, and most
  respectfully inscribed to His Excellency, Henry
  A. Wise, Governor of the State of Virginia. By V.
  Busch.

Conductor   V. Busch.

*First Grand Festival of the Three United Singing Societies
of Richmond, 1856.*[50]

... Consisting of FORTY MEMBERS!
  and assisted by the THEATRE ORCHESTRA
            and the ARMORY BAND ...
      AT METROPOLITAN HALL

              Programme:
              First Part

Overture—Semiramis   Rossini.
Chorus—Hail, Hail   Winter.
Chorus—Joy, Joy   Grager.
Hanseader Grand March   Gungl.

              Part Second

Overture, Oberon   C. M. Von Weber.
Festival Chorus, composed expressly for
    the occasion by   F. Reichert.
Solo Quartet—Canon   Issenhover.
Mountain Chorus   Kucken.
Grand Opera Medley   Labitzky.

<hr>

50. *Ibid.,* May 26, 1856.

A Concert by the Richmond Amateur Instrumental Club given in Metropolitan Hall, 1857.[51]

Conductor and arranger of the Music, Mr. V. Busch.

PROGRAMME:
Part 1st.

1. Overture to the Opera of "La Dame Blanche," by Boieldieu.
2. Barcarole from the opera of Masaniello, by Auber.
3. Romance: "The Last Greeting," sung by a member of the Club, by Schubert.
4. Waltz, composed by a member of the Club.
5. Romance. "In after years," composed for voice and piano by Jno. J. Fry.
6. Sounds from the Swiss Mountains. Pastorale, by Coeckel.
7. Prayer and Chorus from the 1st act of the Opera of "Il Puritani," by Bellini.

Part 2nd.

1. March of Homage, composed and dedicated to H. M. Oscar I, King of Sweden and Norway, by Busch.
2. Ave Maria by Schubert.
3. Ballad, "I'm Dreaming, Oh, I'm Dreaming," sung by a member of the Club, by Robinson.
4. Gallop ("Beta Phi Lambda,") composed for the Piano, by E. R. Archer.
5. "Sounds from Home," by Gungl.
6. The Serenade by Schubert.
7. Introduction from the 2nd Act and Cavatini "Casta Diva" from the 1st Act of the Opera of Norma, by Bellini.

A vocal and instrumental concert by Richmond musicians given in 1857.[52]

GRAND SACRED CONCERT, at STEINLEIN'S HALL!

---

51. *Ibid.*, February 10, 1857.
52. *Ibid.*, December 19, 1857.

. . . To be given by AN EFFICIENT ORCHESTRA
under the direction of Prof. J. A. Rosenberger.

Programme.
Part I.

No. 1. Overture from Bohemian Girl, by
         Balfe. . . .   ORCHESTRA
No. 2. Trompete Solo from Cavatine Nebucodonosor,
         By Verdi. . . .   Mr. BAIER
No. 3. Potpourri, from Lucia di Lammermoor, ORCHESTRA
         By Donizetti. . . .
No. 4. Clarinette Solo. By Joan Muller. . . . Mr. BAUMANN
No. 5. Serenade. By Schubert. . . .   Mr. KRAUSSE
No. 6. Overture—Don Juan. By Mozart. . . . ORCHESTRA

Part II.

No. 7. George Kunkel's Overture, by
         J. A. Rosenberger. . . .   ORCHESTRA
No. 8. Chorus, from the Creation,
         by Haydn. . . .   CECILIA SOCIETY
No. 9. Potpourri, from the Daughters of the Regiment.
         By Donizetti.   ORCHESTRA
No. 10. Flute Solo. By Kummer. . . .   J. A. ROSENBERGER
No. 11. Anvil Chorus. By Verdi. . . .   ORCHESTRA
No. 12. Overture, from Zampa. By Herold. . . .

A concert by Miss Anna Vail given at Corinthian Hall, 1858.[53]

. . . Assisted by Mollenhauer, violinist and Theo. Schreiner,
pianist and composer—pupil of Liszt.

Programme:
Part First

1. Solo—Piano—Fantasie on Hungarian Airs   Liszt.
         SCHREINER

---

53. *Ibid.*, April 26, 1858.

2. Solo-Violin—Adagio and Rondo	Paganini.
MOLLENHAUER	
3. Grand Cavatina—Betty	Donizetti.
Miss ANNA VAIL	
4. La Sylphide—Grande Fantasie	Mollenhauer.
MOLLENHAUER	
5. Ballad—The Spanish Gipsies	Griffiths.
Miss ANNA VAIL	

Part Second.

1. Solo—Piano—Sonate Pastorale Andante	Beethoven.
SCHREINER	
2. Scena and Cavatina, from the Opera	
Lucia di Lammermoor	Donizetti.
Miss ANNA VAIL	
3. Solo-Violin—Duett played on one violin	Paganini.
MOLLENHAUER	
4. Ballad—We met by chance	Kucken.
Miss ANNA VAIL	
5. Solo-Piano Forte—Polka de Concert	Schreiner.
SCHREINER	
6. The Witches' Dance	Paganini.
MOLLENHAUER	

Joseph P. Hanlon's concert at the Mechanics' Hall, 1859.[54]

GRAND GIFT CONCERT

Part I.

Song—Banks of the Blue Mozelle	Mr. J. P. Hanlon.
Song—Rocked in the Cradle of the Deep	Mr. J. C.
Song—Shells of Ocean	Mrs. A. O. G.
Duett—All's Well	Mr. J. P. H. & E. B.

---

54. *Ibid.*, June 28, 1859.

Song—The Dearest Spot on Earth   Miss R. B.
Trio—N. Y. Boat Glee   Messrs. J. P. H., W. M., E. M.
Song—Sailor Boy's Grave   Mr. J. P. H.

Part II.

Quartette—I Forget the Gay World
Duett—Minute Gun at Sea   Mr. J. P. H. & E. M.
Song—Annie Laurie   Miss R. B.
Song—Humorous   Mr. R. H. S.
Song—The Blind Boy   Mr. J. P. H.
Trio—A Little Farm Well Tilled   Messrs. J. P. H., W. M.,
and E. M.

Concert by the Richmond Philharmonic Association given at the Mechanics' Hall, 1860.[55]

PROGRAMME:
Part I.

1. Overture—Tancredi, Orchestra   Rossini.
2. Glee—Four Voices   Beethoven.
3. Duo—Violin and Piano, from Don Giovanni   De Beriot.
4. Der Wanderer—Song   Schubert.
5. Aria—from Romeo, Orchestra   Bellini.

Part II.

1. Hungarian March—Orchestra   Gungl.
2. Quartette—2 Violins, Viola and Violoncello   Haydn.
3. Glee—Four Voices   Eisenhofer.
4. Trio—Piano Forte, Violin and Violoncello   Reissiger.
5. Overture—Masaniello, Orchestra   Auber.

A. GEBHARDT   Conductor.

---

55. *Ibid.,* February 2, 1860.

A later concert by the Richmond Philharmonic Association given at the Mechanics' Hall, 1860.[56]

. . . Assisted by several LADY ARTISTES of our city.

PROGRAMME:
Part First

1. Overture—Barbier von Seville	Rossini.
2. Concerto—for Clarionette	
3. Duetto—for Piano—Semiramide	Rossini.
4. Solo—Violin	
5. March—"Hanseaten"	

Part Second

1. Overture—Zampa	Herold.
2. Song—from the Magic Flute	Mozart.
3. Solo—for Bassoon	C. M. von Weber.
4. Cavatina—Sonnambula	Bellini.
5. Medley—Trovatore	Verdi.

A. GEBHARDT, Conductor

A Soiree Musical given at the Richmond Female Institute, 1860.[57]

Wednesday Evening, June 27th, 1860.

Programme:
Part I.

1. Chorus.—Glad notes of Joy are ringing,	Wm. Mason.
2. Duo—Vocal. Alpine Morning,	Kucken.
3. Overture.—Tancredi. Piano—Three Performers,	Rossini.
4. Cavatine.—Alfin Brillar,	Ricci.
5. Solo and Chorus.—La Carita,	Rossini.

---

56. *Ibid.*, March 9, 1860.
57. The Virginia Historical Society, Richmond, Virginia.

6. Duo—Piano. Valse de Concert,   Lysberg.
7. Trio—Vocal. La Sera,   Lucantoni.
8. Solo—Vocal. Valse di Bravura,   Venzano.
9. Duo—Piano. Variations—Lucia di Lammermoor,   Bruner.
10. Chorus.—Bohemian Girl,   Balfe.
11. Song.—The Switzer's Farewell,   Crosby.
12. Variations.—Lucrezia Borgia, Four Pianos—
      Eight performers,   Czerny.

Part II.

1. Solo and Chorus.—Touch the Soft Harp Gently,   Wurzel.
2. Duo—Vocal. Parigi, O Cara—LaTraviata,   Verdi.
3. Duo—Piano. Variations de Bravoure—Il Pirata,   Hunten.
4. Duo—Vocal. Giorno D'Orrore—Semiramide,   Rossini.
5. Solo and Chorus.—Arranged from Massaniello,   Rossini.
6. Duo—Piano. Rondo Brillante—Linda di Chamounix, Krug.
7. Cavatina.—Non fu Sogno—I Lombardi,   Verdi.
8. Chorus.—Ernani,   Verdi.
9. Duo—Piano. Fantasie on March from Wm. Tell,   Hunten.
10. Terzetto—Vocal. Lift thine Eyes to the
      Mountains—Elijah,   Mendelssohn.
11. Solo—Vocal. Maritana,   Wallace.
12. Divertissement. La Fille du Regiment,
      Four Pianos—Eight performers,   Czerny.
13. Finale.—The Mountaineer,   Swiss Melody.

A concert given in Monticello Hall, 1861.[58]

By the UNITED MUSICIANS OF RICHMOND. . . .

PROGRAMME
Part I.

1. Overture—Yelva   By Reissiger.
2. Solo, for Clarionette   By Mueller.

---

58. *Dispatch*, February 11, 1861.

3. Waltz   By Jos. Gungl.
4. Solo, for Bassoon
5. March, (from the Prophet,)   By Meyerbeer.

Part II.

1. Medley, (from Lucia,)   By C. M. Weber.
2. Solo, for Trompete   By Warg.
3. Ann QUADRILLE   By Joh. Strauss.
4. Medley, (from Daughter of the Regiment,)   By Donizetti.

After the concert, there will be a BALL.

A Vocal and Instrumental Concert given at Metropolitan Hall, 1861.[59]

The Committee of the St. Charles Hospital have the pleasure to announce to the citizens of Richmond that the following ladies and gentlemen have, in the kindest manner, volunteered their services in the aid of the sick and wounded soldiers!
TWO LADY AMATEURS
  Mons. D'ALFONCE,
    Mr. EGGELING,
  Mr. HERMAN BISHOP (Of the Jeff. Davis Flying Artillery,)
    Mr. F. N. CROUCH,
    Mr. B. KRAUSE

The CONCERT to be under the direction of F. W. ROSIER.

PROGRAMME:
Part I.

1. Patriotic Song. "God will Defend the Right."

---

59. *Ibid.,* September 25, 1861.

Dedicated to the defenders of Southern soil, by a young
lady of Virginia, Lady Amateur (pupil of Mr. Rosier,)
and Chorus.
2. Song. "The Wanderer." Mr. F. N. Crouch.   Schubert.
3. Duette from "The Magic Flute." Miss H. and
   Mr. Eggeling.   Mozart.
4. Solo, Violin. "Sounds from Home." Mr. Bishop   Bishop.
5. Song. "The Old Sexton." Mr. Eggeling   Russell.
6. Song. "The Soldier Tired." Lady Amateur,
   (pupil of Mr. R.)   Arne.
7. Ballad. "Kathleen Mavoureen."   Crouch.

Part II.

1. Solo, Piano Forte. Mr. H. Bishop.
2. Song, from "Der Freischutz." Miss H.   Weber.
3. Soldier's Song. Mons. d'Alfonce.
4. Song. "Napolitative." Lady Amateur
   (pupil of Mr. R.)   A. Lee.
5. Solo, Clarionet. Mr. H. Bishop.
6. Irish Ballad. Mr. F. N. Crouch
7. Trio from "The Magic Flute." Miss H.,
   Mr. B. Krausse, and Mr. Eggeling.   Mozart.
8. "The Marseillaise." Mons. D'Alfonce.

A concert given in the African Church, 1861.[60]

GRAND CONCERT

The entire proceeds to be given to the
FIRST MARYLAND REGIMENT
at the
AFRICAN CHURCH
. . . .

COMMITTEE:

---

60. *Ibid.,* October 24, 1861.

Mrs. President Davis,	Mrs. Wirt Robinson,
Brig. Gen. Winder.	W. H. Macfarland, Esq.,
Rev. Dr. Reid,	Rev. Dr. Moore,
Rev. Dr. Burrows,	Rev. Dr. Peterkin,
Rev. George Woodbridge,	Rev. Dr. Duncan,
James Beale, M.D.	Chas. S. Mills, M. D.

———

MADAME M. D'ESTVAN,
MISS L. DE LACY,
A LADY AMATEUR,
PROF. JOHN HEWITT,
F. N. CROUCH,
F. W. ROSIER.

———

PROGRAMME:
Part I.

1. Patriotic Song, (written and composed by Prof. Hewitt,)
"Give our Flag to the Breeze."
F. N. CROUCH.
2. Serenade   Schubert.
LADY AMATEUR, pupil of Mr. Rosier.
3. Song—"The Heart Bowed Down." (From the
Bohemian Girl.)   Balfe.
4. Venetian Gondolier's Song   Stigelli.
MADAME M. D'ESTVAN.
5. Song—"Friend of the Brave." (Poetry by Campbell.)
F. N. CROUCH.   Callcott.
6. Song—"The Nightingale."   Lethe.
LADY AMATEUR, with obligato Violoncello
accompaniment
7. Kathleen Mavourneen, (by desire,)   Crouch.
F. N. CROUCH.
8. Glee—Men's Voices   Bishop.
MYNHEER VON DUNK.
9. Chorale Song   Prof. Hewitt.

Part II.

1. Patriotic Song, by desire, (Written and composed by a young lady of Virginia.) "God will defend the right."
   LADY AMATEUR AND CHORUS.
2. Song—"The Gallant Comrade." (Words written for this occasion by F. W. R.)   Muller.
   F. N. CROUCH.
3. Arietta—"Isolina."   Stigelli.
4. Song "Oh, would I were a boy again."   Rome.
   Mr. R., Gentleman Amateur.
5. Duett—"I would that my love."   Mendelssohn.
   MAD. M. D'ESTVAN and Miss DE LACY.
6. Song—"The Wanderer," (by desire)   Schubert.
   F. N. CROUCH.
7. Song—"The Soldier Tired." (by desire)   Arne.
8. Irish Ballad   F. N. Crouch.

Concert by the Richmond Philharmonic Association, 1861.[61]

GRAND VOCAL AND INSTRUMENTAL CONCERT
by the
RICHMOND PHILHARMONIC ASSOCIATION
to take place at
FRANKLIN HALL
(formerly Trinity Church)
On Tuesday Evening, November 12, 1861,
for the benefit of the WIVES AND CHILDREN
of the Richmond Volunteers.

PROGRAMME:
Part First

1. Overture   Orchestra.
2. "Two Roses"—Chorus, Male Voices   Werner.

61. *Ibid.*, November 12, 1861.

3. Duetto—"Guarda che bianca luna"   Campana.
     Mad. ESTVAN and Miss LACY.
4. Mynheer Van Duneck   Bishop.
     Solo and Chorus, Male Voices.
5. Aria   Concone.
     MADAME ESTVAN.
6. Chorus from Norma—Male Voices   Bellini.

Part Second

1. Overture.   Orchestra.
2. "I Puritani,"—Solo for Flute   Bellini.
     Mr. WILDT.
3. i. "Sevuol ballare;" ii. "La vendetta"—
     from Figaro's Wedding   Mozart.
     Mr. ERICSSON.
4. "Hark Above Us."—Chorus, Male Voices.   Kreutzer.
5. "Hunter's Song"—Duetto   Kucken.
     Mad. ESTVAN and Miss LACY.
6. "Southern Anthem"—Solo and Chorus.   O. A. Ericsson.

O. A. ERICSSON   Conductor.
Madam Estvan and Miss Lacy have kindly consented
to assist The Association for the above benevolent
purposes.

*Madame Bertha Ruhl's first formal concert in Richmond,
1863.*[62]

EXCHANGE HOTEL
Grand Vocal & Instrumental CONCERT

MADAME RUHL,
The Southern Cantatrice, from New Orleans,
a refugee and Exile . . . assisted by

---

62. *Ibid.*, September 25, 1863.

MISS ROSA FAY, of New Orleans
HERR H. BRAUN, the distinguished
violinist and Violoncellist, late of the French Opera of
New Orleans,
CHARLES THILOW, the accomplished
Pianist of this city.

Programme:
Part I.

No. 1. Piano Solo, "La Campanella"   Taubert.
          C. W. Thilow
No. 2. Casta Diva   Bellini.
          Madame Ruhl
No. 3. Solo Violin, French air, with brilliant variations
                                                      De Beriot.
          Herr Braun
No. 4. Sacred Song, "When from the Sacred Garden" Bishop.
          Madame Ruhl
No. 5. Solo Violoncello, "souvenir de Bellini"   Patti.
          Herr Braun
No. 6. Duett, "Juanita"   Mrs. Norton.
          Mad. Ruhl and M'lle Rosa Fay

Part II.

No. 1. Grand Duo Piano, Il Diavolette   Sanfiorenzo.
          C. Thilow and H. Braun
No. 2. Patriotic Song, the Soldiers' Grave   Schreiner.
          Madame Ruhl
No. 3. Solo Violoncello, Lucrezia Borgia   Braun.
          Herr Braun
No. 4. Grand Capriccio Piano   Wollenhaupt.
          C. W. Thilow
No. 5. Cavatina, "Robert, Robert"   Meyerbeer.
          Madame Ruhl
No. 6. Duo Concertante Piano and Violin, "Lucia" De Beriot.
          Herr Braun and C. W. Thilow

Herr Herman Braun's benefit concert, 1863.[63]

EXCHANGE HOTEL   GRAND CONCERT

Benefit of HERR HERMAN BRAUN. . . . assisted by Madame Bertha Ruhl, M'lle Rosa Fay, Mr. Charles Thilow, Messrs. F. and Charles Sibert and several of the best Amateur Singers of this city.

PROGRAMME.
Part I.

1. Grand Solo—Piano	Thalberg.
Mr. Ch. Thilow.	
2. Solo Violoncello—Home, Sweet Home, with	Braun.
brilliant variations	
Herr Braun.	
3. Grand Cavatina—Der Freischutz	Von Weber.
Mad. Ruhl.	
4. De Beriot's 6th Air—Violin	De Beriot.
Herr Braun.	
5. Duett Vocal—My Mountain Home	Verdi.
Mad. Ruhl and Amateur.	
6. Souvenir de Favorita, Violoncello	Singuleur.
Herr Braun.	

Part II.

1. Scene de Bal—Duett, Piano	Fesca.
2. German Song—Marie	Abt.
Madame Ruhl.	
3. Spanish Fantasi	Bohrer.
Herr Braun.	
4. We meet by chance—Tenor	Kucken.
5. Robert toi que J'aime (by request)	Meyerbeer.
Mad. Ruhl.	
6. Duett, Piano—Carnival de Venice	Ernst.
7. Duett, Song—I Know a Bank	Horn.

---

63. *Ibid.*, October 5, 1863.

8. Grand Duo Brilliant—Piano and Violin from
     William Tell   **Benedict.**
          Braun and Thilow.

*A vocal and instrumental concert for the benefit of the poor
and soldiers' families, under the direction of the Army Committee of the Young Men's Christian Association, given at the
African Church, 1863.*[64]

PROGRAMME:
Part I.

1. Trio—Piano, Violin, and Violoncello   **Reissiger.**
     J. Reinhardt, E. Loebmann, and C. W. Thilow.
2. Duet—"Oh, Maiden Fair"   **Paisiello.**
     Miss Dale and Rosier.
3. Cavatina—"Di Piacer," from La Gazza Ladra   **Rossini.**
     Madame Ruhl.
4. Quatuor for two Violins, Viola, and Violoncello—
     "Hymn for the Emperor"   **Haydn.**
     E. Loebmann, A. Gebhardt, F. W. Rosier,
     C. W. Thilow.
5. Song—"The Soldier Tired of War's Alarms."   **Arne.**
     Miss Rosetta Dale.
6. Quartette—"Come Where, my Love"   **Forster.**
7. Song—"La Serenade"   **Schubert.**
     Madame Ruhl.

Part II.

1. Duet—Piano, Nottivino Tremola   **Thalberg.**
     C. W. Thilow and J. Reinhardt.
2. Song—"Non fu Sogno," from I Lombardi,   **Verdi.**
     Madame Ruhl.
3. Duet—"Non fu Sogno," from I Lombardi   **A. R.**
     Madame Ruhl and Mr. A. R.
4. Trio—Piano, Violin, and Violoncello   **Reissiger.**

64. *Ibid.*, October 22, 1863.

Reinhardt, Loebmann, and Thilow.
5. Ballad—"Had I Met Thee,"
   Miss Rosetta Dale.
6. Song—"Then You'll Remember Me,"   Balfe.
   Major M.
7. German Song—"Scheiden und Leiden"   Truhn.
   Madame Ruhl.

Madame Ruhl and Charles Thilow's benefit concert, 1864.[65]

Exchange Hotel, Grand Vocal and Instrumental concert! . . .
   Benefit of Mad. Ruhl, and Charles W. Thilow,
   Assisted by Miss Rosa Fay, of New Orleans,
   Mr. Kisnich, J. Reinhardt.

1. Grand Overture   Mendelssohn.
   C. W. Thilow and J. Reinhardt.
2. Scena and Cavatina—Ernani involami   Verdi.
   Mad. Ruhl.
3. Duo Violin and Piano—I'Lombardi   Singelee.
   Mr. Kisnich and C. W. Thilow.
4. Song—Rataplan   Malibran.
   Mad. Ruhl.
5. Souvenir di Hensitt—Tarantella   Fesca.
   C. W. Thilow and J. Reinhardt.
6. Duet—Juanita   Mrs. Norton.
   Mad. Ruhl and Miss Rosa Fay.

                    Part II.

1. Grand Gallop—Diavoletto   Sanfiorenzo.
   C. W. Thilow and J. Reinhardt.
2. Grand Valse—The Forest Fairy   Venzano.
   Mad. Ruhl.
3. Solo—Violin—Grand Concerto   De Beriot.
   Mr. Kisnich.

---

65. *Ibid.,* January 5, 1864.

4. Duet—Gondoliers Evening Song   Glover.
   Mad. Ruhl and Miss Rosa Fay.
5. Grand Sinfonie—Scherzo   Beethoven.
   C. W. Thilow and J. Reinhardt.
6. Song—Scheiden—Leiden   Truhn.
   Mad. Ruhl.

A concert given at the Second Baptist Church, 1864.[66]

CONCERT
         for the benefit of Refugees, at
                The Second Baptist Church. . . .

                  Programme—Part First.

Solo—Alpine Horn   Proch.
Solo—Ballad
Duett—Una Notri d'amore   Arditi.
Solo—Il due Foscari   Verdi.
Solo—Clarionet   Baermann.
Duett—Holy Mother Guide His Footsteps   Wallace.

                      Part Second.

Duett—Norma   Bellini.
Solo—Piano—Mose in Egitto   Rossini.
Solo—Sky Lark   Benedict.
Duett—Serenade   Schubert.
Duett—Clarionet and Voice
Chorus—Miserere Trovatore   Verdi.

A concert given by Charles Thilow, 1864.[67]

Exchange Hotel.
               A Grand Classical Concert
_____
   66. *Ibid.,* April 29, 1864.
   67. *Ibid.,* April 29, 1864.

will be given by C. W. Thilow. . . . Mr. Thilow will be kindly assisted for this occasion by Mad. Ruhl, Messrs. F. Seibert, H. Schneider, J. Kessnich, J. Reinhardt.

Programme:
Part I.

1. Grand Overture—Yelva   Reissiger.
    C. W. Thilow and J. Reinhardt.
2. Solo, violin—Souvenir de Halevy   Artot.
    Mr. J. Kessnich.
3. Solo, Soprano—Judith   Concone.
    Mad. Ruhl.
4. Solo, Violoncello—Souvenir de Puritani   Piatti.
    Mr. C. W. Thilow.
5. Solo, Clarionetto—Fantasie   Barmann.
    Mr. H. Schneider.
6. Lied—Soprano and Violoncello Obligato   Linder.
    Mad. Ruhl and C. W. Thilow.

Part II.

1. Solo, Violin—Premier Concerto   F. David.
    Mr. J. Kessnich.
2. Grand Scene and Aria—Der Freischutz   Weber.
    Mad. Ruhl.
3. Grand Solo, Violoncello—Le Desir   F. Servais.
    Mr. C. W. Thilow.
4. Lied—Soprano and Violoncello Obligato   Proch.
    Mad. Ruhl and C. W. Thilow.
5. Grand Trio—Piano, Clarinetto and Violoncello—
        Les Huguenots   Meyerbeer.
    Messrs. Thilow, Schneider, and Seibert.
6. Grand Dramatic Song—Erlkoenig   F. Schubert.
    Mad. Ruhl.

A concert given by the Post Band, 1864. [68]
GRAND VOCAL AND INSTRUMENTAL CONCERT BY
THE POST BAND (formerly Smith's)
Assisted by a full orchestra and the following acknowledged
talent:
>Madame RUHL, Mademoiselle BLANCHE MIDDLE-
>TON, Messrs. KESSNICH, SCHNEIDER, REINHARDT,
>SMITH, &c., &c. . . . at the Exchange Hall. . . .

Programme.
Part First

1. OVERTURE— (Tubel)   FULL BAND.
2. CLARIONETTO SOLO— (Carl Maria von Weber)
                                               SCHNEIDER.
3. CAVATINA— (Ernani, fly with me)   MAD. RUHL.
4. VIOLIN SOLO— (Brillante)   KESSNICH.
5. SOUNDS FROM HOME— (as performed by Gungl)
                                          FULL ORCHESTRA.
6. THE LAST OF THE NARRAGANSET— (Waltz by
   Gungl)
                     Part Second

1. OVERTURE— (Zampa, Herold)   ORCHESTRA.
2. FLUTE SOLO— (Kummer)   ROSENBERGER.
3. CASTA DIVA— (Norma)   MAD. RUHL.
4. QUARTETT— (Die Kapella Kreutzer. . . .)
5. BASSOON SOLO— (Schneider)   RITTERSHAUS.
6. WEDDING MARCH FROM MIDSUMMER NIGHT
   (Mendelssohn)   FULL BAND.

*A concert given by Miss Blanche Middleton and Mr. F. N.
Crouch, 1864.* [69]

Miss BLANCHE MIDDLETON and Mr. F. N. CROUCH,
>(who appears before his Richmond friends after a three
>years' absence in camp) assisted by Mr. J. Reinhardt and

---

68. *Ibid.,* December 16, 1864.
69. *Ibid.,* December 20, 1864.

Amateur Friends, will give a GRAND VOCAL CONCERT on . . . December 20, 1864.

PROGRAMME
Part First

1. National Song—"God will defend the right"   Rosier.
   Miss BLANCHE MIDDLETON and Chorus
2. Scena from Maritani—"Let me like a Soldier fall"   Wallace.
3. Glee—Three Voices—"Breathe soft ye winds"   Webbe.
   F. N. CROUCH and Amateurs
4. Scena—"France, I adore thee"   Auber.
   Miss BLANCHE MIDDLETON
5. Old English Ballad (1620) —"Sally in our alley."   Carey.
6. Song—"Mother, oh sing me to rest"   Keller.
7. Duet—"When thy bosom heaves the sigh"   Braham.
   Miss BLANCHE MIDDLETON and Amateurs

Part Second

1. Christmas Carol (1600).
   Miss MIDDLETON, F. N. CROUCH and Amateurs
2. "Kathleen Mavoureen"   Crouch.
   F. N. CROUCH
3. "Dermot Asthore" (answer to the above)   Crouch.
   Miss BLANCHE MIDDLETON
4. Glee—three voices—"Mynheer Von Dunk"   Bishop.
   F. N. CROUCH and Amateurs
5. Song—"The Standard-Bearer"   Lindpaintner.
   F. N. CROUCH
6. "Who will care for mother now?"   Thompson.
   Miss BLANCHE MIDDLETON
7. "Laughing Trio"   Martini.

Part Third

1. Duet—"I've wandered in dreams"   A. J. Wade.
   Miss BLANCHE MIDDLETON and F. N. CROUCH
2. "Black-Eyed Susan"
   F. N. CROUCH
3. Duet—"Softly sighs the evening breeze"
   Miss MIDDLETON and F. N. CROUCH

4. Irish Ballad—"Oh, Molly Bawn"   Lover.
   F. N. CROUCH
5. New Song—"You can never win us back"   J. E. Smith.
   Miss BLANCHE MIDDLETON
6. Duet—"Could a man be deceived?"   Corfe.
7. Finale—Irish Ballad
   F. N. CROUCH

A concert given by the Nineteenth Georgia Band, 1864.[70]

METROPOLITAN HALL. GRAND VOCAL AND IN-
STRUMENTAL CONCERT by the NINETEENTH GEOR-
GIA BAND assisted by Mad. Ruhl and Messrs. H. Schneider,
J. Kessnich, and O. L. Siegel. . . .

PROGRAMME:
Part First

1. March-Tancredi   Rossini.
   FULL BAND
2. Ballad
   Mr. C. KESMODEL
3. Piano Solo—Grand Polka de Concert   Wallace.
   Mr. GEORGE W. CHASE
4. Canzone—Stride la Vampa (Trovatore)   Verdi.
   Madame RUHL
5. Flute Solo—Variations—Sur un Air Tyrolean   Boehm.
   Mr. C. L. SIEGEL
6. Comic Song
   Mr. R. H. NASH

Part Second

1. Pot Pourri—Favorite Airs
   FULL BAND
2. Duet—Sila stan shesta— (soprano and tenor)   Verdi.
   Madame RUHL and Mr. C. KESMODEL
3. Violin Solo—First Concerto   De Berriot.
   Mr. J. KESSNICH

70. *Ibid.*, December 22, 1864.

4. Ballad—Brightest Eyes   Stigelli.
        Madame RUHL
5. Comic Song (in character)
        Mr. R. H. NASH
6. Les Clochettes—Polka   Labitzky.
        FULL BAND

Mr. J. Kessnich's concert, 1865.[71]

A Grand Concert . . . at Metropolitan Hall, by

Mr. J. KESSNICH, assisted by

Madame RUHL, Professor THILOW, Professor SCHNEIDER, Professor REINHARDT, and a FULL ORCHESTRA, composed of the members of the Armory and Post Bands.

PROGRAMME.
Part I.

Overture (Yelva)   Reissiger.
        FULL ORCHESTRA
Casta Diva
        MADAME RUHL
Dreams on the Ocean   Gungl.
        FULL ORCHESTRA
Violin Solo (Beethoven's Waltz, with variations)
        J. KESSNICH
Anvil Chorus (Trovatore)   Verdi.

Part II.

Overture (Zampa)   Herold.
        ORCHESTRA
Air from Ernani   Verdi.
        MADAME RUHL
Concert Quadrille (Bohemian Girl)   Strauss.
        ORCHESTRA

---

71. *Ibid.,* January 26, 1865.

Potpourri for string quartette   Strauss.
Finale (Lucia di Lammermoor)
        FULL ORCHESTRA

Mr. Heinrich Schneider's concert, 1865.[72]

GRAND CONCERT

Mr. SCHNEIDER, assisted by Madame RUHL, Messrs.
THILOW, KESSNICH, REINHARDT, and FULL OR-
CHESTRA . . . at the African Church. . . .

Part First

1. Overture—"Martha"   Flotow.
        ORCHESTRA
2. Aria—"Robert, Robert, &c."   Meyerbeer.
        Madame RUHL
3. Clarionet Solo   Baermann.
        H. SCHNEIDER
4. Trio   Reissiger.
    Messrs. THILOW, KESSNICH and REINHARDT
5. Aria—"Maritana"   Balfe.
        ORCHESTRA

Part Second

6. Festival Overture   Kalliwoda.
        ORCHESTRA
7. Cavatina—"Nell," from "Betty"   Donizetti.
        Madame RUHL
8. Violin Solo—"Souvenir de Bellini"   Artot.
        Mr. KESSNICH
9. Echo Song, with Clarionet Obligato   Bishop.
        Mr. KESSNICH
10. Cavatina—"Ernani Involami"   Verdi.
        ORCHESTRA

_____
72. *Ibid.*, February 7, 1865.

Bibliography

Newspapers

Enquirer (Richmond). 1804–1865.

Examiner (Richmond). 1847–1865.

Religious Herald (Richmond). 1825–1865.

Richmond Compiler. 1813–1853.

Richmond Dispatch. 1850–1865.

Richmond Sentinel. 1863–1865.

Richmond Whig. 1824–1865.

Virginia Argus (Richmond). 1796–1815.

Virginia Gazette (Richmond). 1780–1781.

Virginia Gazette (Williamsburg). 1736–1780.

Virginia Gazette, or, the American Advertiser (Richmond). 1782–1786.

Virginia Gazette and General Advertiser (Richmond). 1790–1809.

Virginia Gazette, and Richmond and Manchester Advertiser (Richmond). 1793–1795.

Virginia Gazette, and Weekly Advertiser (Richmond). 1787–1789. 1793–1795.

Virginia Independent Chronicle (Richmond). 1786–1790.

Selected Publications

Allen, Harvey. *Israfel, The Life and Times of Edgar Allan Poe.* New York: Farrar and Rinehart, 1934.

Ames, Susie M. *Reading, Writing and Arithmetic in Virginia, 1607–1699.* Williamsburg: Virginia 350th Anniversary Celebration Corp., 1957.

Andrews, Matthew Page. *Virginia, The Old Dominion.* Richmond: The Dietz Press, Inc., 1949.

The Army and Navy Prayer Book. Richmond: Diocesan Missionary Society of the Protestant Episcopal Church of Virginia, 1864.

Bailey, James Henry. *A History of the Diocese of Richmond.* Richmond: Whittet and Shepperson, 1956.

Bailey, James Henry. *History of St. Peter's Church.* Richmond: Lewis Printing Co., 1959.

Bio-Bibliographical Index of Musicians in the United States of America Since Colonial Times. Washington, D.C.: Music Section, Pan American Union, 1956.

Blanton, Wyndham B. *The Making of a Downtown Church.* Richmond: John Knox Press, 1945.

Bondurant, Agnes M. *Poe's Richmond.* Richmond: Garrett and Massie, Inc., 1942.

Bradbury, William B. *Oriola: A New and Complete Hymn and Tune Book for Sabbath Schools.* Cincinnati: Moore, Wilstach, Keys and Co., 1860.

Bradbury, William B. *The Singing Book for Boys' and Girls' Meetings.* New York: Ivison and Phinney, 1854.

Brawley, B. J. *History of the English Hymn.* New York: Abington Press, 1932.

Brigham, Clarence S. *History and Bibliography of American Newspapers.* 2 vols. Worcester, Massachusetts: American Antiquarian Society, 1947.

Broaddus, Andrew. *The Dover Selection of Spiritual Songs.* Richmond: Drinker and Morris, 1828.

Broaddus, Andrew. *The Virginia Selection of Psalms, Hymns, and Spiritual Songs.* Richmond: Robert I. Smith, 1836.

Browne, C. A. *The Story of Our National Ballads.* New York: Thomas Y. Crowell and Co., 1919.

Burton, Lewis W. *Annals of Henrico Parish, Diocese of Virginia, and Especially of St. John's Church.* Richmond: Williams Printing Co., 1904.

Cappon, Lester J., and Duff, Stella F. *Virginia Gazette Index.*

2 vols. Williamsburg: The Institute of Early American History and Culture, 1950.

Chappell, William. *Popular Music of the Olden Time*. 2 vols. London: Cramer, Beale, & Chappell, 1859.

Chappell, William, ed. *National English Airs*. 2 vols. London: Chappell (Music-Seller to Her Majesty), 1840.

Chappell, William. *Old English Popular Music*. 2 vols. London: Chappell and Co., 1893.

Chase, Gilbert. *America's Music*. New York: McGraw-Hill Book Co., Inc., 1955.

Chestnut, Mary Boykin. *A Diary from Dixie*. New York: Peter Smith, 1929.

Christian, W. Asbury. *Richmond, Her Past and Present*. Richmond: L. H. Jenkins, 1912.

Cotter, John L., and Hudson, J. Paul. *New Discoveries at Jamestown*. Washington, D.C.: U. S. Government Printing Office, 1957.

Davison, Archibald T. *Protestant Church Music in America*. Boston: Unitarian Laymen's League, 1921.

Dichter, Harry, and Shapiro, Elliott. *Early American Sheet Music, Its Lure and Love, 1768–1889*. New York: R. R. Bowker Co., 1941.

Dunford, Frank B. *History of Central Methodist Church*. Richmond: W. M. Brown and Son, 1942.

Eckenrode, H. J. *et al.*, eds. *Richmond, Capital of Virginia*. Richmond: Whittet & Shepperson, 1938.

Ellinwood, Leonard. *The History of American Church Music*. New York: Morehouse-Gorham Co., 1953.

Elson, L. C. *History of American Music*. New York: The Macmillan Co., Revised by Author Elson, 1925.

Engel, Carl, ed. *Music from the Days of George Washington*. New York: Alfred A. Knopf, 1931.

Everett, L. C. *Everett's Sabbath Chime*. Richard: George L. Bidgood, 1860.

Everett, L. C., and Everett, A. B. *The New Thesaurus Musicus*. Richmond: Published by the Authors, 1858.

Ezekiel, Herbert T., and Lichtenstein, Gaston. *The History of the Jews of Richmond*. Richmond: Herbert T. Ezekiel, 1917.

Farish, Hunter Dickinson, ed. *Journal & Letters of Philip*

Vickers Fithian. Williamsburg: Colonial Williamsburg, Inc., 1957.

Fisher, George D. *History and Reminiscences of the Monumental Church, Richmond, Virginia, from 1814 to 1887.* Richmond: Whittet & Shepperson, 1880.

Fisher, Miles Mark. *Negro Slave Songs in the United States.* Ithaca, N. Y.: Cornell University Press, 1953.

Fisher, William Arms. *The Music That Washington Knew.* Boston: Oliver Ditson Co., Inc., 1931.

Flournoy, Mary H. *Essays on American History.* Washington, D. C.: Peabody Press, 1956.

Foote, Henry Wilder. *Three Centuries of American Hymnody.* Cambridge: Harvard University Press, 1940.

Fox, Adam. *English Hymns and Hymn Writers.* London: Jarrold and Sons, Ltd., 1947.

Freedley, George, and Reeves, John A. *A History of the Theatre.* New York: Crown Publishers, Inc., 1955.

Frost, Maurice. *English and Scotch Psalm and Hymn Tunes C. 1543–1677.* London: Oxford University Press, 1953.

Gaines, Richard Heyward. *Richmond's First Academy.* Richmond: Virginia Historical Collections, 1891.

Hamilton, J. D. de Roulhac. *The Best Letters of Thomas Jefferson.* Boston: Houghton Mifflin Co., 1926.

Harland, Marion. *Marion Harland's Autobiography.* New York: Harper and Brothers Publishers, 1910.

Harvie, Mrs. John B., ed. *Beacon on A Hill.* Richmond: The Williams Printing Co., 1955.

Harwell, Richard B. *Confederate Music.* Chapel Hill: The University of North Carolina Press, 1950.

Harwell, Richard B. *Songs of the Confederacy.* New York: Broadcast Music Inc., 1951.

Hewitt, Barnard. *Theatre U.S.A. 1668 to 1957.* New York: McGraw-Hill Book Co., Inc., 1959.

Hewitt, John Hill. *Shadows on the Wall.* Baltimore: Turnbull Brothers, 1877.

Howard, John Tasker. *The Music of Washington's Time.* Washington, D. C.: United States Constitutional Sesquicentennial Commission, 1937.

Howard, John Tasker. *Our American Music*. New York: Thomas Y. Crowell Co., 1956.

Howard, John Tasker. *A Program of Early American Piano Music*. New York: J. Fischer and Brother, 1931.

Howard, John Tasker. *A Program of Early and Mid-Nineteenth Century American Songs*. New York: J. Fischer and Brother, 1931.

The Hymnbook. Philadelphia: John Ribble, 1955.

Hymns of the Spirit. Boston: The Beacon Press, 1951.

Jackson, George P. *White and Negro Spirituals*. New York: J. J. Augustin, 1944.

James, W. C., compiler. *Leigh Street Baptist Church, 1854–1954*. Richmond: Whittet and Shepperson, 1954.

Johnson, Asa. *A History of Clay Street M. E. Church (South) Richmond, Virginia 1844–1918*. Richmond: Whittet and Shepperson, 1919.

Kennedy, John P. *Memoirs of the Life of William Wirt*. Philadelphia: Lippincott and Co., 1860.

Koch, Adrienne, and Peden, William, eds. *The Life and Selected Writings of Thomas Jefferson*. New York: Random House, Inc., 1944.

Lang, Paul Henry. *Music in Western Civilization*. New York: W. W. Norton and Co., Inc., 1941.

Law, Andrew. *The Art of Singing; in three parts—1803—I. The Musical Primer, II. The Christian Harmony, III. The Musical Magazine*.

Law, Andrew. *A Collection of Hymn Tunes from the most Modern and approved Authors*. [ca. 1783.]

Law, Andrew. *Harmonic Companion, and Guide to Social Worship*. 1819.

Little, John Peyton. *History of Richmond*. Richmond: The Dietz Printing Co., 1933.

Lomax, John A., and Lomax, Alan. *American Ballads and Folk Songs*. New York: The Macmillan Co., 1957.

Lutz, Francis Earle. *A Richmond Album*. Richmond: Garrett and Massie, 1937.

Magri, F. Joseph. *The Catholic Church in the City and Diocese of Richmond*. Richmond: Whittet and Shepperson, 1906.

Manly, B. Jr. *Baptist Chorales*. Richmond: T. J. Starke, 1859.

Mason, Frances Norton, ed. *John Norton & Sons, Merchants of London and Virginia*. Richmond: The Dietz Press, 1937.

Maurer, Maurer. "The Library of a Colonial Musician, 1755," *The William and Mary Quarterly*, III (October 1950), 39–52.

Maurer, Maurer. "The 'Professor of Musick' in Colonial America," *The Musical Quarterly*, XXXVI (October 1950), 511–24.

Metcalf, Frank J. *American Psalmody 1721–1830*. New York: C. F. Heartmann, 1917.

Metcalf, Frank J. *American Writers and Compilers of Sacred Music*. New York: The Abingdon Press, 1925.

McCartney, E. M. *Virginia Composers*. Petersburg, Virginia: Virginia Publishing Co., 1936.

McCutchan, Robert Guy. *Hymn Tune Names*. New York: Abdington Press, 1957.

Minnigerode, Meade. *The Fabulous Forties 1840–1850*. New York: G. P. Putnam's Sons, 1924.

Moffat, Alfred, compiler and arranger. *The Minstrelsy of Ireland*. London: Augener & Co., 1897.

Mordecai, Samuel. *Richmond in By-Gone Days*. Republished from the Second Edition of 1860. Richmond: The Dietz Press, 1946.

Morgan, Edmund S. *Virginians at Home*. Williamsburg: Colonial Williamsburg, Inc., 1952.

Musical Library. 4 vols. London: Charles Knight, 1834–36.

The New Psalms and Hymns. Richmond: Presbyterian Committee of Publication, 1901.

O'Dell, George C. D. *Annals of the New York Stage*. Vols. III–IV. New York: Columbia University Press, 1928–1931.

O'Neill, Francis. *Irish Folk Music*. Chicago: The Regan Printing House, 1910.

Padover, Saul K. *The Washington Papers*. New York: Harper Brothers, 1955.

Page, Thomas Nelson. *Social Life in Old Virginia*. New York: Charles Scribner's Sons, 1897.

Pell, Edward Leigh, ed. *A Hundred Years of Richmond Methodism*. Richmond: The Idea Publishing Co., 1899.

Pittman, J.; Brown, Colin (music ed.); and Mackay, Charles

(poetry ed.) . *Songs of Scotland*. London: Boosey & Co., 1877.

Pollard, Julia Cuthbert. *Richmond's Story*. Richmond: Richmond Public Schools, 1954.

The Presbyterian Hymnal. Richmond: Presbyterian Committee of Publication, 1945.

Richmond City Directory, 1819, 1852, 1855, 1856, 1858–59, 1860, and 1862.

Riley, Edward M., and Hatch, Charles E., eds. *James Towne in the Words of Contemporaries*. Washington, D. C.: Government Printing Office, 1955.

Rosenberg, Charles G. *Jenny Lind in America*. New York: Stringer and Townsend, 1851.

Routley, Erik. *The Music of Christian Hymnody*. London: Independent Press Limited, 1957.

Sacred Songs for Family and Social Worship: Comprising the Most Approved Spiritual Hymns, with Chaste and Popular Tunes. New York: American Tract Society, 1842.

Shay, Frank. *American Sea Songs and Chanteys from the Days of Iron Men and Wooden Ships*. New York: W. W. Norton and Co., 1948.

Simkins, Francis Butler; Hunnicutt, Spotswood; and Poole, Sidman. *Virginia*. New York: Charles Scribner's Sons, 1957.

Smith, Lucy. "Music of the Early Colonies." *Daughters of the American Revolution Magazine*, XCIII (June-July 1959): 557–58.

Sonneck, O. G. *Early Concert Life in America. 1731–1800*. Leipzig: Breitkopf and Haertel, 1907.

Sonneck, O. G. *Early Opera in America*. New York: G. Schirmer, 1915.

Sonneck, O. G. *Miscellaneous Studies in the History of Music*. New York: The Macmillan Co., 1921.

Sonneck, O. G. *Suum Cuique*. New York: G. Schirmer, 1916.

Southgate, Charles. *Harmonia Sacra*. New York: Edward Riley, n.d. [1820].

Stanard, Mary Newton. *Richmond, Its People and Its Story*. Philadelphia: J. B. Lippincott Co., 1923.

Stevenson, Arthur L. *The Story of Southern Hymnology*. Roanoke, Va.: The Stone Printing and Manufacturing Co., 1931.

Sweet, William Warren. *Virginia Methodism, A History*. Richmond: Whittet and Shepperson, 1955.

Troubetskoy, Ulrich, ed. *Richmond, City of Churches*. Richmond: Whittet and Shepperson, 1957.

The Vocal Standard, or the Star Spangled Banner. Richmond: J. H. Nash, 1824.

Walker, Ernest. *A History of Music in England*. 3d ed. revised and enlarged. London: Oxford University Press, 1951.

Weddell, Alexander Wilbourne, *et al. Richmond Virginia in Old Prints*. Richmond: Johnson Publishing Co., 1932.

Weddell, Elizabeth Wright. *St Paul's Church*. Richmond: The William Byrd Press, Inc., 1931.

Weeks, Nan F., compiler. *Grace Baptist Church, Richmond 1833–1958*. Richmond: Garrett and Massie, Inc., 1959.

West, Georgia C., compiler. *Gifts to Centenary*. Richmond: Centenary Methodist Episcopal Church, South, 1937.

White, Blanche Sydnor, compiler. *First Baptist Church, Richmond, 1780–1955*. Richmond: Whittet & Shepperson, 1955.

Willison, George F. *Behold Virginia: The Fifth Crown*. New York: Harcourt, Brace and Company, 1952.

Wright, Louis B., and Tinling, eds. *The London Diary and Other Writings of William Byrd*. New York: Oxford University Press, 1958.

Wright, Louis B., and Tinling, eds. *The Secret Diary of William Byrd of Westover*. Richmond: The Dietz Press, 1941.

Unpublished Material

"Minutes of the First Baptist Church, Richmond City Book 4," 1851–1860.

Montague, Richard A. "Charles Edward Horn: His Life and Works." Ed. D. dissertation, School of Music, The Florida State University, 1959.

"Record Book, St. John's Parish, 1785–1887."

Shockley, Martin Staples. "A History of the Theatre in Richmond, Virginia, 1819–1839." Ph. D. dissertation, Department of English, University of North Carolina, 1938.

Index

Abella, Sig., 202
Abercrombie, John J., 99
Academy of Sciences and Fine Arts, 57, 60, 69–72, 79
accordion, 139, 139 fnt., 149, 188
African Church, *see* Baptist Church, First African
Alberti, 41; Francis, 49
Albites, Sig., 204
Allen: 196; Harry, 190
amateur musical society, Richmond, 81, 84, 95; *also see* Concordia Singing Society, *Gesangeverein,* Musical Amateur Club of Richmond, Quartette Club, Richmond Academy of Music, Richmond Amateur Instrumental Club, Richmond Philharmonic Association, Richmond Sacred Music Society, Singing Society of Virginia, Turner Society, Virginia Verein Club
amateur musicians, 24, 26–27, 32, 33, 35, 41–43, 48–50, 79–81, 84, 91, 94, 110, 117, 119–121, 154, 155, 163–165, 170–172, 176, 204, 219–223, 227, 228–230, 232, 233, 242, 244, 250, 251, 254

American Company, the, 46, 47, 68, 79
Amphitheatre, 143, 193
Anderson, A., 188
Andre, 154
anthem, 129, 130, 170
Appy, 211
Arditi, Signor L., 186
Armbrecht, 184, 233
armonica, 35
Arne, Thomas, 38, 75, 76, 77, 111, 230
Arnold: the Herren, 159–160; Samuel, 75, 76, 77
Arth, 151
Artot, Monsieur J., 160
Astor Place Opera, the, 199
Athenaeum, 214
Auber, 145, 186
Avison, 129

Baccherini, 37
Baier, 222
Bailey, Mrs., 160
Baker: A., 100, 114–114; J., 189
Balfe, 186, 230
ballads: 145, 156–158, 161, 164; singing of, 24, 40, 55, 95–97, 188,